Hippocrene Insider's Guide to
PARIS

Hippocrene Insider's Guide to
PARIS

Elaine Klein

HIPPOCRENE BOOKS
New York

Library of Congress Cataloging-in-Publication Data

Klein, Elaine.
    Hippocrene insider's guide to Paris / Elaine Klein.
        p.   cm.
    ISBN 0-87052-876-9
    1. Paris (France)—Description—1975-Guide-books.
    I. Title.
    DC708.K55   1990
    914.4'3604839—dc20   90-47658
                                         CIP

For information, address:
Hippocrene Books, Inc.
171 Madison Ave. New York, NY 10016

All photos by Mokhtar Moktefi.

Printed in the United States.

to Mokhtar

Contents

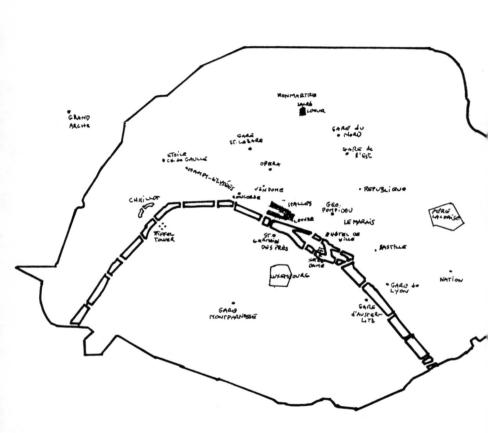

GRAND
ARCHE

MONMARTRE
SACRÉ
COEUR

GARÉ DU
NORD

GARÉ
ST·LAZARE

GARÉ de
L'EST

ÉTOILE
CH·DE GAULLE

CHAMPS·ELYSÉES

OPERA

RÉPUBLIQUE

VÉNDOME

PÉRÉ
LA·CHAISE

CHAILLOT

CONCORDE

HALLES

GEO·
POMPIDOU

LE MARAIS

LOUVRE

EIFFEL
TOWER

ST·
GERMAIN
DES PRES

L'HOTEL DE
VILLE

BASTILLE

NATRE
DAME

LUXEMBOURG

NATION

GARE de
LYON

GARE
MONTPARNASSE

GARE
D'AUSTER-
LITZ

Introduction

This guide was conceived one Sunday morning in the Luxembourg Gardens. A friend and I were watching the miniature sailboats and military vessels skim across the pool behind the French Senate: a submarine submerged, a battleship fled, the siren of a fireboat bleated. The operators around the edge of the basin were at war in remote control.

We lingered, delighted with the scene and the ritual pleasantries. My friend commented: "If you have never watched the ships playing around the fountain at the Luxembourg Gardens, you do not know Paris."

It occurred to me that no guide describes this very Parisian happening. From there, the realization that the modern traveler has a need for a new kind of guide to Paris—less official, less monument-oriented—was the next step I took.

This guide, while not overlooking the major museums and famous landmarks, is an approach to a more intimate view of Paris. Its intent is to take you by the hand and lead you through the narrow streets of Old Paris and along the boulevards, in and out, familiarly, of the chic shops. It will seat you comfortably at chosen cafés and restaurants. It will help you live something of the real life of the city and succumb to its charm. It wants you to eat fantastic food, shop happily, sleep well, move about with pleasure and ease, fill your eyes and your heart, and have a memorable time doing it.

CHAPTER 1

Paris: A Little Bit of History

The first Parisians were members of a Celtic tribe called the Parisii. They settled on what is today the Ile de la Cité in the middle of the third century B.C. The island was a natural shelter ideally situated at the junction of three major rivers: the Seine, the Marne and the Oise. Blessed with a climate tempered by the Gulf Stream, Lutetia, as it was called by the Romans, benefitted from an abundance of good agricultural lands and nearby stone quarries.

The settlement became permanent. When the Roman conquerors arrived in 52 B.C., room was made for a new city on the Left Bank. In true Mediterranean style the Romans covered the hilltops with forums and temples and constructed arenas, markets, baths and theatres close to the river Seine. A nine-mile-long aqueduct brought in water from the South.

As the Roman Empire declined, the great centers of southern Europe lost their luster. Merovingian king Clovis made the northern isle on the Seine his capital in 508 A.D. For those who followed, it was at the least a major residence if not a capital in the modern sense.

Paris entered the Middle Ages as a vast trading center with a massive port covered with boats. A powerful guild of fluvial merchants governed the city until well into the 17th century, giving it its motto, *fluctuat nec mergitur* (it floats yet does not sink), and a coat-of-arms: a ship with a silver sail.

Following the death of Charlemagne, the Treaty of Verdun, in 843, divided his empire into three parts, each governed by one of his grandsons. The Frank princes proved to be poor military leaders incapable of exercising royal authority. In 885–886, Paris was subjected to an interminable siege by the Vikings. The city was saved *in extremis* by Eudes, Count of Paris. On February 29, 888, an assembly of counts, lords, and bishops elected Eudes to the throne of West Francia; Paris was on the way to becoming a legend.

The first really Parisian king was Philippe Auguste, who came to power in 1179. He built solid ramparts and roads. He paved streets. He laid down regulations for commerce and trade, strengthened the administration, and formally recognized the University of Paris. Notre Dame was under construction. Noblemen built mansions, extending the city on the Right Bank, which by then harbored four-fifths of Paris's population. Construction of the first Louvre, at the time a fortress donjon, was begun in 1200.

The Hundred Years War (14th–15th centuries) and the English occupation of Paris reduced the city to poverty and devastation.

It was only in the year 1500, when Paris had recovered from the marasmus of war, that concern for the city's appearance was recorded. Architectural ordinances were adopted. François I made Paris his official residence and undertook to reconstruct the Louvre on a grander scale. Paris also was to have a city hall befitting its new role as a political center and center of learning. Another disaster was, however, in the wings: religious dissension. The Catholic League led the city to rebellion against the humanist views of the intellectuals and the monarchy. Thousands of Protestants were massacred and King Henri III forced to flee. With Henri of Navarre, he laid siege to Paris. Mortally wounded during the siege, Henri III formally recognized Henri de Navarre as his heir to the throne. In 1594 Henri de Navarre, accepting conversion to Catholicism, entered the city in ruins to become France's crowned king, Henri IV. He immediately put the population to work on immense public works projects: the Pont Neuf, the Louvre, the Tuileries Castle, roads, the Place des Vosges, and the Place Dauphine, at whose entrance his statue stands today. Between 1600 and 1640 some sixty convents and monasteries opened doors.

Louis XIV, the Sun King, and Anne of Austria, the Queen Mother, were in dread of Paris and ordered the construction of the palace of palaces at Versailles. Although Paris was abandoned by the monarch, his brilliant secretary of state, Colbert, left an indelible mark. On the Left Bank wide boulevards were to ring the quarter from the Invalides to Austerlitz; the Invalides, the Observatory and the Salpetrière Hospital were built. On the Right Bank there were the addition of a colonnade to the Louvre, the tracing of the Tuileries Gardens, the Place des Victoires, and the Place Vendôme. The city opened westward.

Louis XIV set up residence at Versailles in 1677 and government in 1682. Versailles versus Paris: the city—brilliant, intellectual, artistic, and scientific capital—faced the court.

Louis XV and XVI stayed on at Versailles. Paris continued to grow at a rapid pace. In the middle of the 18th century, the Place de la Concorde was laid out and trees were felled for the opening of the Champs-Elysées. New bridges crossed the Seine. Theatres, hospitals, the Law Courts, and the Pantheon came off the drawing boards. In 1783 the height of buildings was limited by law. Speculators and promoters, taking advantage of higher rents and an overwhelming demand, were quick to put up new housing and business sites.

In the second half of the 18th century, however, impoverishment of the burgeoning city was to lead to an economic crisis that brought the monarch and the populace into open conflict. The French Revolution of 1789 banished the former, but the city did not rise easily from its wounds. Famine and rationing were soon its lot. Paper bills became worthless.

Napoleon, in 1799, faced the problems of Paris with the intention of making the city the capital of Europe. His reign was marked by the building of new bridges and a multitude of Roman-style buildings and monuments: the triumphal arches, the Madeleine Church, and the arch-covered Rue de Rivoli. Significant were the measures he took to organize the provisioning of the city. Markets, slaughterhouses, and grain storehouses were constructed. A water canal, riverside quays, and sewers were dug. Cemeteries were moved to the outskirts and houses received numbers.

People poured into Paris from the countryside during the reigns of Napoleon and the Bourbon kings that followed. Class divisions were remarkable. On the one hand the city's old central neighborhoods were teeming with a destitute population crowded into insalubrious tenements where malady, alcoholism, and prostitution were rank. Cholera took 44,000 of Paris's 700,000 inhabitants in 1832. On the other hand, in the western sector of the city, construction financed by the banks was under way. A new bourgeoisie had come to the forefront with the birth of industry. Fashionable quarters rose off the ground: Rue François Ier, the Madeleine, St. Georges, and Europe. A new Stock Exchange opened in 1826. Gas lighting of the streets was introduced in 1829. It was the golden age of theatre and café life.

The Revolution of 1848 that overthrew King Louis Philippe prompted a number of large public works projects with a dual purpose: to meet the needs of a desperate population and provide quick and easy control of a potentially revolutionary class. Prefect of Paris Baron Haussmann, given full authority by new Prince-President Louis Napoleon, demolished entire districts to cut the great avenues. Steel was used for the construction of railway stations and market halls. Stone apartment buildings lined the new avenues. Parks at Boulogne and Vincennes were delineated and landscaped. For twenty years the city expanded, encompassing the suburbs of Auteuil, Passy, and Montmartre. The first department stores came into existence.

In 1870 Louis Napoleon, now Emperor Napoleon III, after a series of military adventures including the unsuccessful attempt to create a Latin Catholic Empire in Mexico under the puppet emperor Maximilian, declared war on Prussia. It proved a disaster.

The emperor was overthrown and the Republic once again proclaimed. However, the Franco-Prussian War continued. Paris surrendered after a bitter winter siege of four months. France suffered a humiliating defeat.

The working population of the city, now quartered miserably on the periphery and excluded from the rich, bourgeois center, rose in revolt in March 1871. This was the Paris Commune. But direct democracy was short-lived; the Versailles Army regained its foothold quarter by quarter, street by street. A very bloody week ended in the assassination of 30,000 insurgents and the deportation of as many more. Monarchy, however, was done.

The advent of the Third Republic endowed Paris with the Sacré Coeur in expiation of the Commune's "sins," the Great Exhibition of 1889 graced her with the Eiffel Tower, the exhibition of 1900 added the Grand and Petit Palais and the Alexander III Bridge. The métro was built in the 1890s.

Paris became the art capital of the world. The gentle hill of Montmartre, covered with windmills, a village, orchards, and an old church, had attracted penniless artists in search of cheap lodgings. Montmartre became the center of art and bohemia. Today a miniature vineyard remains as testimony to that bucolic past.

In the 1920s and 1930s, the artistic and intellectual circles emigrated to Montparnasse on the Left Bank. After the Second World War, St. Germain–des–Près was the chosen spot.

World War I and the Great Depression hit the city hard. A

popular front came to power in 1936. Many social reforms were adopted; however, the experience was brief. In 1939 war struck again. Paris was occupied by the Nazis from 1940 to 1944.

In the postwar period the city has seen numerous realizations: the UNESCO palace, the Montparnasse Tower, the towers and the double arch of the Défense to the west, the Georges Pompidou Center, and the Forum complex of the Halles. Within little more than ten years time, four major museums have been created: the National Museum of Modern Art at the Pompidou Center, the Picasso Museum, the Museum of Science and Technique at La Villette, and the Orsay Museum. The Arab World Institute on Quai Saint-Bernard is now a reality. The new Opera House at the Bastille recently has opened.

The known history of Paris covers twenty-three centuries. From the small Celtic tribe on a little island on the river to today's ten million inhabitants of Greater Paris, much blood and water have passed under the bridges of the Seine. Paris has been marked and swayed by people and events, both tragic and munificent. The varied waves of immigration from the provinces, the different regions of Europe, and the former overseas colonies have provided her with energy renewed at each turning. The result is a veritable capital of art, fashion, science, and technique; a political and economic metropolis unique to France and the world.

CHAPTER 2

Practical Information and Hints

(Prices, obviously, are subject to change.)

Transportation

From and to the airports

Regular taxi service between central Paris and Roissy-Charles de Gaulle: 150 to 220 francs, and Orly: 120 to 170 francs.

That is the approximate metered fare. There is a baggage charge for more than two bags. Add 10 percent tip.

Limousines are three or four times more expensive than taxis.

Air France buses Roissy-Porte Maillot or Etoile: 36 francs.
Air France buses Orly-Invalides terminal: 29 francs.

Bus and train (RER) Roissy-Gare du Nord, Chatelet, St.
Michel: 27.50 francs. Orly-St. Michel: 22 francs.

City bus 350   Roissy-Gare de l'Est and Gare du Nord
         351   Roissy-Place de la Nation
         215   Orly-Place Denfert-Rochereau
         183A Orly-Porte de Choisy
         285   Orly-Porte d'Italie

For all the city buses, six bus tickets.

In the city

Taxis—All are metered. Add 10 percent tip. Usually only
    accept three passengers. You can reserve a taxi one
    day for next day early morning call.

Bus and métro

Métro—First train at 5:30 A.M.
    Last train between 12:30 and 1 A.M.

Buses— First bus about 7 A.M.
    Last bus between 8:30 and 9 P.M. for most
    lines.
    Lines with black number marked on white
    disc operate on Sundays; some of the latter
    run until 12:30 A.M.

Tourist passes valid on both buses and métro. On
sale in most métro stations.

3-day pass: 70 francs
5-day pass: 115 francs

1 month pass: 173 francs—valid from first to last day of month. Identity photo required.

Carnet of 10 tickets: 31.20 francs. Métro—1 ticket; buses—1 or 2 tickets depending on distance.

NB Neither these passes nor ordinary bus-métro tickets are valid for Versailles and Défense.

City, suburbs and airports (including Versailles and Défense)

Tourist passes

3-day pass: 135 francs
5-day pass: 170 francs

Trains—There are six railway stations in Paris, serving different regions of France and Europe:

Gare du Nord	Information: 4582-5050
Gare de l'Est	day and night
Gare St. Lazare	
Gare de Lyon	Reservations: 4565-6060
Gare d'Austerlitz	8 A.M.–8 P.M.
Gare de Montparnasse	

Hotels—Paris Tourist Office, 127 Avenue des Champs-Elysées, tel. 4520-8898. 9 A.M.–10 P.M. Monday through Saturday; 9 A.M.–8 P.M. Sundays and holidays. Winter closing time, weekdays: 8 P.M.; Sundays 6 P.M.

There are hotel information counters at the Gare du Nord, Gare de l'Est, Gare de Lyon, Gare d'Austerlitz.

Counter also at Air France Invalides terminal, Quai

d'Orsay. In halls at Roissy and Orly airports are hotel telephones.

Changing Money—Banks generally pay better rates than foreign exchange offices and hotels. Beware of high commissions and service charges.

Banks are generally open Monday to Friday 9 A.M.–4:30 P.M. Exchange offices are open Saturdays, some even on Sundays, and have longer business hours.

Post Office—Post offices are open from Monday to Friday 9 A.M.–7 P.M. Saturdays 9 A.M.–12 noon. The main post office, 52 Rue du Louvre, métro Louvre, is open day and night.

Mail can be addressed to you, care of American Express, 11 Rue Scribe, 75009 PARIS (métro Opéra).

Museum Passes—Sixty museums and public monuments in Paris and suburbs can be visited with the Museum Pass, sold in museums, métro stations and travel agencies. Direct admission, no waiting.

1-day pass: 50 francs
3-day pass: 100 francs
5-day pass: 150 francs

Museums are closed on Mondays or Tuesdays. Free entry or reduced prices on Sunday at most major museums. Reduced rates in some museums for children and senior citizens.

Shopping—Department stores are open from 9 A.M. to 6:30 P.M. Mondays through Saturdays. Usually one late closing a week.

Other shops generally are open from 10 A.M. to 7 P.M. Art galleries sometimes are closed mornings.

Small food stores often are closed Mondays and open Sunday mornings. *Charcuteries* are open on Mondays. Food store hours are 9 A.M. to 1 P.M. and 4 to 7:30 or 8 P.M.

Supermarkets do not close between 1 and 4.

In most quarters there are a few food shops open until 9 or 10 P.M.

Most bakeries are open from 8 A.M. to 8 P.M.

Outdoor markets have their days or their mornings, although there are a few that are open every day except Sunday afternoon and Mondays. The all-day outdoor markets are open from 9 A.M. to 1 P.M. and from 4 to 7:30 P.M.

Tipping—Generally speaking, there is no need to tip in restaurants, cafés, tea shops; the tip is included on your check. If you are pleased with the service, you can leave a few coins.

Hotels add a service charge to cover tipping. However, in the more expensive establishments, the staff seem to expect an additional something for carrying a bag, room service, etc. It is really up to you.

Telephone—Dial 19 for long distance calls; after dial tone, dial country code, area code and your correspondent's number.

Country codes: Canada   1
               Ireland   353
               U.K.   44
               U.S.A.   1

For France, outside the Paris region, dial 16, wait for dial tone, dial 8-digit number. For Paris, 8-digits only.

Collect calls are called P.C.V. in French.

Reduced rates apply for Europe from 9:30 P.M. to 8 A.M. weekdays; from 2 P.M. on Saturdays and all day Sundays and holidays.

For Canada and the U.S.A. (except Alaska and Hawaii), reduced rates are in effect from 8 P.M. until 2 P.M. the next day and all day Sundays and holidays.

Telephone booths in Paris are operated with *télécartes*. Different denomination telecards can be bought at railway stations, post offices, and tobacco counters in cafés. There are few coin phones. Operator assistance is available at most post offices.

Electrical Appliances—Voltage in France is 220. If your electric shaver or dryer is not equipped with an adapter, nor with a European "male" plug, these can be purchased at either of the following department store basements:

Samaritaine, 19 Rue de la Monnaie, métro Pont-Neuf or Louvre

Bazar de l'Hôtel de Ville, 52 Rue de Rivoli, métro Hôtel-de-Ville

Automobile Hazards—While the French seem to park just anywhere, this is not actually so. They avoid pedestrian crossings, carriage-doors, and intersections. Underground parking lots or garages are the safest. However, if you park in the street and find your car has disappeared, have your hotel check with the *fourrière*, a car pound on the edge of town, before reporting to police.

Embassies —*Canada:* 35 Avenue Montaigne, tel. 4723-0101
and
Consulates *Ireland:* 4 Rue Rude, tel. 4500-2087

U.K.: Embassy—35 Rue du Faubourg St. Honoré, tel. 4266-9142
Consulate—16 Rue Anjou, tel. 4266-9142

U.S.A.: Embassy—2 Avenue Gabriel, tel. 4296-1202
Consulate—2 Rue St. Florentin, tel. 4296-1202

Medical—American Hospital, 63 Boulevard Victor Hugo, Neu-
Services illy, tel. 4747-5300
British and American Pharmacy, 1 Rue Auber, tel. 4742-4940
Pharmacie Anglaise des Champs-Elysées, 62 Avenue des Champs-Elysées, tel. 4225-2513 and 4359-2252

French drug stores and pharmacies give advice on non-prescription medication. It is not rare to find English-speaking personnel.

Airlines—Air Canada, 24 Boulevard des Capucines, tel. 4742-2121

Air France, 119 Avenue des Champs-Elysées, Invalides Air Terminal, Quai d'Orsay and many others, tel. 4535-6161

Air Inter, 49 Avenue des Champs-Elysées, Invalides Air Terminal, Quai d'Orsay, and many others, tel. 4539-2525

American, 108 Rue du Faubourg St. Honore, tel. 4289-0522

British Airways, 91 Avenue des Champs-Elysées, tel. 4778-1414

Continental, 92 Avenue des Champs-Elysées, tel. 4225-5928

Eastern, 92 Avenue des Champs-Elysées, tel. 4225-3750

Pan Am, 1 Rue Scribe, tel. 4266-4545

TWA, 101 Avenue des Champs-Elysées, tel. 4720-6211

Churches—American Cathedral in Paris (Episcopal), 23 Avenue George V, tel. 4720-1792

American Church in Paris, 65 Quai d'Orsay, tel. 4705-0799

Saint George's, 7 Rue Auguste-Vacquerie, tel. 4720-2251

Saint Michael's, 5 Rue d'Aguesseau, tel. 4742-7088

Scots Kirk Manse, 10 Rue Thimonier, tel. 4878-4794

Saint Joseph's, 50 Avenue Hoche, tel. 4227-2856

Book Shops—Albion, 13 Rue Charles V, tel. 4272-5071

Brentano's, 37 Avenue de l'Opéra, tel. 4261-5250
Galignani, 222 Rue de Rivoli, tel. 4260-7607
Shakespeare and Co., 37 Rue de la Bûcherie, tel. 4354-3262
W. H. Smith and Son, 248 Rue de Rivoli, tel. 4260-3797

CHAPTER 3

Old Paris 'Round and About Notre Dame

Notre Dame de Paris

If you come upon Notre Dame from across the front square, the great Gothic cathedral appears curiously small and squat. When it was originally conceived in the 13th century, it was hemmed in on all sides by houses and shops and one arrived in front of it, properly, very close to the facade. It was Baron Haussmann who destroyed most of the buildings on the island and created the oversized square or parvis in the 19th century.

Notre Dame took 182 years to build. Begun in 1163 under Louis VII, it was completed in 1345. It was the result of a collective effort. While the King, noblemen, clergy, and various corporations financed the project, local craftsmen contributed their labor under the guidance of the master builders.

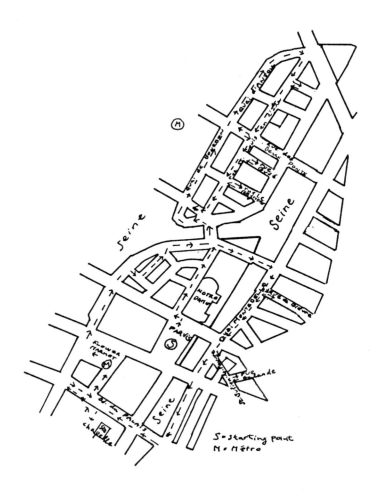

Notre Dame
Ile de la Cité

Métro: Cité
Bus: 47, 24, 27, 21, 38, 85

Sainte Chapelle
Boulevard du Palais

Open from 10 A.M. to 5 P.M. every day
Evening concerts 9 P.M.

Ile St. Louis

Métro: Pont Marie
Bus: 67, 86, 87

Time: Almost all day

Notre Dame has been the scene of many an historic event. Henry VI of England was crowned here in 1430. Mary Stuart was enthroned upon her marriage to François II of France. During the French Revolution all but the great bell was melted down and the church was used to store food, wine, and forage. For Napoleon and Josephine's coronation in 1804, immense tapestries were hung to mask the disrepair. Afterwards it fell into disuse. Some years later Victor Hugo's *The Hunchback of Notre Dame* aroused popular interest. In 1841 architect Viollet-le-Duc was entrusted with its restoration. We can thank him for the delightful gargoyles that cover the cathedral.

Notre Dame survived, unharmed, the Paris Commune and World War II. It is the zero point from which the streets of Paris and the roads of France part.

Facade

The facade is rich in sculpture and symbolism. Try to evoke the stone imagery as it was in the Middle Ages, painted with bright colors against a gilt background. For a largely illiterate population, these representations were the story of the Bible in figurative form.

Of the ground-level portals, the Virgin's Portal on the left is interesting for its statuary depicting the occupations, month by month, of the rich and poor of the time. The wrought-iron work of the doors themselves is magnificent.

The gallery of figures just above the portals represents the kings of Judea. At the time of the French Revolution, they were mistaken for the kings of France and beheaded! Though since replaced, the original heads were discovered by chance in a private cellar, in 1975, and are now on display at the Cluny Museum.

Above center is the rose window, the largest of its time. The next level is a delicate lacelike gallery of stonework supporting two towers, one of which (the south tower) contains Emmanuel, a bell weighing over thirteen tons that is rung on great occasions. Three hundred eighty-seven steps climb to the tower platform.

Access is on the north side of the church, to your left as you face it (9 A.M.–4 P.M. in winter, to 5 P.M. in summer).

Inside

The immediate impression is one of immensity, a never-ending Gothic mall or promenade: here the shop; then the chapels; there a bank of white tapers, the amazing pillars of which the largest measure 16 feet in diameter. And, of course, the windows of blue, lavender, purple, and turquoise splashed with reds and greens and yellows. The resplendent rose windows at either end of the transept are from the 13th century, as is the one above the entrance to the cathedral. The other stained glass windows date from different periods: the clear glass with fleur-de-lis from the 18th century; the monotone glass from the 19th; the modern windows, recognizable by the abundant use of lead fillers and their abstract design, were made in 1965 in scrupulous respect of the ancient manufacturing techniques.

Take your time inside Notre Dame. Amble. Let its feeling pervade and take hold. Some of the chapels include statues that appear as black silhouettes against the glass windows; in others old brass oil lamps are suspended from on high. On the outside of the chancel or choir are remarkable naive stone screens from the 14th century of scenes from the life of Christ. The treasury, which can be visited from 9 A.M. to 5 P.M. except Sundays and holidays, contains various religious objects and relics—including a fragment of what we are told is the true cross of Jesus and his crown of thorns.

Outside

Along the north side (left as you face the cathedral) is the richly decorated Cloister Portal. As you move past the red door, you will arrive at John XXIII Square, where you have a wonderful view of the choir end of the cathedral with its intricate gables and pinnacles, gargoyles, and most important, the 14th-century flying buttresses. Introduced by Jean Ravy, the buttresses give the cathedral its air of lightness and fineness. The main problem to be resolved by the early builders was that of the relationship between weight and balance. With the introduction of the flying buttresses—the first ever—Notre Dame became a model for succeeding Gothic monuments. The weight of the framework and ceilings was borne by these outside structures. In shifting weight from the walls to the buttresses, the window openings could then be enlarged and the walls themselves lightened.

Above the original 13th-century roof, Viollet-le-Duc reconstructed the spire using 500 tons of oak and 250 tons of lead. It rises 295 feet (90 meters) off the ground. The architect may be winking at you: he actually placed himself among the evangelists and apostles visible on the roof.

On Sunday afternoons at 5:45 P.M. you can listen to the cathedral's organ in concert; it is the largest organ in France. (There is no entry fee.)

A President's Home

Leave Notre Dame from the rear and cross the Pont de l'Archevêché (to your right if your back is to the cathedral) to the Left Bank. Turn right on the Quai de Montebello. The first street on your left will be the Rue de Bièvre. Go down to number 22, which is the private home of President François Mitterand. Although his presidential activities require his presence at the Elysées Palace, it is well-known that he often steals away from officialdom to his unassuming Parisian residence.

St. Julien-le-Pauvre

Go back to Quai de Montebello and to your left for three very short blocks to René Viviani Square and St. Julien-le-Pauvre, the oldest church in Paris (depending upon how you reckon the facts). Begun two years after Notre Dame, it was finished in 1220, 125 years before the cathedral. The church at St. Germain-des-Près actually is older than St. Julien, but at the time St. Germain was outside the city limits in the middle of fields.

The church has several claims to firsts. As the headquarters of the Latin-speaking clerics, it was, in fact, here that the Latin Quarter literally was founded. In the 13th century it became the official seat of the newly chartered University of Paris. With its fame came fortune, and the church built a series of underground cells to house more than one hundred monks. Little by little, however, the church fell into decline. By the 16th century there no longer were any monks. The students, furiously opposed to a newly elected university rector, smashed the place to bits. The church was closed. In the 17th century the hospital Hôtel Dieu became owner and did sufficient restoration for it to be used as a chapel.

During the French Revolution it served to store salt, as a fairground for wool merchants, and as a flour granary.

In 1889 the unused church was given to the Greek Catholic community by the Archdiocese of Paris. Sunday services (10 A.M. and 6 P.M.) are in Greek; the liturgy is sung at 11 A.M. by the church choir.

As you approach the church through the little park, you will see a false acacia or black locust tree, the Robinia, on two cement props. It was planted in 1601 by French botanist Jean Robin and is considered to be the oldest tree in Paris. The large-bottomed ash tree is from the same period.

Enter the church from the front. Very much the country church, it has a great deal of charm. The style is typical of the transition from Romanesque to Gothic architecture.

Across the street from the church entrance, number 14, is the *Tea Caddy*, founded in 1928 by Miss Kinklin, who was the English governess at the Rothschild's. This was her retirement gift. It is still a very English tea shop and serves light lunches, pies, scones, muffins, and homemade jams. It is open from 12 NOON to 7 P.M. and closed on Tuesday.

The *Satay*, next door, is comfortable and relaxing. It boasts good cakes, tea, and old-fashioned chocolate. Open 4:30 P.M. to 2 A.M. and closed Sundays.

If you backtrack past the entrance to the church, and make the first left, you will find *Le Chat Huant* (Rue Galande), two adjacent shops with a fine selection of handicrafts: jewelry, hand-woven bags, batiks, and all sorts of tea things.

Now back to the river front. On your left is *Shakespeare and Co.*, the book shop of English-speaking Bohemia, owned and run by George Whitman, goatee and all. A place to browse, relax, and exchange thoughts and information, it is open from noon to midnight; poetry readings occur Mondays at 8 P.M. Tea is served on Sunday. Shakespeare and Co. is an institution in Paris, located at zero kilometer, as its proud stamp announces.

Now go along the quay, to the left, past all the book and print vendors, until you reach Place St. Michel. Turn right and go over the bridge. On the left-hand side of the street, in the middle of the block, is the entrance to the Law Courts and la Sainte Chapelle.

La Sainte Chapelle

Louis IX or St. Louis was a pious king. He learned that Baldwin, a French nobleman who became Emperor of Constantinople, was prepared to sell the "True Crown of Thorns" in order to settle some debts. The price was high and many doubted its authenticity, but St. Louis would not be dissuaded.

When the crown arrived in France at Sens, some seventy miles from Paris, the king and his brothers carried it, barefoot, to Notre Dame. There it awaited the Sainte Chapelle, designed by Pierre de Montreuil and completed in record time in 1248. The chapel adjoined the royal palace at the Conciergerie. It is the epitome of Gothic art.

There are in fact two chapels: a lower one intended for the palace servants and an upper one for the royal family.

In your haste to see the upstairs marvels, do not neglect the lower chapel. Here you can obtain a close view of the Gothic arches and the ceiling of midnight blue studded with gold stars. You are walking on the tombstones of generations of the chapel's clergymen.

Mount the staircase to the upper level and behold!

The stained glass windows retrace episodes from the Old Testament. They are read from bottom to top and from left to right. These are the oldest stained glass windows in Paris; most date from the 13th century, and some were repaired in the 19th. One of the windows recounts the story of the crown's voyage, from its purchase by two friars weighing out gold to the barefoot royal brothers transporting it to Paris.

While one may regret the absence of tapers or oil lamps, the burst of glory of the reds and blues is evident. The more delicate greens of the rose window are best appreciated from the opposite end of the chapel. Note the one small window at eye level on either side. Also note the wonderful polychrome ceiling and pillars as well as the inlaid floor patterns. The relics of the chapel were displayed on the baldachin above the gilded platform, while St. Louis followed proceedings from a private chapel separated from the main one by a latticed window. Story has it that the God-fearing man lived in dread of assassination.

As you come out of the Sainte Chapelle, notice the entryway and harmonious upper loggia. Back off from the building, in front and on the side, to get a glimpse of the delicate stone structure on high. Also observe the portion of a fleur-de-lis-covered wall beyond the entrance to the chapel.

The Sainte Chapelle is open daily from 10 A.M. to 5 P.M. Try to pick a sunny day. Evening concerts are at 9 P.M.

When you leave the Sainte Chapelle, go left to the corner. There you can check the time on the oldest clock in the city just as Parisians have since 1370. This is the corner tower of the Conciergerie, St. Louis's fortress residence, transformed into a prison in 1392. During the French Revolution 2600 prisoners went from here to the guillotine, including Marie Antoinette, and later, Danton and Robespierre.

We now shall cross the Boulevard du Palais and return, right, to the esplanade called Rue de Lutèce, first left. This esplanade has been laid on the surface of a Roman forum. Julius Caesar once tred here!

Just beyond the Art Nouveau, turn-of-century métro exit "Cité" is the Flower Market.

Flower Market

Wend your way in and out of the world of gardenias, jasmine, roses, and azaleas.

Leave the market on the far side; cross over the Rue de la Cité at the corner with the Seine. As you advance on the street along the river front, you will see to your left the tall St. Jacques Tower, all that remains of a church destroyed during the Revolution. It was a major stopover for pilgrims on the road to Santiago de Compostela in Spain. The tower is now a weather station. Every morning a meteorologist climbs the many hundred steps to the top to take readings.

A little further on you will have a glimpse of the blue and green industrial tubing of the Pompidou Center. Closer to the Seine, you will be greeted by a wide view of City Hall.

At Rue de la Colombe, the first street on your right, turn in. The *La Colombe* restaurant has a unique décor. Unfortunately, the food is not up to the surroundings. Across the street, located in a 15th-century residence, is *L'Embellie*, one of the most beautiful dining rooms in the quarter. The food is recommended.

Continue on the Rue des Oursins, which runs parallel to the quay. At the end of the street is a completely renovated medieval townhouse. Observe the stained glass windows, wrought-iron window grating, and heavy spiked, wooden door.

Up the steps, over the bridge on the left to the Ile St. Louis.

Ile St. Louis

Until 1614 there were two islands. A channel between them was then packed with fill and stone bridges were built connecting with the shore on either side. Land was parcelled out and residences constructed. They were completed in 1664 and little has changed since. There is rare unity of style, called Classic; much of the work was done by architect Louis Le Vau.

If the weather is right, you can drop down to the water level where there are park benches. On the street level, skirt around to the left of the mini-park. A walk along the poplar-lined riverfront is pleasant. There are many lovely buildings, and you may get a glimpse of some interesting courtyards.

At number 17 Quai d'Anjou is the *Hôtel de Lauzun* or *Lansan*. In 1845 the Haschich Club established its seat here. Among its members were Charles Baudelaire, Alexander Dumas, and Eugène Delacroix. Now owned by the City of Paris, the residence is used to house official guests. The interior is lavish. On the outside the water mains and balcony are especially decorative.

The *Hôtel Lambert*, number 1 Quai d'Anjou or 2 Rue St. Louis-en l'Isle, is one of the most beautiful private homes in the city. It once was the residence of Michèle Morgan. Today it belongs to the Rothschild family.

Turn in to the Rue St. Louis-en-l'Ile. On the corner of the first street on the left, 3 Rue des Bretonvilliers, masterful renovation has just been completed on the manor house. Further down Rue St. Louis-en-l'Ile is *St. Louis Church*. On the wall along the street-side aisle is a plaque inscribed in 1926: "In grateful memory of Saint Louis in whose honor the City of Saint Louis, Missouri, USA, is named."

Across from the church at number 24 is the *Bamyan Gallery* of ethnic jewelry and artifacts from Afghanistan. At number 32 *Jacqueline Lemoine's Gallery* specializes in fine watercolors.

There are many agreeable tea shops and snack places in this street. One is the tea and chocolate shop *La Charlotte de l'Ile* at number 24.

At number 26 is *Odysse*, travel books and guides specialists, with another shop at number 35 of the same street. The line outside *Berthillon*, at 31 Rue St. Louis-en-l'Ile, is for the best ice cream in town.

Turn right at the Rue des Deux Ponts. Number 33 is *Les Fous de l'Isle,* a tea salon and restaurant. Everything is made on the premises. Saturday and Sunday brunches cost 98 francs at this writing, 120 with a Bloody Mary.

Back to our main street and to the right. *Yamina's* silk shop at number 56 is a refreshing stop, with gay prints and solids, beautifully cut garments, as well as scarves and ties.

If the door to number 51 is open, take in the courtyard. *Pylones,* a few doors down, has novel ideas for gifts: latex bracelets and earrings, suspenders and visor caps, for example.

Turn left at Rue Le Regrattier. At number 16 is *Aux Décors de Martres,* exclusive agent for charming Martres handpainted dishware. Martre is near Toulouse in the Southwest, and the designs, which are very similar to Provençal, date from the 18th century.

Back on the center street, at the end of which is Rue Jean du Bellay. To the right a little shop called *Vertige* is a treasure house of copies of mechanical toys from our childhood.

Along the way

Restaurants
Atelier du Maître Albert
Auberge des Deux Signes
Le Bistrot de Clémence
Brasserie de l'Ile St. Louis
La Bûcherie
Chieng Mai
L'Embellie
Au Franc Pinot
Le Monde des Chimères
Wally

Tea, Snacks, Ice Cream, Pastry
Al Dar (Oriental pastry)
Berthillon (ice cream)
La Charlotte de l'Ile
Coco Passion

La Cuisine Gourmande (takeout)
La Flore en l'Ile
La Fourmi Ailée
Les Fous de l'Ile
Le Satay
Tea Caddy

Beer, Wine Bars, Cafés
Brasserie de l'Ile St. Louis
L'Ecluse
Au Franc Pinot

Hotels
Hôtel Le Colbert
Hôtel des Deux-Iles
Hôtel Esmeralda
Hôtel des Grandes Ecoles
Hôtel du Jeu de Paume
Hôtel de Lutèce
Hôtel du Lys
Nôtre-Dame Hôtel
Hôtel du Vieux Paris

CHAPTER 4

The Little Streets Behind St.-Germain-des-Près

In 542, Childebert, son of the first Christian king of France, went to war against his brother-in-law, the Visigoth king of Spain. While laying siege to Saragossa, Childebert espied an elaborate ceremony centered around gold relics and a tunic said to have belonged to Saint Vincent. Childebert lifted the siege in exchange for the relics.

St. Germain the Golden, as it then was called, was built to house the cherished booty. Set outside the city limits, in the middle of green fields, it could be seen from afar: a magnificent basilica of marble columns and gilded rafters; golden mosaic and shining copper completely adorned its exterior. So it remained for 300 years until Norse invaders reduced it to ruins. The Vikings, it seems, took it to be all gold. . . .

St. Germain-des-Près (of the Fields) was rebuilt on the old

S = starting Point
M = Métro

Métro: St. Germain-des-Près
        Mabillon

Bus: St. Germain-des-Près—39, 48, 63, 86, 95
         Rue du Four—70, 96, 87

Eugène Delacroix Museum: 10 A.M.–5:15 P.M.
                          Closed Tuesdays

Time: Almost all day

foundations in the Romanesque style between 990 and 1021, with some of the original marble columns. Today's tower and belfry date from that time, making it the oldest church of Paris. The choir was added in the 12th century.

In the 13th century cloisters, dormitories, a refectory, a vast library, and the lovely Chapel to the Virgin, in the Gothic style, were built adjacent to the church. All have disappeared.

As one of the 17,000 Benedictine abbeys of Europe, St. Germain-des-Près owed allegiance to the Pope alone and rivalled in power the City of Paris. Its lands extended to the west, far into today's suburbs.

Monastic power came to an end with the French Revolution. On June 6, 1789, the people of Paris attacked the abbey's prison to release twenty soldiers who had been jailed for their refusal to fire on workers. In 1792 the church was turned into a warehouse for saltpeter.

Two years later an explosion of fifteen tons of powder in the refectory destroyed many of the abbey's buildings and shook the church to its foundations. Thanks to writer Victor Hugo, it was not razed but rather was repaired and reconstructed in the 19th century.

As you enter St. Germain-des-Près, you pass between fine marble columns on either side. The ceiling, walls, and columns of the interior are painted in dark polychrome, deep greens and wines, with a dark blue star-studded ceiling. The effect, by contrast to the rough-stone country exterior, is most unexpected.

The murals above the nave are by Hippolyte Flandrin (19th century). There is the lovely *Jesus Entering Jerusalem* at the beginning of the choir on the north (left) side.

A few of the stained glass windows are noteworthy, in particular the two in the last chapel on the right behind the choir. A plaque to the philosopher Descartes can be seen in the third chapel from the end on the same side.

On the outside of the church, to the south and to the north, are two squares, zones of quiet and repose in the heart of an active quarter. On the right, just beyond the métro entrance, is

Félix Desruelles Square. To your left is a stone trough with figures of a shepherd and woman against a backdrop of ivy. To your right, beyond the benches and the children's sand pit and slide, there is a fairly good view of the brick and stone abbatial palace, a magnificent example of 16th-century architecture.

In the Laurent Prache Square, to the left of the church, is a statue by Picasso dedicated to his old friend and companion, poet Guillaume Apollinaire. A number of Gothic vestiges of the Chapel to the Virgin form a background to the square.

We will leave here through the Rue de l'Abbaye, alongside Laurent Prache Square. As you walk down the street, look ahead and upwards at the overlapping buildings and terraces that form a lightly nuanced quilt pattern.

On the left, *La Galérie de la Hune* at number 14 is a reputable gallery for contemporary prints (Lalanne, Kozo, Masurovsky, Piza, etc.).

At number 10 is a sales outlet for posters, books, and catalogues of French national museums. Posters are 25 and 35 francs. Playing cards for a French family game—the rules are in English as well—are decorated with reproductions of major works of art from either the Louvre or the Orsay Museum. An educational gift at 50 francs a deck.

In this street and along our itinerary are showrooms for fine decorator fabrics and wallpapers by Rubelli, Manuel Canovas, Dollfus Mieg, Zumsteg, Etamine, Liberty of London, Pierre Frey, Voghi, and Nobilis.

Our first left takes us into Place Furstenberg, a gem of a square, often seen to typify Paris in lieu of the Eiffel Tower. On summer evenings musicians settle down here under the lavender-flowered pawlonia trees for impromptu open-air concerts.

In the far left-hand corner of the square is the old stable entrance to the *Eugène Delacroix Museum*, open from 10 A.M. to 5:15 P.M. It is closed Tuesdays and costs 10 francs.

Before proceeding, glance behind you at the abbatial palace facade. This is one of the rare uses of brick in the city.

The little street leading out of the Place Furstenberg boasts two fine antique shops: *Yveline* and *Aux Armes de Furstenberg*, the latter for scientific instruments and military objects.

We will take the tiny Rue Cardinal to the right just after *Sophie Canovas's* chic bedroom shop. On your left is the back entrance to *Liberty of London*. Liberty sells dressmaking cotton by the yard (roughly $15 a yard at today's exchange rate). They carry a number of pretty gift items as well: a jewel roll for 150 francs, a stuffed frog for 60 francs, change purses, toilet bags, and so forth.

On your right as you go along Rue Cardinal is an attractive Scandinavian household shop, *Torvinoka*. At the corner with Rue de l'Abbaye, a "macrobiotic" vegetarian restaurant, the *Guenmaï*, is open for lunch from 11:45 to 3:30.

On the corner opposite *Claude Murat's* amazing lamp shop, is *l'Echaudé*, a good restaurant with a very pleasant décor.

Now turn left into the Rue de l'Echaudé. At number 15 is one of the best dealers in prints of old masters in the quarter, *Arsen Bonafous-Murat*. Browsing is welcomed.

Across the way is *Cipango*, a jewelry shop, which sells one-of-a-kind pieces.

We turn left at Rue Jacob into two blocks of superbly stocked and reputable antique shops, art galleries, wallpaper and fabrics showrooms, and specialized bookshops.

Etamine, at number 3, has a delightful collection of English stencilled wallpapers. *Pierre Madel*, at number 4, sells classic hand-wrought iron pieces for the fireplace as well as articulated bronze lamps.

Jean-Marc Braun, in a slip of a shop at number 6, specializes in antiques of the late-18th and 19th centuries, typically French. Jean-Marc's prices are the best in the quarter, and you are assured of a warm welcome.

Next door, *La Galérie Furstenberg*, known for its editions of prints by Dali and Leonore Fini, now is turning to works of young artists, including the very agreeable sculpture of Jean Michel Fichot.

In the lovely courtyard of number 12 is *Mohanjeet*, an Indian dress shop. Perhaps this is the place to say that the street-side fronts of French houses often are misleading, because the cool, elegant, or sometimes run-down facades can conceal inner courtyards of great charm. Inevitably , most doors now are coded and closed to the public, even in the daytime. When they are not, do not hesitate to venture inside. There are many pleasant surprises behind the "coach door," as the French call the wide carriage-size entrances.

L'Entr'acte (meaning Intermission), at number 14, is a pleasant café open every evening from 7 P.M. until 2 A.M. Although it is not a private club—you need only ring to enter—its customers are habitués who gather here nightly. The banter is gentle and the drinks amusing: the Bagdad Café is a jigger of gin, a dash of black currant liqueur and grapefruit juice. Or try a Droopy or a Bambi, a Superman or a Tom and Jerry. Drinks start at 50 francs.

Across the way is *Antoinette*, with naive art. At number 11 is *Le Petit Atelier*, a language and theatre studio run by Sylviane Mahsias, a Barnard-trained French woman. Originally devoted to teaching English to small children through theatre work, the studio now has expanded to classes for professional actors. It is such a delight on certain afternoons to watch little tots on stage spouting their lines in English.

Now cross the street to number 20. Ring the buzzer and push hard on the heavy door to the street. Pass into the long cobblestone courtyard and advance slowly toward the elegant two-story house in the rear. Gone are Parisian urbanity, the bustle of city streets and the aggressiveness of their dwellers. At the end of the country-style lane, on your right, high iron gates open onto a garden built around a temple to friendship, a vestige from the days following the French Revolution when shrines were no longer dedicated to the gods. The house itself is occupied by Michel Debré, former French premier under Charles de Gaulle, and now a member of the French Academy. Our interest in his house, however, is because of its former occupant, Nathalie Clifford Barney, an extravagant American who prior to World War I and during the period between the two great wars played host to one of the most exciting literary and artistic salons of the city. Colette was a frequent visitor and, so the story goes, could be seen dancing nude in the house and through the gardens on a summer afternoon.

Well known for her lesbian friendships as well as for her support of artists in need (and somewhat less well known as a poetess), Nathalie Barney has remained a legend, witness to which has been paid by a number of recent books.

As you come back on to the street, look up at numbers 11 and 13. These lovely houses date from the 17th century. On the facade are two *mascaron* or masks from the 18th century. If you tip your head at the right angle, you may get a glimpse of the ceilings of the mezzanine and second floors. Their painted rafters have survived the ages, preserved in plaster coatings. Now that beams are fashionable, the plaster has been peeled off and the beautiful old designs rediscovered.

To your right is *Maud Bled's* shop, a rare high temple of Art Deco featuring objects, jewelry, and small pieces of furniture of the 1920s and 1930s.

Next door is another antique shop of marvels. *Huguette Bertrand's* specialties are old tools, traditional French crafts and curios. Admirers of her shop check her window frequently for her latest finds.

The second door down is *La Maison Rustique*, an exceptional bilingual (French and English) source of cookbooks, wine books, herb books, and how-to-do-it books on everything from tapestry to organic gardening.

The *Rotisserie of the Abbey*, also at number 22, nightly recreates the atmosphere of medieval times in its 13th-century vaulted cellar. Costumed troubadours and magicians add to the flavor of "traditional" fare of flaming steaks and skewered meats and to the sounds of guitars and mandolins.

Directly across the street, at number 13, *Martine Jeannin* has a fine selection of games, French Provincial Furniture and objects of charm (18th and 19th centuries). Both she and her daughter Ivy speak fluent English.

Galérie Jacob, at number 28, deals in sober, agreeable, contemporary painting.

At the corner of the Rue Bonaparte are the several interlocking boutiques of *Madeleine Castaing*, whose reputation is international. Furniture and curios from the 19th century are her specialty. Now in her nineties and a small, tottering woman supported by canes, Madame Castaing can be spotted up and down the street, easily recognizable by her black woolen leggings and mouse-blond wig.

Across Rue Jacob at the corner is Simrane, which specializes in cushions, quilts, tablecloths, etc. of Indian-made, hand-blocked cotton.

Across Rue Bonaparte is the *Aubusson* tapestry shop featuring reproductions of well-known artists such as Folon and Toffoli. At certain times of day you can watch the weaver at work in the window of the shop reproducing a masterpiece from a work of art. Two floors of tapestry can be visited.

Let us follow Rue Bonaparte to the left (if you are on the Aubusson side of the street), or to the right (if you are back at Madame Castaing's shop). *Bulloz*, at number 21, is a photo library for works of art and history. Reproductions of masterpieces of many countries, as well as photos to be used as décor, are on sale. Photos for murals run about 300 francs ($50) a square meter.

At number 13, *l'Ile du Démon* has a good collection of ethnic jewelry and objects at reasonable prices.

Cross the street to enter the School of Beaux-Arts. Saunter straight across the cobbled square toward the far building. Eye the columns, bits of sculpture, and ceramic inlay on your way. Is this Paris? or are we in the heart of Italy? Turn left in front of the far building. Past the capitals imbedded in the walls, on the loggia to the left, see a sculpture of a wooden horse and child rider, in all innocence. Then head down to the right. If it is a good day, students will be hammering on plaster and stone in the alleyway. They are used to observers.

Now retrace your steps to the other side of the "far" building:

there are friezes and statues along the way. Is the painted bikini and bra still visible on one of them? In front of you is a flagpole donated in 1931 by grateful American students. Now wend your way to the right and once again to the right, where you should come upon "the courtyard of the mulberry tree," a convent cloister of burnt sienna, mosaic floors and memorials to the war dead, plus a statue of a *poilu*, a World War I soldier.

The School of Fine Arts was originally the Brothers of Charity Hospital. It was built in the 16th century for Marie de Médicis, when she came from Florence to marry Henri IV. She staffed it with Italian doctor- and pharmacist-priests. The hospital was removed a few years later, but it remained a convent until the French Revolution.

For a time it served as a museum for the art treasures saved from destruction during that period of revolutionary and anti-clerical fervor. In 1858 it opened as the School of Beaux-Arts.

Upon leaving the school, we shall go straight ahead down the Rue des Beaux-Arts, which itself literally is one long art gallery, showing everything from primitive to modern art in the series of shops on either side.

At number 13 is l'*Hôtel*, the very unique inn in which Oscar Wilde lived and died in 1900. The fixed-price dinner is an excellent value and the winter garden setting astounding. Stop in for just a look or a drink at the piano bar.

At *number 11* are permanent shows of artwork by Beaux-Arts students. The gallery also is tended by the students, who are ever-ready to help you acquire some of their output.

Number 5, the *Claude Bernard Gallery*, is one of the finest contemporary galleries in Paris.

At the end of the street, we shall turn left into the Rue de Seine. Set back from the street, number 10 is a well-maintained private mansion from the 17th century. A visit to the *Eolia Gallery* is a good excuse for taking a closer look at the courtyard.

A few doors down, at number 6, is the *Roger-Viollet* photo library. All the photos on display in the windows are for sale. Their stock includes reproductions of photos from all over the world, taken as far back as 1850. Prices are roughly 150 francs a print.

After several interesting art galleries, we come to the small, semicircular Honoré Champion Square and its statue of a benevolent Voltaire.

Across the way is a large square with benches, two of which represent open books. On the corner is a prized statue of the child Carolina by Marcello Tommasi (1968), and in the middle of the square are a statue and fountain dedicated to commerce and abundance. At the back end of the square is a good example of *trompe l'oeil*, lattice-work used to mask the plain sides of several buildings.

Now pass through the archway to the Seine, cross over at the light, and go up to the *Pont des Arts* footbridge. There always is something happening on the bridge—occasional vendors of post cards or drawings, a mime show, perhaps a guitar concert. The view is one of Paris's best.

Many European cities are split in two by a river of which the visitor is barely conscious. The Seine is not a divider; it is a wide thoroughfare harmoniously linking the two halves of a great city. Until the 20th century it was a very active port.

As you turn back to come off the bridge, you will be face-to-face with the dome of the *French Institute*. Enveloping arms reach out to you. This is one of the most beautiful buildings of Paris, built in the 17th century. Financed by Cardinal Mazarin and designed by the architect Le Vau, it was intended as a boarding school for sixty "sons of gentlemen" from different regions of France. Its library, built in 1643, is the oldest public library in France.

Today, the institute and its five academies sit here. The best known is the French Academy, which presides over the destiny—and the purity—of the French language. The academy is composed of forty "immortals" who meet every Thursday to continue the updating of the definitive French dictionary. The last edition appeared in 1935 and the next is scheduled for 2050. The "immortals" are self-perpetuating: upon the death of one, the others elect a successor who, ornately attired in a costly full-dress uniform with sword, must sing the praises of his predecessor; this is often an arduous task. The members are drawn essentially from literary, university, and political circles. There has been one woman academician, Marguerite Yourcenar, who was a French novelist elected to membership in 1980. She retreated to the State of Maine and died in 1988. Visits of the institute are on Saturday and Sunday at 3 P.M. Admission is 35 francs.

Now retrace your steps back to the Rue de Seine, and go through the archway. At number 17 is the *Lecomte Gallery*, with an excellent collection of prints from the 18th to 20th centuries.

Let me say here that all along the Rue de Seine are fine art galleries. The ones I have chosen to point out satisfy my tastes, which is not to say the others merit less attention. Among my favorites are the *Resch Gallery*, at number 20, containing the art of the 1920s and 1930s; the *Akka-Valmay Gallery*, number 22, for contemporary art: Kim Hai Lim's apples, Lacombe's heads and shoulders; the *Jacques de Vos Gallery*, number 34, for "art work on paper" and sculpture from the beginning of the century until now. The décor here is special, if hard to take.

If it is time for a halt, there is a popular neighborhood café, *La Palette*, on the corner of Rue Jacques Callot. A drink at *La Palette* on a summer afternoon or evening is always fun. Seat yourself outside at one of the large round tables under the trees and take a drink from the tray circulating on the arm of the lone waiter arrayed in a traditional black vest, black string tie, and long white apron.

A shop with ideas for gifts is *l'Oiseau de Feu* at number 49, overflowing with imports from Eastern Europe. They have handpainted wooden eggs from 30 to 70 francs and magnificent patterned wool shawls from 300 to 900 francs.

The *Galérie-Documents* at 53 Rue de Seine sells posters dating from the turn of the century until now. Most are lithographs; many are rare. Prices range from 50 to 2500 francs.

At number 55 is the *English Theatre*, open from Tuesday through Saturday. Performances are at 8:30 P.M. For reservations call 4326-6351. Special Wednesday and Saturday matinées for children are at 3 P.M.

Jeanne Do's unusual jewelry shop, at number 67, is a mélange of new and old. Even the new has an Art Nouveau or Art Deco look. Jeanne is an adept of Mel Brooks and Woody Allen; her English is "ve-r-r-r-y fluent."

As you approach the corner of the Rue de Buci, you can hear excitement in the air. The street vendors are hawking at one of Paris's liveliest outdoor markets. It is colorful any time, but Sunday mornings are special. There usually are a few musicians on hand. Regular noontime arrivals are an Anglo-American jazz group, a little raggedy, probably intentionally so. The market is closed between 1 and 4 P.M. as well as Sunday afternoons and Monday.

Among the interesting shops around the market are *Le Fournil de Pierre* for bread and cookies (64 Rue de Seine); *La Vieille France* for pastry (14 Rue de Buci); and *La Bonbonnière*, also for pastry, just next door.

At number 10 Rue de Buci is the most popular market *café*. Sunday mornings at a table, sidewalk-side, are ritual.

The *Charcuterie Alsacienne*, alongside the café, features stupendous cold cuts and sausage. Along with the *bakery* at number 6, these are both good stops.

Across the street is *La Grange aux fleurs*, the florist. However, just on the corner of the Rue Grégoire-du-Tours is a *flower vendor*, Monsieur Marcel, an oldtimer known to everyone in the quarter for the freshest cut flowers.

The Rue *Grégoire-de-Tours* is lined with restaurants for every taste.

Continuing on Rue de Buci, you will arrive at an intersection of five streets. Take Rue St. André des Arts, directly opposite, past the *Mazet*, a café frequented by a young guitar-playing crowd. At numbers 59 and 61 is the *Cour du Commerce*, an arcade. Turn in here.

On your left is *A la Cour de Rohan*, a tea shop as a tea shop should be. Today's entry in the guest book on the stand by the door, signed Leïla, states unequivocally: "Just like the Buckingham Palace dining room. Everything is perfect: the music, the setting, the china, the red berry pie with crème fraîche." The odor of chocolate hits you as you mount the stairs to the second floor dining room—it is absolutely devastating. Every Friday from 4 till 6 P.M., Lydia Laurent plays the harp on the landing. A la Cour de Rohan is open for lunch and for tea til 7:30 P.M. except Sunday lunch and Monday. Special jams made from 18th-century recipes are on sale for 28 and 37 francs.

Continue down the passageway, past the bookbinder's and past the ribbon shop. There you have the back entrance to the *Procope Café*, founded in 1686 and just completely overhauled, as well as the back way into the *Pub St. Germain*, famous for its 450 brands of beer. The Procope was one of the very first cafés to serve the "new" brew of yore: coffee.

Turn left opposite the entrance to the Procope and go into the *Cour de Rohan*. As soon as you pass the gate, you will hear the birds. Then you will see the cobblestones and the ivy pots. Look up at the balconies and terraces. Go through to the second court. There is an old well in a corner. Some very lucky people actually live here, in what is left of a 15th-century mansion. It was in this courtyard, incidentally, that Dr. Guillotin did the trial runs on his famous machine—on sheep!

To leave the Cour de Rohan, you can continue on. At the end of the little street, you will find Boulevard St. Germain and just to the right the Odéon métro stop.

You also can turn back and left in the arcade. You will pass the *Bistro Rive Gauche*, an authentic 1900s bistro with continuous service. Then out to Boulevard St. Germain. Across the street is the Odéon métro stop, and to your right on the boulevard, two short blocks away, the St. Germain-des-Près stop.

There are several wonderful cafés along here: *La Rhumerie Martiniquaise*, a sort of theatre box from which to watch the world go by. And, of course, there are *Les Deux Magots*, across from the church, and *Le Flore*, just beyond.

Along the way

Restaurants
Le Bélier-L'Hôtel
Calvet
L'Echaudé St. Germain
Guenmaï (vegetarian)
Katyouschka
Lipp
Naka
Le Petit St. Benoît
Le Procope
Restaurant des Arts
Rotisserie de l'Abbaye
Vagenende

Hotels
L'Hôtel
Hôtel d'Angleterre
Hôtel des Marronniers
Latitudes St. Germain
Madison Hotel
Le Relais Saint Germain
La Villa

Tea, Snacks, Ice Cream, Pastry
A la Cour de Rohan
Baskin-Robbins (ice cream)
La Bonbonnière (pastry)
Charcuterie Alsacienne (takeout)
Dalloyeau
Le Fournil de Pierre (bread and pastry)
Gérard Mulot (pastry, chocolate)
Le Glacier Moderne (ice cream)
L'Heure Gourmande
La Vieille France (pastry)

Beer, Wine Bars, Cafés
Le Chai de l'Abbaye
Les Deux Magots
L'Entr'acte
Le Flore
Le Mazet
La Palette
Pub St. Germain
La Rhumerie Martiniquaise

CHAPTER 5

The Elegance and Charm of the Marais

Itinerary 1

The *Marais* or marshes were originally swampland and forest, traversed by an affluent of the Seine. In the 7th century kings and noblemen would leave their island city on the river to come here to hunt. After drainage in the 13th century, wheat fields, kitchen gardens, vineyards, and windmills covered the area. Monasteries and churches grew up among them. Weavers and drapers set up shop near the Seine. Then wealthy families built "country" estates in the meadows. Coining and money lending were the sources of wealth of many of these gentle folk, among whose indebted clients were kings of France.

In the 14th century the drapers and weavers pushed their

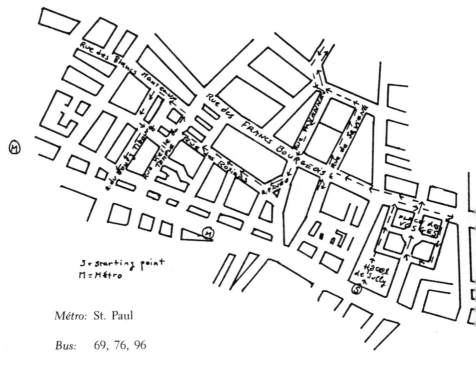

J = starting point
M = Métro

Métro: St. Paul

Bus: 69, 76, 96

Hôtel de Sully: 62 Rue St. Antoine
                            9 A.M.–6 P.M. weekdays
                            10 A.M.–6 P.M. Saturdays and Sundays

Victor Hugo House: 6 Place des Vosges
                            10 A.M. 5:40 P.M. Closed Mondays and holidays.

Carnavalet Museum: 23 Rue de Sévigné
                            10 A.M.–5:40 P.M. Closed Mondays and holidays.

Picasso Museum: 5 Rue de Thorigny
                            10 A.M.–5:15 P.M. 10 A.M.–10 P.M. Wednesdays.
                            Closed Tuesdays.

Key and Lock Museum: 1 Rue de la Perle
                            10 A.M.–12 noon and 2 P.M.–5 P.M. Closed Sundays,
                            Mondays, August, and last week of December.

Time: All day

trades farther north, taking over any vacant land available. At the end of the century, Charles V walled Paris, bringing the Marais within the city limits. The king himself settled here, only too happy to quit an overcrowded and increasingly dangerous Ile de la Cité. His court and notables followed suit; they built grand mansions, so many chateaux in an urban setting. The Rue St. Antoine, which passed through the quarter, was the main thoroughfare out of the city to the east. It was also a high road, wide enough for jousting, games, processions, and ceremonies, which were the amusement of court and kings. This role was taken over by the Place des Vosges at the beginning of the 17th century.

In the 18th century nobility abandoned the Marais for the newly fashionable Faubourgs St. Germain and St. Honoré to the west. Merchants and craftsmen took over the mansions. They became industrial premises; they were split into innumerable rooms, offices, and apartments. Dilapidated and desecrated, they fell to rack and ruin. Many were torn down by speculators.

It was only in the early 1960s that citizens' committees for the defence of the Marais were founded. In 1962, under a law introduced by writer André Malraux, the quarter became the largest "protected" district in France. This measure ensures the perpetuity of the historic monuments and landmarks and guarantees their maintenance and embellishment. With renovation, however, the working-class character of the quarter is being altered. Workers, craftsmen, and ethnic minorities are giving way to a more sophisticated population.

We shall begin our tour of the Marais at 62 Rue St. Antoine (métro St. Paul) at the Hôtel de Sully.

Hôtel de Sully

Built in 1624, this Renaissance chateau was designed by Jean Androuet de Cerceau. The first courtyard is truly lovely; the figures representing the elements and the seasons are fleshy and sensual, the sphinx guards full-breasted. Go through to the orangery. The entrance to the temporary exhibits is to your left. At the end of the garden is a gift shop. In addition to posters, magazines, and books, for 7 francs you can buy post cards with cutouts that become models of Parisian monuments: Sainte Chapelle, Hôtel de Sully, Place des Vosges, St. Germain des Près, a métro entrance.

Go out the back way, at the far right-hand corner, and enter the Place des Vosges.

Place des Vosges

This is Paris's very first square, commissioned in 1605 by Henri IV. The king was an amateur architect and an early urban renewal bug. His project, erected on the grounds of a huge horse market, was to be the elegant center of the city, "in like symmetry," and inhabited on the south side by the king himself. Directly opposite there would be a Milanese silk factory. The remaining space was parcelled out and given free to private owners, provided they maintained the identical style.

The plan was for brick and stone. Unfortunately, bricklayers were a rarity and bricks at a premium. So the majority of the facades were simply wood frames, plastered over and painted to resemble bricks and mortar. Many of today's renovators have laid real brick fronts at great expense.

The southern royal pavilion was too restricted a space for a king, and neither Henri IV nor his successors ever lived in it. The silk factory quickly closed its doors. A matching pavilion for the queen was erected in its place. The beautiful people of that age did settle here and in the quarter generally.

The square itself became the stage for all major public events: tournaments, pageantry, receptions of foreign dignitaries, equestrian ballets, parades, fireworks, and duels. Seventeenth-century high society was lavish, ceremonious, and extravagant. The lovely and clever resident ladies, in addition to a fondness for duels under their balconies, invented the *ruelles*, forerunners of the *salons* of the 18th century. The former were gatherings of socially accomplished wits that took place in the bedroom alcoves of the hostesses!

The square was initially called *Place Royale*. During the French Revolution it became *Place de l'Indivisibilité*, in honor of the Republic, one and indivisible. Finally, it was called the *Place des Vosges* in deference to the region of France that first paid its taxes.

The trees make it difficult to take in the entire square at a glance, and critics would prefer lower-profiled greenery or just grass as it was originally. Should you visit Victor Hugo's home at number 6, you will have an overall view. The statue in the middle of the square is of Louis XIII, who inaugurated it with the celebration of his marriage to Anne of Austria. His father, Henri IV, was assassinated shortly before its completion. On his way through the narrow streets of the quarter in an open carriage for his daily visit to the construction site, he was stabbed to death.

If you begin the tour of the square on the left side, start with number 9, the *Hôtel de Chaulnes*. It is one of the authentic brick facades and has been beautifully restored. Ring the gallery's bell and go into the courtyards where you will find a miniature cobblestone village. *L'Ambroisie*, at the same address, is a three-hat restaurant according to the Gault Millau rating; elegant and refined, the food is delicious and expensive.

Popy Moreni, at number 13, is a swank designer. Down at the corner, at number 19, is *Ma Bourgogne*, home to bistro food at moderate prices.

Musicians and artists often set up to play and sell on the corner at *number 21*. Go into the courtyard. There are a garden and flowers, a small leather factory, and what are certainly charming apartments. The *antique shop*, which spreads out under the arcades, sells a little bit of everything and is not too expensive.

At number 28 is the *Pavillon de la Reine*. Through the glass doors is an attractive new luxury hotel of the same name. At number 26 is an excellent Japanese art dealer, *Janette Ostier*. Next door, *Annamel* specializes in African art. The shop at *number 24* has an exceptional doorway.

Before turning right into the east side of the square, take a look at number 6 Rue du Pas-de-la-Mule. The *Boucherie* is a serious

shop for old musical instruments and their repair. It was originally a butcher's shop, as you will see from the meat hooks and
tiling.

Back to the Place des Vosges. The *Melrose Restaurant*, at
number 18, serves brunch: 100 francs for salmon and champagne; 60 francs for a big breakfast. *Nectarine*, next door, is less
expensive. *Number 16*, you will note, has a real balcony.
Number 14 has one as well. On this side of the building is a
synagogue for eastern European Jews; if you enter from the back
side, Rue des Tournelles, you will be in the oriental half of the
synagogue, the domain of the Sephardic Jews, mainly from
North Africa. The doors often are closed. When they are not,
visitors are welcome.

At number 10 is *Eurydice*, small, pleasant restaurant for cakes
and snacks.

The *Victor Hugo House* at number 6 was the writer's home
from 1832 to 1848 before he left France and went into exile on
the Channel isle of Guernsey. There is a door in the back
through which Hugo would slip out to visit his mistresses. Start
your visit from the top staircase.

Leave the Place des Vosges from the northwest corner, diago-
nally across the square from Hugo's house, and enter the *Rue des
Francs Bourgeois*, named for penniless gentry exempt from pay-
ing their taxes: free bourgeois. At number 23, *Inna Kobja* has
interesting ethnic-inspired women's wear.

At the Rue de Sévigné, take a quick dip left into number 32 to
visit *Jean-Pierre Besenval's* shop of painted furniture from Alsace.
His shop is open every day except Monday from noon to 7 P.M.

Backtrack now, on to the corner of the Rue de Sévigné, near
the Rue des Francs Bourgeois, to the Carnavalet Museum.

Carnavalet Museum

The museum is devoted to the history of Paris; the building
itself is part of that history. The original Renaissance structure
dates from 1544, another was added by architect François Man-

sart in the 17th century. It was restored by Baltard in the 19th century. In 1989, the City of Paris annexed the Hôtel Le Peletier de Saint-Fargeau next door and redecorated the two chateaux.

The Marquise de Sévigné, the famous author of letters who vividly depicted life in 17th-century France, lived at the Hôtel Carnavalet from 1677 to 1696. The lion guards and statues of the seasons are by Jean Goujon.

In this part of the museum are collections covering the period up to 1789; in the Le Peletier half are collections from the French Revolution to the present day.

There is a certain thrill in viewing Paris through time, in recognizing this street, that square, the river, and the bridges. One of the most moving paintings of Paris I have ever seen, Albert Marquet's *Notre Dame in the Snow* (1910), is here.

There are so many musts at Carnavalet: among the canvases are Marcel Gromaire's *Place Blanche*; Pierre Sicart's *Le Pigall's in the 20s*; Paul Signac's *Pont des Arts*; Stanislas Lépine's *Pont des Arts*; and the last scene from *Panorama of the Century* by Henri Gervex and Alfred Stevens for the Universal Exhibition of 1889, at which President Sadi Carnot inaugurated the centennial of the Revolution.

Also note Siebe Ten Cate's *The Carrousel Quadrangle and the Ruins of the Tuileries*, Luigi Noir's *Effect of Snow, at Night*, Alfred Smith's *End of the Races at Auteuil*, *Cocteau* by Foujita, and *Natalie Barney* by her friend Romaine Brooks.

The cradle of Napoleon III is a stunner. However, nothing is more evocative of a period—the turn of the century—than Georges Fouquet's jewelry shop conceived by Alphonse Mucha: it is animal, vegetable, and mineral ravishment. And view the extravagance of José Maria Sert's ballroom for the Wendel manor house.

Visiting Marcel Proust's bedroom, the very bed in which he wrote *Remembrance of Things Past*, is stirring. Imagine Anna de Nouailles in her so-feminine alcove, receiving, in the fashion of 17th-century ladies.

In another vein are the paintings of the Declaration of Human

Rights and the beautiful marquetterie armoire as well as the gouache cut-outs by Le Sueur depicting the story of the revolution. Do not forget to view, in certain rooms, the heavy brocade tapestries, the crystal chandeliers, and the marble floors. The courtyards and gardens also warrant a visit.

Across the street from the museum, at number 44, is the small art gallery of *Luc Chomel*. Chomel exhibits his own work; the most recent are joyful, bright, abstract gouaches. They start at about 2500 francs ($400) framed. He also organizes shows of good, contemporary French artists.

Next door, number 46, *La Maison des Bonbons*, is the candy shop of our memory. Anne Dalloz, the proprietor, will make you most welcome.

There is a nice park on the corner of Rue de Sévigné and Rue du Parc Royal. Behind the park is a row of 17th-century buildings. Number 8, the former *Hôtel Duret de Chevry*, has been bought by the St. Raphaël aperitif people. The gates usually are open and you can wander into the courtyards.

Turn right at the Rue de Thorigny. Number 5 is the *Hôtel Salé* or *Picasso Museum*. This chateau was built in the 17th century by a man whose money derived from the salt tax. The local populace nicknamed his mansion the "Salty House"; the name has stuck. This is a very complete collection of Picasso's works, from 1901 to 1975. A penetrating self-portrait dates from 1908. The very beginnings of cubism, in ochre and earth colors, are here, as are *Fernande*, sculpted in 1909, and *Olga* in black (1917). *The Reading of a Letter* (1921) is moving. Note the marvelous *Village Dance* of 1922, he in a blue suit, she in an orange beret, and *Two Women Running on the Beach* (1922). Sculptures of the 1930s: whittled wood of elongated bodies, the bronze *Lady in the Leaves*, the *Nanny-goat* with pottery udders, the *Woman Reading*, the long-tailed *Guenon*, and the *Crane* are particularly evocative of Picasso's feeling and humor. The superb portraits of *Dora Mear* from 1937 grace the walls. A *Pregnant Woman* in bronze from the 1950s and ceramics also are featured.

Turn right when you leave the museum; you will run smack

into the *Key and Lock Museum*. This was the home, designed for himself, of Libéral Bruant, architect of the Invalides.

Facing the Key and Lock Museum, go left, take your second right, Rue Payenne. *Number 13* is an ivy-covered country manor house with a tree in the corner and a lovely staircase and ramp. At number 11, the *Swedish Cultural Center* organizes regular art exhibits. At the corner of the Rue des Francs Bourgeois, number 20 is a comfortable tea and gift shop named *Marais Plus*.

Continue on the Rue Payenne, which changes its name to Rue Pavée. On your left is the 16th-century *Hôtel de Lamoignan* with its outside watchtower. It is now the seat of the Paris Historical Library.

Take your first right onto Rue des Rosiers. You have just entered the Jewish Quarter.

Jewish Quarter

This quarter has known many ins and outs. Jews were expelled from the city in 1182, were recalled in 1198, and expelled again in 1306. In those days Rue Ferdinand Duval was named Rue de la Vieille Juiverie (Street of the Old Jewry). Banishment from Paris lasted officially until the French Revolution (1789). Actually, a first small community of Sephardic Jews from Portugal and Avignon appeared on the Left Bank during the 17th century. On the eve of the Revolution, they numbered 500.

During the 19th century Jewish families settled around Place St. Paul, then called Place des Juifs (Jews Place). They arrived from eastern France in 1870, from Russia and Poland at the turn of the century, and from Germany during the rise of Hitler. More recently, in the 1950s and 1960s, Sephardic Jews from North Africa settled in Paris when Tunisia, Morocco, and Algeria won their independence from France, with whom they had sided.

Number 3, *Le Loir dans la Théière* (Dormouse in the Teapot) is another comfortable tea shop.

Have you ever experienced an Oriental steam bath? This is

your chance—the *Hammam Saint-Paul* at number 4 is open from 10 A.M. to 8 P.M. Women go on Wednesdays and Fridays; men on Thursdays and Saturdays. For 90 francs you are supplied with sarong, robe, and sandals.

At number 7 is *Jo Goldenberg's* high temple of eastern European specialties. This delicatessen and restaurant has moderate prices. All up and down Rue des Rosiers are vendors of *fellafel* and other Middle-Eastern dishes. Regular fellafel is 15 francs; super is 20 francs.

Number 27 has been a *pastry shop and bakery* for 125 years. It now is run by Sacha Finkelsztajn and specializes in Central European breads and sweets: homantash, strudel, babka, honig lekel—all too good to be true.

Chez Daisy, at number 54, is a good sit-down cafeteria for Oriental hommus, fellafel, and thina.

At the end of the street is Rue Vieille du Temple. On the left-hand corner, try *The Pacific and East Company–British Colonies* for a real English breakfast on Sundays and other days from 11 A.M. to 5 P.M.

Across the way, at number 47, is the *Hôtel Amelot de Bisseuil,* built in the 17th century. Playwright Pierre Augustin Caron de Beaumarchais (the *Barber of Seville* and the *Marriage of Figaro*) lived here. In 1776 he founded the House of Rodriguez-Hortalez and Co. as a front for the collection of funds from the French and Spanish governments; they were used to buy arms for the American colonies during the Revolutionary War. Note the decorated doorway. If open, you can visit the courtyards. The second one contains a sundial and bas-relief of Remus and Romulus.

Take your first left on Rue des Blancs Manteaux and then the second left onto *Rue Aubriot,* a charming little street of wonderful old houses and doorways. At number 3 ring the bell and take a glance at the storybook courtyard. At number 4 look up at the mascaron (or head) above the doorway.

At the end of the street, turn left a few yards and right into the Rue Bourg-Tibourg. *Mariage Frères,* on your left, is the oldest tea merchant in Paris, with 300 varieties of teas. Expensive tea and cakes are served in the pretty back room.

Across the way, at number 31, is one of the rare *Greek restaurants* on this side of the Seine. The food is good and moderately priced, the décor attractive. In the window is a picture of the owner, George, with Robert Mitchum and his wife taken in 1986. According to George, two bottles of claret, one of burgundy, one of Dom Perignon, and much Armagnac bit the dust before the evening was out.

At *number 14*, look up and see the edge of the woods on the rooftop. *Number 12* is *Le Coude Fou*, one of the top wine bars of the city. *Number 8* is a sweet-smelling scent, porcelain and picture frame shop.

Across the little square and a few blocks to your right is the Hôtel de Ville métro stop.

Along the way

Restaurants
L'Ambroisie
Coconnas
Esther Street
La Guirlande de Julie
Jo Goldenberg
Piccolo Théatre
Au Tibourg

Tea, Snacks, Ice Cream, Pastry
Chez Daisy
Chez Marianne
Eurydice
Finkelsztajn (pastry)
Galérie Gourmande
Le Loir dans la Théière

La Maison des Bonbons (candy)
Marais Plus
Mariage Frères
The Pacific and East Company
Le Petit Salé (pastry)

Beer, Wine Bars, Cafés
Le Coude Fou
La Tartine
Verre à Soif

Hotels
Hôtel des Chevaliers
Hôtel de Sévigné
Grand Hôtel Jeanne d'Arc
Pavillon de la Reine

Itinerary 2

The *Saint Gervais-Saint Protais Church*, at the beginning of Rue François Miron, is a grand 16th-century Gothic church that is practically invisible behind its facade. The facade, added in the early 17th century, is Renaissance in style. In medieval times Parisians gathered regularly out front under the elm. It was there that justice was meted out.

Inside are wonderful, flamboyant Gothic arches and pillars, good paintings, and stained glass. The oldest organ in Paris, dating from 1601, was played continuously by members of the Couperin family from 1656 to 1826. Perhaps you will be lucky enough to hear it played now.

Go out the back door of the church situated to the left of the nave; go right in the Rue des Barres. You will pass in front of a timber-framed edifice, once a *charnal house* and now a student dormitory and hotel. At number 6 is the *Ebouillanté* tearoom and luncheonette. The atmosphere is relaxed and friendly. Try a Tunisian *brik* and gaze at the buttress heights of St. Gervais.

On leaving here go down the steps and to your left. Then go left into the Rue du Pont Louis-Philippe. There are several fantastic paper shops in this street. *Melodie's Graphiques* carries Florentine imports of bookbinder's themes and flowers and birds (number 10); *Calligrane*, two shops at 4 and 6, has Italian imports; *Paper +* (number 9), also two shops, sells, in addition to beautiful writing papers, sheets of recycled paper of many nuances.

An interesting photo gallery, *Agathe Gaillard* at number 2, has some of the best for sale: Cartier-Bresson, Marc Riboud, and Robert Doisneau.

Opera

Place de la
BASTILLE

Henri IV

BOULEVARD

RUE SAINT-ANTOINE

Rue St-Antoine

R. CHARLES

R. ROUSSONNIER

MIRON

Rue François

RUE de RIVOLI

R. du Jouy

CITY HALL

Métro: St. Paul, Pont Marie, Hôtel de Ville

Bus: 67, 69, 76, 96

Time: Half day

S = starting point
M = métro

There is a pretty Japanese shop with interesting ideas for gifts at number 11.

Le Grenier sur l'Eau at number 14 is charming. The dinner menu is 126 francs. The price also is right at *Le Gournaudin*, number 18. *La Perla* at the corner of Rue François Miron, with Mexican specialties, is a neighborhood hangout. Chile con carne is 36 francs, caesar salad 19, and margaritas 40.

Turn right on the Rue François Miron. There is a clever *hat shop* at number 21, owned by designer Miyoko Gushiken.

The *Hôtel de Beauvais* (number 68), designed by Lepautre, was once an elegant mansion. Mozart spent the winter here in 1763–1764 when he was eight years old. It is now unsightly and awaits restoration. We should note in passing that this site was offered to de Beauvais in 1654 by an ever-grateful royal family. His wife, Catherine, age forty, was lady-in-waiting and closest confidante to Anne of Austria. The duty of divesting Louis XIV, aged 16, of his virginity, fell to Catherine.

Backtrack a few doors and turn left into the Rue de Jouy. At number 7 is a mansion designed in the 17th century by Le Vau. It is now the seat of the *Administrative Court of Paris*.

Continue into the Rue Charlemagne; just to the right in the Rue Fauconnier is a superb *town house*.

At the end of Rue Fauconnier, one of the two authentic medieval castles left in Paris stands: *l'Hôtel de Sens*, now a library for the Art Deco period, was built in 1475. At the end of the 16th century, it was a gathering place for the clergy in support of the Catholic League. The league gained its infamy from the lead it took in the massacre, in one night, of thousands of Protestants. Henri IV, a Protestant, laid seige to Paris and entered the city victorious in 1594 to become king of France. Monsignor de Pellevé literally died of apoplexy within the castle walls on hearing that a Te Deum was being sung at Notre Dame in honor of the new king.

Take the Rue de l'Avé-Maria to the Rue des Jardins St. Paul. Between this street and the next is the *St. Paul market* of antiques cum flea market, which winds in and around the two streets.

At the top of the Rue des Jardins St. Paul, there are a lovely *fountain of cherubs* and a tastefully renovated building to the right. Go down the Rue St. Paul toward the Seine to the Rue Charles V on the left. Number 14, *L'Excuse*, is an attractive and not expensive restaurant. The impressive doorway of number 12 was the entrance to the residence of a famous poisoner of members of court, the *Marquise de Brinvilliers*. At number 10 is the *English Institute* of the University of Paris, another wonderful courtyard. Across the street at number 13 is a friendly English book store, the *Albion*.

At the end of the street, turn left into the Rue du Petit Musc. At the corner with the Rue St. Antoine is the *Hôtel de Mayenne*, now being restored.

Take Rue St. Antoine to the right until you reach the Bastille.

The Bastille

The prison-fortress is no longer. On July 14, 1789, the Bastille was seized by the people of Paris and dismantled stone by stone the following day. Some stones became road marks, others were sculpted and sold as souvenirs of the French Revolution. Among the Bastille's famous prisoners were the *Man in the Iron Mask*, Voltaire, and the Marquis de Sade. The bronze column in the middle of the square, topped by a statue representing liberty, is dedicated to the memory of the Parisians killed during the popular uprisings of 1830 and 1848.

The square is the home of the very new *Popular Opera*, which features two theatres, one with 2700 seats and a moveable orchestra pit; the other is completely transformable. The opera also has a 500-seat amphitheatre.

Along the way

Restaurants
Bofinger
Courrier Sud

L'Excuse
Le Gournaudin
Le Grenier sur l'Eau
La Perla

Tea, Snacks, Ice Cream, Pastry
L'Ebouillanté

Hotels
Le Fauconnier
Hôtel des Célestins
Hôtel de Fourcy
Hôtel Maubuisson
Hôtel du 7ème Art

Itinerary 3

Our starting point today is in the Rue des Francs Bourgeois at the corner of the Rue Payenne or Rue Pavée.

The *Hôtel d'Albret* at number 31 has been totally renovated to house the Cultural Affairs Division of the City of Paris. Among its numerous claims to renown is the meeting here of Madame de Montespan and the young widow Scarron, whom the former engaged as governess to her eight illegitimate children by Louis XIV. Four years later, the children had been recognized officially and the widow Scarron had become a member of the monarch's court. Then, in 1684, as Madame de Maintenon, she secretly married the king! Prior to remodeling, the Hôtel d'Albret was a factory for lighting fixtures.

At number 41 Rue des Francs Bourgeois is the *Kwok On Museum* of Asian treasures. Mr. Kwok On of Hong Kong was a rabid collector of artifacts of the Chinese opera. His and other fascinating pieces evoking Asian theatre in general are on permanent exhibit here.

Next door, at number 43, is the tearoom *Les enfants gâtés*. It features a relaxed brunch on Saturday and Sunday and is open noon until 7 P.M. every day.

The *Dômarais* at 53 bis presents nouvelle cuisine in an old domed chapel. It is closed Saturday, Sunday, and Monday at lunchtime.

Just next door is the *Municipal Pawnbroker's Office*, located on the site of a former convent. Sales of unclaimed objects, advertised at the entrance, are held regularly.

The *Soubise Palace*, number 60, opens onto an elegant courtyard designed on the site of a former riding academy. In the 16th

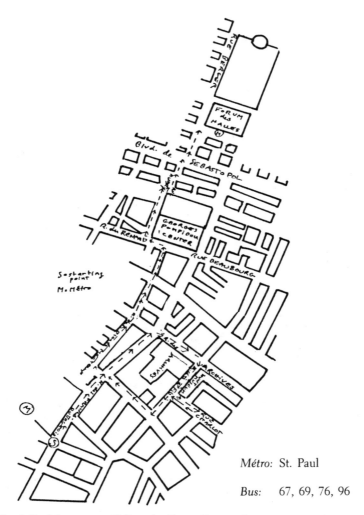

Métro: St. Paul

Bus: 67, 69, 76, 96

Kwok On Museum:	41 Rue des Francs Bourgeois 10 A.M.–5:30 P.M. Closed Sundays and Mondays.
Museum of the Hunt and of Nature:	60 Rue des Archives 10 A.M.–12:30 P.M. and 1:30 P.M.–5:30 P.M. Closed Tuesdays and holidays.
Georges Pompidou Center:	120 Rue St. Martin 12 noon–10 P.M. weekdays; 10 A.M.–10 P.M. Saturdays and Sundays. Closed Tuesdays.
Time:	All day

century it was the residence of "Scarface," the Duke of Guise, backer of the Catholic League who organized the St. Bartholomew massacre of the city's Protestants.

In 1697 the palace was purchased by the Princess of Soubise with the generous assistance of Louis XIV, her royal lover. The mansion then was transformed considerably and embellished.

In 1808 the National Archives took over and assembled the official papers of the French Empire here. Today, as the Museum of French History, there are six billion documents on file in this building and in a half dozen other noble residences surrounding the palace. Among the documents is the report of the French police officer who accompanied Thomas Paine on the day of his arrest (Doc F7 4774 64). Paine was taken into custody at dawn on December 18, 1793, by two officers who had orders to confiscate any dangerous manuscripts. His most important document, *The Rights of Man*, was just next door. In order to gain time, recover the document, and put it into safe hands, Paine convinced his captors that he needed breakfast. He invited them to join him. The breakfast lasted three hours and included several bottles of good wine. He then persuaded the officers to let him stop by the Rue Jacob to say good-bye to a friend. He slipped the famous document to the latter while the officers had their backs turned.

Other documents at the archives include Marie Antoinette's last letter before going to the scaffold, Louis XVI's diary, and his will as well as Napoleon's.

Turn right on Rue des Archives. At number 60 is the *Hôtel de Guénégaud*, which has become the *Museum of the Hunt and of Nature* thanks to the efforts and contributions of a modern-day hunt enthusiast. Built by the architect Mansart in 1648, it is a jewel. Whatever your opinion of hunting, it is worth the visit, if only for Monet's painting *The battue hunt*. On show is a rare collection of hunting rifles and paraphernalia. Stuffed animals from Alaska include a giant brown bear, a polar bear, and a caribou. The first semi-automatic Winchesters are on display, as well as a copy of Old Betsy, Davy Crockett's .41 caliber rifle. See the bill for Napoleon's hunting costume from Monsieur Bastide.

From the upstairs window you will discover a French formal garden.

On leaving the museum, take the Rue des 4 Fils. In the first street on your left, 11 rue Charlot, is *Indiens d'Amérique*, a book shop devoted to material on North and South American Indians. You'll get a very friendly welcome.

Go back to Rue des 4 Fils, turn left and then right at the Rue du Vieille-du-Temple. At number 87 is the *Hôtel de Rohan*. It shares the gardens of the Soubise Palace. The stables on the right are crowned by the magnificent *Horses of the Sun* by Le Lorrain.

Continue down the street until you reach the Rue des Blancs Manteaux; then turn right. You will arrive, face on, at the Georges Pompidou Center.

Georges Pompidou Center

The center has been the object of both violent attack and passionate defense; Parisians are definitely not indifferent to the modern "inside-out" structure designed by architects Renzo Piano and Richard Rogers. No one, however, can dispute the fact that the multifaceted center, free of the weight of history, receives through its doors not only museum habitués but curious, first-time museumgoers. Its success has outweighed expectations by far: it attracts six million visitors a year.

Inaugurated in 1977, the center comprises the Modern Art Museum, a public library, a children's library and workshop, the Center for Industrial Creation, and all sorts of distinctive temporary exhibits.

But as you will quickly see, not all activity is within the center. The famous slanting esplanade is invaded daily by myriad groups of musicians, dancers, fortune tellers, jugglers, and poets, among others. There is a wonderful view of Paris from the top floor.

You will leave the esplanade through the Rue Aubry-le-Boucher, crossing Boulevard Sébastopol and continuing on Rue Berger to the Halles.

The Halles

For those of you who never knew the old Paris central market that stood on this terrain until 1969, the large mall will be just another modern glass structure, more or less appealing. For the rest of us, the Halles is a wound on our nostalgic past. It was Paris's digestive tract: a horn-of-plenty, wholesale food supplier to every store, restaurant, canteen of the city, as well as a retail outlet for one and all. It was absolutely unique—high in color and personality, couched under Baltard's steel umbrella roofs. The restaurants around the Halles—some of which still exist— catered to the late night crowd of theatre and party goers just as the drivers and market people were downing the early day's first coffee or glass of red.

The Halles today is a luxury mall as well as a hangout for a young crowd from the suburbs. Since it is a major métro exchange point between east-west and north-south, there is much traffic.

Along the way

Restaurants
Les Bourgeoises
Au Cochon d'Or des Halles
Dômarais
L'Escargot Montorgueil
La Fermette du Sud-Ouest
Gros Minet
Joe Allen
Le Louchebem
Pharamond
Au Pied de Cochon

Tea, Snacks, Ice Cream, Pastry
Les Enfants Gâtés
Les Mille-Feuilles

CHAPTER 6

The Luxembourg Gardens on a Sunday Morning or at Any Other Time

The Luxembourg Gardens is one of the most satisfying ambles in Paris. It is a place of beauty, variety, peace, and even participation. One actually can become an actor in a Renoir, a Dufy or a Seurat painting. Picture it now in your mind's eye: ladies wheeling baby carriages, small children with balloons on strings, sailboats whisking across the pool, athletic young men and women at tennis or on the run, groups of happy loungers and strollers.

In the background are great chestnut trees trimmed square, giant flower pots overflowing with yellow and orange chrysanthemums in October and yellow and white nasturtiums in

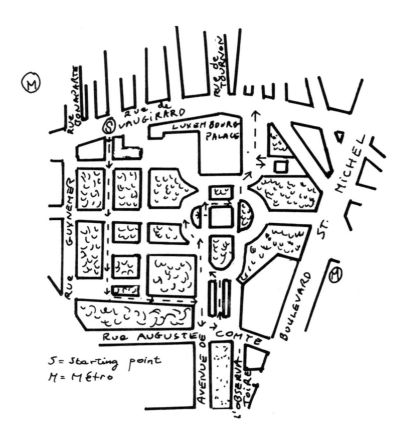

Métro: St. Sulpice, Luxembourg, Notre-Dame des Champs

Bus: 21, 27, 38, 58, 82, 84, 85, 89

Time: Half day

July. Beds of bright fuchsia-colored tulips, others of purple pansies and pink begonias are planted when the first leaves appear in mid-April. Outsize peonies glorify the gardens in early May. Orange trees blossom and bear fruit, pots of odorous pink petunias surround Marie de Médicis's pool and fountain in midsummer.

Throughout the park there is stately statuary: those of the *grandes dames* of France, spaced on the terraces above the pool, overlook the formal lawns and flower beds *à la française*. On a dewy morning the grassy patches are dotted with sea gulls having made the long wing from the English Channel over 100 miles away.

The gardens are not on the tourist track, but they are nonetheless central to the existence of thousands of Parisians.

✻   ✻   ✻

There are many entrances to the Luxembourg Gardens. All are valid. The one I am most used to and perhaps most fond of is the one on Rue de Vaugirard to the right of the museum (as you face it). The museum organizes interesting temporary shows.

On your right, past the trinket vendor's stall and the big floppy chestnut tree, is a spectacular statue of a male figure reclining on a stone embankment and framed in veritable tree foliage, an ideal companion for a photo portrait.

On your left is the entrance to the exhibition hall where occasional shows are organized, including the local garden club's floral arrangements and prize fruit shows in the fall.

Continuing down the pathway from the gate, on your left is a large, open kiosk where the chess, domino, and card players gather in the afternoon. The stakes are not high and they will let you in if you are game.

Just behind here is a hedge-enclosed area of sandpits and benches for very small children and their moms. Along the wall of the exhibition hall, on your left, loll the sun seekers of a good day, their feet up, books overturned in their laps.

Back to our pathway. Up ahead are four tennis courts open to the public. (There are six in all in the gardens.) The price is roughly two dollars for a half-hour. To play, sign up at the first little green garden house on the left-hand side of our same pathway (after the open playing field). Names are called every half-hour. I will not even attempt to enumerate the exceptions to this simple system: sign up, wait your turn, pay and play for one half-hour at a go. Don't be discouraged, you *can* play. Avoid weekends, however.

On every first and third Sunday of the month at 10 A.M., the field is laid out for amateurs of *jeu de paume*, the ancestor of tennis as it surfaced in the French monasteries of the 13th century. Played with a very long racquet with a small head and a ball composed of many layers of cloth sewn together in a compact, roundish shape, the game so overwrought French priests and monks that in 1245 the Archbishop of Rouen forbade the clergy to continue playing it. At about the same time, royalty adopted it. It seems that King Louis X was so weakened by a marathon match at the Vincennes Palace on the outskirts of Paris that he contracted pneumonia and died!

Along our pathway on the right are romantic spaces of lawn, trees, flowers, forsythia and other shrubbery, benches, gravel walks and statues, including a model of the Statue of Liberty by Bartholdi.

Beyond the green tennis house is a large area for small children. There are afternoon puppet shows at 2:30 and 3:30 Wednesday, Saturday, and Sunday afternoons; sandpits, swings, seesaws, a merry-go-round, mazes, and obstacle courses. There also are pony, donkey, and cart rides for the children in front of the tennis courts.

As we continue on our path, we run straight into the pétanque-bowls courts. Afficionados—all men, generally from the South of France—can be found on the three large courts and two smaller ones in the afternoon.

On your right a little further on is a tiled pavilion housing the Association of Auditors of the Luxembourg Courses. They organize regular sessions on trees, plants, mushrooms, floral art, gardening, and beekeeping. Be careful. A little behind you, in the shaded area, are twenty active hives.

Pick up our path again. As it bears left, you will discover a small, experimental orchard filled with more than three hundred varieties of apple and pear trees, most of which are espaliered, and which bear such evocative names as the *Belle of Berry*, *Superfine Butter*, *Winter Royal*, and *American Beauty*. I can only wish you the delight of being in Paris at the end of April or beginning of May when they are all in pink and white bloom.

As we continue onward, lovely tall trees, including some California sequoias, colorful flower beds, and lawn in the English fashion stretch gently downhill.

At last we come to a large rectangular open area of grass. To our right are the sedate buildings along the Avenue de l'Observatoire leading to the domed observatory, the oldest astronomical establishment of its kind, cornerstoned on the first day of summer 1667. The Meridian of Paris runs through the center of the building. Although Greenwich was chosen over Paris as the reference mean, the Observatory does house the International Time Bureau, which sets universal time from clocks installed in cellars 92 feet below ground, maintained at a constant temperature of 53° Fahrenheit (11.86° Centigrade). For the sake of precision, we note that the Paris Meridian is 2°20′14″ East of Greenwich.

On Sunday mornings at 11, calisthenics enthusiasts fall in behind several instructors between the green plots here at the south end of the gardens. Each participant holds high a balancing rod.

Now let's turn left and follow the lawns in the direction of the Senate building. We will be approaching the pool with fountain. Stay on the upper terrace and skirt the balustrade to the left. If you have made your Luxembourg visit on a Sunday morning, you will first encounter a group of Spanish gentlemen who ritually gather here after church. You will recognize them as they alone in all the gardens will be wearing brimmed hats, two-piece suits, and ties.

Just beyond them are numerous, small groups of reverent amateurs of *tai chi* and *tai chi chuan*, the Chinese arts of corporal harmony. In and among the giant horse-chestnut trees, the exaggerated slow-motion gymnastics appear more like ballet and poetry than martial arts.

Let us now go down the steps to the lower level. At the pool, concentrated marine activity is at its height at about noon. A torpedo patrol boat flying the American flag, every bit handmade, is on the lookout for enemy subs (kit models). A resplendent lobster and crab smack, replete with traps and slickers, and a fireship with siren, water pumps and hoses, both handwork, skirt the danger zone on alert. Old and young are here every Sunday, rain or shine, to guide their models by remote control around the pool and underwater.

If there is sun, on any weekday you can count on groups of students and office workers flocking to the traditional pale green iron chairs set at a distance all around the basin. Lunch in a bag and a book in hand, they stretch out and absorb the warm rays. It's beach time in central Paris!

Up the steps on the opposite side of the pool and off to the left is a pleasant, painted chalet, an outdoor café, for a cool drink or coffee and a snack. Just behind it is an old-fashioned bandstand.

Also in the rear of the café is a lovely statue of the Greek actor lined up with the Pantheon as background—a favorite spot for photos.

Now go down again a few steps to the blissfully peaceful Marie de Médicis pool and fountain surrounded by tall plain trees and stone flower pots. This is a moist, poetic spot to linger in and contemplate.

If you are a jogger, there is an outside track about one and one-half miles long that takes you all around the Luxembourg Gardens.

The palace, built for Marie de Médicis upon the death of her husband, King Henri IV, was completed in 1625. Thomas Paine, the American revolutionary, was imprisoned here in December 1793. As an American citizen, he was convinced his stay would be short. However, the U.S. Minister to France, Gouverneur

Morris, detested Paine and all he stood for. He claimed that Paine, on becoming a member of the French Assembly, had renounced his American citizenship. When orders arrived for the execution of 150 prisoners, including Paine, X's were marked on the cell doors. Paine at the time was seriously ill with fever; the guards took kindly to him and allowed him to open his door. The X was thus safely on the hidden side. The next U.S. Minister, James Monroe, intervened on his behalf. He was released in November 1794.

The palace now houses the French Senate and can be visited on Sundays at 9:30 and 11:30 A.M. and 2 and 4:30 P.M. There are many fine paintings by Delacroix.

Along the way

Restaurants
Le Chat Grippé
Chez Marie
Polidor
Boulevard St. Michel (fast food)

Tea, Snacks, Ice Cream, Pastry
Dalloyeau
In the gardens

Beer, Wine Bars, Cafés
La Gueuze
In the gardens
Au Petit Suisse

Hotels
Atelier Montparnasse
Grand Hôtel des Principautés Unies
Hôtel du Danemark
Hôtel Elysa-Luxembourg
Hôtel Sainte Beuve

CHAPTER 7

The Louvre Museum and Mini-Guide of the Louvre

You have before you the *Great Louvre:* the Renaissance exterior of a palace of kings and the 20th-century version of an Egyptian tomb. The royal abode cum museum took 800 years to be completed. The glass and metal pyramid, respecting exactly the angles and form of those constructed along the Nile 4600 years ago, is symbolic of the modern Louvre, of the fact that each civilization nurtures the next.

As we descend through the pyramid to the underground concourse of the new Louvre, on all sides we view the old like so many rushes of a travelogue. Instinctively, we are delving into the world of imagery and imagination. The Louvre is indeed the

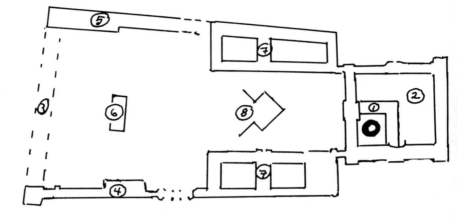

1—original donjon fortress
2—*cour carrée* (quadrangle)
3—Tuileries castle site
4—Grand Gallery
5—Gallery Rue de Rivoli
6—Carrousel Arch
7—Napoleon III extensions
8—I. M. Pei pyramid

Métro: Palais-Royal

Bus: 21, 27, 39, 48, 72, 76, 81, 95

Museum hours: 9 A.M.–5:45 P.M. Thursdays, Fridays, Saturdays, and
Sundays.
9 A.M.–9:45 P.M. Mondays and Wednesdays.

Medieval Louvre and Bookshop: 9 A.M.–10 P.M.
Temporary shows: 12 noon–9:45 P.M.

Closed Tuesdays.

Time: One to two days

story book of man's past as portrayed in works of art and architecture.

The Past

The original Louvre was a donjon fortress (1) built in 1200 by King Philippe Auguste to protect the city from the west, its weakest point of entry. The foundations of the original walls, moats, and donjon actually can be visited! The excavations carried out under the *cour carrée* (2) for the creation of the new Louvre have revealed the ancient structures. A footwalk leads you in and around them. The fortress in its totality occupied less than one-quarter of the present *cour carrée*.

In the 14th century, Charles V built a protective wall around Paris. The fortress then was well within the city limits and could no longer discharge its defensive role. The king transformed the original structure and made it a medieval residence. Later kings, however, shunned the Louvre and it reverted to a role of prison and arsenal. In 1527 François 1, eager to gain the sympathy of the people of Paris, moved in. He had the donjon dismantled and leveled off the courtyard. In 1546 he entrusted architect Pierre Lescot and sculptor Jean Goujon with the construction and decoration of new west and south wings.

In the second half of the 16th century, Catherine de Médicis launched the project of a chateau in the Tuileries (3), so-called because of the tile kilns that abounded there. Then Henri IV imagined an extravagant project, known as the Grand Design, which would link the Tuileries Castle and the Louvre Palace around gardens and pavilions, enclosed on all sides. He began with the long gallery (4) on the Seine stretching from the castle to the palace. The ground floor was occupied by shops and workshops; living quarters were just overhead on the mezzanine.

Louis XIII had a central pavilion built by Sully and extended the west wing of the *cour carrée*. This part of the Louvre now had its present dimensions.

Interior embellishment, architectural improvements, and ad-

ditions were stepped up under Louis XIV. However, in 1682, he
and his government had abandoned Paris for the new palace at
Versailles. Work stopped. Empty apartments were rented out. An
artists' colony settled in the galleries. Taverns and entertainers'
shacks leaned against the walls of the palace. Private homes
covered the area between the Tuileries Castle and the Louvre, as
well as along the classic colonnade created by Perrault in 1667 on
the outside facade of the *cour carrée,* to the east.

It was Napoleon Bonaparte who emptied the Louvre of tenants
and interlopers; he started construction of a gallery along the Rue
de Rivoli (5) leading from the Tuileries Castle towards the palace.
The Carrousel Arch (6) was erected during his reign to celebrate
his victories. In 1810 Napoleon's marriage to Marie-Louise was
sealed in what is known as the Square Room at the near end of
the Grand Gallery.

Following the emperor's banishment in 1815, work again
ceased. In 1852 the decision to complete the palace on all sides
was taken by Napoleon III, who came closer to the Grand Design
than any of his predecessors. The northern gallery (7) was termi-
nated and new inner wings and courts created (7). The Louvre
was the world's largest palace.

Then, in 1871, during the Paris Commune insurrection, the
Tuileries Castle was set afire and destroyed. The pavilions at the
far end of the two long galleries were rebuilt, but the castle link
was dismembered once and for all. In recent years, Maillol's
statues of sturdy females have lined this passage.

Until the 1980s no further major work was undertaken. In the
meantime, the Louvre had become one of the world's greatest
museums.

From Palace to Museum

François I (16th century) was the first collector. He purchased
twelve paintings by Italian masters—Titian, Raphael, da Vinci—
including the Mona Lisa. In the 17th century Louis XIII's collection numbered over 200 canvases. By 1715, at the end of Louis

XIV's reign, 2500 paintings were scattered throughout the various royal estates.

While the Louvre served as venue for the annual show of the Academy of Painting and Sculpture under Louis XIV, it was only after the French Revolution, in 1793, that the Grand Gallery was opened to the public. The idea of presenting the Crown's paintings to the nation was born around 1780. Louis XVI's buildings director, Count d'Angiviller, prepared for the opening of a gallery of the Louvre and stocked the royal collections. Many of the Dutch masters were purchased by him, as well as *The Young Beggar* by Murillo.

Under Napoleon I, the museum was to become the richest repository of major art works in the world. Napoleon's agents were constantly on the lookout for art treasures to enrich the collection. Also, art tributes were demanded of the vanquished of the Napoleonic wars. At one time the Carrousel Arch was crowned by the four gilt-covered bronze horses of St. Mark's Square in Venice. Like many trophies of the wars, they were returned to their place of origin following the defeat of 1815.

French archaeological expeditions have been a principal source of numerous outstanding pieces. Donations and legacies account for thousands of others. Between 25,000 and 30,000 objects are now on display. Several hundred thousand more are in storage.

The Present

Conceived as a palace of impressive proportions, the Louvre was ill-prepared for its role as a modern museum equipped to receive over 10,000 visitors on an average day. Those who have been here before will pay witness to a musty, unwelcoming edifice. Its exceptional works of art were sometimes difficult to find and very often impossible to see because of fading or no light. Chilling in the winter and stuffy in the summer, to visit the Louvre was a must—but always a feat. Visitor's reception areas were nonexistent. The presentations were poorly planned, artistically and otherwise; the distances to be covered discouraging. Basic restructuring was required.

I. M. Pei, an American architect, was entrusted with this mighty task. A museum specialist responsible for the additions to the Boston Museum of Fine Arts and the National Gallery in Washington, D.C., Pei has created a veritable city under the Louvre's two large courtyards. The new central pyramid and its three miniature likenesses (8) inundate with light the underground concourse and the broad avenues leading in different directions to the exhibits. These have been totally redeployed in renovated grand rooms and halls. The décor of the salons and galleries is now as much a part of the displays as the works of art on show.

Pei's genius has instilled new life into the Louvre. The visitor is aware, the very moment he steps inside the pyramid, that a memorable experience awaits him on the lower level. He is descending airily, not in a shaft to a subway station or to a labyrinth, but to a city within—smooth, rational, and beautiful. Nothing is ajar; this new Louvre is in itself a work of art with enhancing volumes, shapes, colors, transitions, and amenities.

The first phase was completed in 1988. A second phase, including, under the Carrousel Arch, a giant underground parking area for tourist buses and private cars, a mall, warehouses, and roadways to service the museum, will be completed in 1992. The Richelieu wing of the museum will be open to the public in 1993.

The Richelieu wing has long been a thorn in the side of French public life. Seat of the Ministry of Finance since 1871, that key personage, the finance minister, enjoyed residence here in the luxurious apartments of the Duke of Morny. A new ministry finally was constructed in the eastern part of the city and has been occupied by ministry personnel for several years. However, the departure of the minister from the majestic locale was more difficult to achieve. His apartment and offices were only vacated in 1989, after the socialists return to power.

Mini-Guide of the Louvre

A thorough visit of the Louvre would require a week or more. A minimum visit takes a full day. Whatever your schedule, chart your itinerary in advance. An orientation leaflet in English is distributed free-of-charge at several points on the concourse. One possibility simply would be to see what pleases you, including those particularly well-known art pieces: winged victory of Samothrace, Venus de Milo, Mona Lisa, the Egyptian seated scribe, Hammurabi's code of laws, and so forth.

Another possibility would be to give preference to the Louvre's most unique exhibits: the antiquities. Cassettes in English can be rented on the Sully mezzanine. The various exhibits are well explained in wall displays and information sheets placed in the exhibit halls. Unfortunately, these are in French. For your guidance a mini-historical guide follows, beginning with the antiquities and ending with the paintings.

Mesopotamia

The vast plain between the Tigris and Euphrates Rivers—today's Iraq—is the birthplace of the peoples of Semitic languages and institutions. Fertile, and irrigated, this plain has been traveled by nomadic herdsmen since time immemorial. In the years around 9000 B.C., in the Kurdistan hills to the northeast of the plain, some became sedentary. They invented pottery about 6000 B.C. and gradually migrated north to what would become Assyria and then south to the future country of Sumer, where the first-known cities grew.

The decisive event to occur about 4000 B.C., in the Sumerian city of Uruk, was the appearance of the written word.

Sumer gradually dominated all of Mesopotamia. Temples were built; pious statuary abounded; writing developed. The first known page of history is the *Vulture Stele* (2450 B.C.), which recounts a battle arising out of a border dispute at Lagash.

In 2340 B.C., Sargon of Kish in the north conquered Mesopotamia; Akkad became his capital. The archaic Sumerian language then was replaced by the Semitic language, although Sumerian ideograms remained in use. Art forms turned to recording royal battles, the masterpiece being the *Stele of Narâm-Sin* illustrating the Monarch's victory over mountain people.

These same mountaineers were to destroy the Akkad Empire in 2200 B.C. The Sumerian cities became independent vassal states, among them Lagash, ruled by the pious Prince Gudea. A code of laws originated. Expeditions to Lebanon for wood and cut stones; to Oman for stones, copper, and gold; and to India were recorded. At Ors, a brilliant dynasty reigned, leaving masses of literature. Sumer had reached its apogee. This is known as the neo-Sumerian period. Toward the year 2000 B.C., Sumer was invaded by the Amorites, nomads from the west, and by Elamite mountain people from the east. Its civilization, however, was adopted by the conquerors. In the 19th century B.C., the Amorites settled in the small city of Babylon in Akkad. The sixth king, Hammurabi (1792–1750 B.C.), reunited southern Mesopotamia. In so doing the Mari Kingdom and its palace, situated at the western limit of the Euphrates (now Syria), were destroyed. Babylon, however, became one of the most glorious cities of the Ancients.

Mesopotamia gradually declined. At the beginning of the 16th century, the Hittites of Anatolia invaded the territory, founding the Kassite dynasty, of which little is known. The Kassites in turn were defeated by the Elamites in 1160 B.C. The latter transported the artistic treasures of Mesopotamia to their capital city of Susa (now Iran) on the edge of the plain, where they were discovered in 1901 by French archaeologist Jacques de Morgan. Babylon itself never has been found.

Babylonia waned while Assyria in the north spread its wings. In the 9th century B.C., Assyrian monarch Ashurhasirpal II established his capital at Calah (Nimrod). The palace was imperial, decorated in stone with portals of carved animals and ogres. In the 8th century B.C., Sargon II built his palace in Khorsabad. It was the discovery of the latter, in 1843, which marked the beginnings of archaeological research in Mesopotamia. Its dimensions and its decoration were colossal. The fresco of the transport of Lebanese cedar for its construction is a brilliant demonstration of the times.

In the 7th century B.C., Sargon II's successors moved the capital to Nineveh. The Ashurbanipal palace represents both a library of encyclopedic proportions and the epitome of Assyrian art. The reliefs of the palace are classified among the sculptural marvels of all time. The empire was to vanish in 612 B.C.

Babylonia managed to last for a few more decades, during which time its capital was restored on a grand scale. In the center of the city, the 275-foot-tall tower of Babel was erected.

Babylonia fell to the Persians in 539 B.C. Then came the turn of the Greeks to dominate the "country between the two rivers," as they called Mesopotamia. Unfortunately, their curiosity did not extend to the thousands upon thousands of cuneiform texts. Their message was to remain hidden until the 19th-century European expeditions.

Iran

Ancient Iran covered a vast territory stretching from the central Asian steppes to the Persian Gulf, from the Indus to the Zagros Mountains north of the Mesopotamian plain. Settlement began in the Zagros valleys. Little by little, villages appeared in central and southeastern Iran around 6000 B.C., where the people exploited copper mines and invented colored pottery.

In about 4000 B.C. Iranian Susa became an urban center. Its painted ceramics were of great beauty; the decorations were either geometric designs or stylized animals.

In a second stage, Susa came under Mesopotamian domination. Although written language had not yet appeared in Susa during this period (between roughly 3500 and 3000 B.C.), the centralization of the administration required an accounting system. Envelope balls in which small accounting tokens were placed and then tablets for accounting circulated. Alabaster and other statuary proliferated. The human figure and daily life were illustrated as never before. Also, the first castings for metalwork were devised, an excellent example being the small gold dog on display.

At the same time, the nomadic mountain population of the upper valleys of Luristan (to the north) produced the first decorated bronzes, in the form of stylized weapons and tools. An independent civilization in the Gorgan plain of northeastern Iran forged the techniques of precious stone cutting; in the southeast, a seminomadic population exploited the copper mines and a green stone called chlorite. Susa, trundled between Sumer and the Elamites for centuries, truly blossomed as part of the Elamite Kingdom in 2000 B.C. Then, inexplicably, in the 18th century B.C., the northern regions of the Elamite country once again slumbered and became nomadic.

Several centuries later the north revived. This renaissance was perhaps because of an immigrant population. Indeed, along the Caspian, the tombs of nomad potentates have been uncovered, revealing richly decorated gold and silver vases reminiscent of the Assyrian and Babylonian civilizations.

In the middle of the 13th century, King Ontash-Napirisha founded, near Susa, a new city dominated by a tower several stories high and temples devoted to divinities of the different provinces. Their furnishings demonstrated unique artistry in metalwork, Queen Napir-Aso's statue being one example.

In the 12th century B.C., the Elamites conquered Babylonia and returned to Susa with an amazing booty of art objects. These generations demonstrated great aptitude for enamel work: the 12th century lion, as well as the facade of the Inshushinak Temple, are outstanding examples of technical prowess.

Babylon riposted at the end of the century, whereupon Susa sank into oblivion for almost five centuries. During this time, the Luristan mountain population, once again nomadic, had resuscitated the tradition of decorated bronzes. In Media monumental architectural constructions evolved in a style that would be continued by the Persians. In 646 B.C. the Assyrians destroyed Susa.

The Persian Darius (522–486 B.C.) revived Susa and made it his winter capital. The art of the Persian palaces was non-religious, the intention being to manifest royal power. Walls were enameled, illustrating the Persian people in arms; note the wonderful archers.

The Persian Empire was destroyed in 331 B.C. by Alexander the Great, who imposed Hellenism throughout the Orient. Then the Parthians overthrew the Greeks. In the 3rd century A.D., the Sassanids were to impose, in art as in religion, a form of Persian nationalism. They maintained and developed the Elamites' taste for richly decorated gold and silver objects and jewelry, a tradition they passed on to the Muslim princes after the Arab conquest.

The Levant

The City of Byblos on the Levantine coast established close trade ties with Egypt in the third millennium B.C. The pharaohs bought famous Lebanese cedar and timber for the construction of their temples and palaces. Among the many objects found in the royal tombs of Phoenicia is the Egyptian gold pectoral of the falcon.

During the second millennium, the small Levant kingdoms sought Egyptian protection from invaders. Requests for aid inscribed on terra cotta tablets have been uncovered, written with cuneiform script in the diplomatic language of the time, Akkadian (of Mesopotamia). The Levantine traders required a more readily usable script than the cuneiform, and during the second millennium developed the process that would lead to the invention of the alphabet. On the statue of Pharaoh Osorkon, around the Egyptian cartouche, is a dedication in primitive Phoenician letters.

The Assyrian dynasties of the 9th century B.C. provided another wealthy clientele for Phoenician craftsmen. Artisans produced masterpieces in ivory for the decoration of ceremonial couches and chairs and precious coffers, often adding color and touches of gold. Certain monarchs later would be stigmatized in the Bible for the insolent luxury of their "houses of ivory." The *Lady at the Window* is characteristic. The gold and silver bowls discovered in Cyprus were prized not only by the royal Assyrians but also by a Greek and southern Italian clientele. The decorative motifs were generally Egyptian.

The art of glassmaking has been traditional to the Near East and Egypt since the second millennium. From the Levant it travelled to the Greek islands and later to Italy. Blown glass originated in the Levant shortly before the Christian era.

During the period of Persian domination, the merchant kingdoms of the Levantine coast continued to prosper. The wealth of their tombs is proof. Sarcophagi, like the one in marble on display, were ordered from Greece.

Between the 9th and 7th centuries B.C., the Phoenicians embarked on a policy of expansion and colonization in their quest for new markets. They set up counters in Cyprus and Carthage (on the Tunisian coast). Carthage in turn procured satellite regimes in Malta, southern Italy, Sicily, Sardinia, and Spain.

Ugarit

Since its discovery in 1929, French archaeological teams have explored Ugarit almost without interruption. Located on the Mediterranean shores of Syria, directly opposite Cyprus, Ugarit—or Ras Shamra as it is called today—immediately posed an enigma. Its texts were written in a language unknown until the time of this discovery. A rapid deciphering of the cuneiform letters has revealed one of the most ancient known alphabets, dating from the 14th century B.C.

The site was first occupied in the seventh millennium. In the beginning of the second millennium, it boasted a large urban population. Destroyed by an earthquake in the 14th century B.C., it was completely rebuilt only to be destroyed again and plundered in the 12th century by invaders—"people from the sea." Ugarit then was abandoned until the 6th century B.C.

The city itself was surrounded by ramparts. The palace and its dependencies, which occupied one-fourth of the total area, were several stories high and looked onto courtyards and gardens. A sophisticated hydraulic system ensured the water supply and a giant main carried used waters outside the city limits.

The Temple of Baal, a high tower visible from the sea, was the sanctuary of the God of the Storm, who is pictured on the stele on display. In other sanctuaries offerings of liquids were made in funneled vases called rhytons.

Music played an important role in the life of the community. Cymbals, tambourines, lyres, and lutes accompanied voices that declaimed poetry and religious chants. The instruments were of Mesopotamian origin, except for clappers from Egypt.

Ugarit was a prosperous commercial port. Oil, wine, painted Grecian urns, amber from the Baltic, copper, and semiprecious stones were imported. Caravans of laden donkeys crossed the mountains into Mesopotamia. Copper was treated and crafted in Ugarit and made into weapons sold to Egypt and the Hittites. Another specialty of the city was chariots for combat; observe the old hunting bowl on display.

Families dug their tombs under their houses. Each tomb contained many luxury items: jewelry, objects of ivory or faience, and dishware made of precious metals or Egyptian alabaster. Apparently, wealth was fairly distributed throughout the society.

Islam

Islam was born in Arabia in the 7th century A.D. with the revelation of the Koran to the Prophet Muhammad. After his death in 632 the following four caliphs (lieutenants), chosen from among his closest companions, embarked on a policy of conquest. They triumphed over the Byzantines, then the Sassanids (Iran).

The first Muslim dynasty was founded in 661. It was called the *Umayyad Caliphate* in honor of Omayya, an ancestor of the Prophet's tribe. Its capital was Damascus. During the reign of the

Omayyads, Islam swept across North Africa, parts of southern Europe and Spain, and east as far as Chinese Turkestan.

Its rule represented a period of transition for art. Nevertheless, the very first mosques, in Jerusalem and Damascus, rivalled easily the religious edifices of the preceding era. The Great Mosque of Damascus would, in fact, serve as the prototype of the mosque: a vast prayer room opening onto a courtyard surrounded by porticos. Tastefully decorated in marble, mosaic, gold leaf, and rich color, the mosques represented the glory of Islam and contrasted sharply with the severity of the lay edifices of the time.

The Arabic language and Arabic script were sacred because of their past as the vehicles of the revelation, which explains the extraordinary development of calligraphy in art.

In 750 A.D. the *Abbasids*, descendants of Muhammad's uncle, Abbas, overthrew the Omayyads. They founded the cities of Samarra and Baghdad; the latter became one of the great economic and intellectual capitals of the world. However, Spain, most of North Africa, and eastern Iran defied the Baghdad administration. At the end of the 9th century, Egypt, too, was independently governed. The Abbasids were dispossessed of political power in the 10th century by Iranian and later Turkish military leaders. Their religious supremacy, however, went unchallenged until the Mongol invasion of Baghdad in 1258.

Although the circular city of Baghdad has completely disappeared, the Okhaydu Palace and the archaeological remains of Samarra confirm the splendors of Abbasid art and architecture. Mosques and palaces were immense; symmetry was more apparent than real. Stone, stucco, and wood were carved in depth, creating nuances of light and shade; the Samarra doorway is typical. Stylization, as can be seen on the Egyptian wood panel, was common. Potters innovated with the use of cobalt blue as well as monochrome and polychrome lusters on faience and new glazing techniques. See the *science plate*. Engraved bronze objects in a variety of shapes were other examples of the ingenuity of the craftsmen.

One of the greatest edifices of that era was the Great Mosque of Cordoba in southern Spain. Carvers of ivory in Cordoba and Cuenca excelled in the creation of rectangular as well as cylindrical boxes called pyxides.

The *Fatimids*, so-called after Fatima, the Prophet's daughter, seized power in North Africa in 910. In 969 they conquered Egypt and founded Cairo. They were builders, their best-known edifices being the al-Azhar Mosque-University (970) and the fortified wall around Cairo (1087). Art was original and sensitive, reflecting the refinement of Fatimid society. Rock crystal objects, in great vogue in Egypt, also were highly prized by the crusaders, who brought them back to Europe. Glassmaking, while a traditional craft, was intensified. Bowls, cups, perfume bottles, and makeup containers were made. Ivory was finely chiselled and often perforated; animal motifs dominated, many times with a touch of humor. Similar patterns were used for lustered ceramics. During the 12th century stylization of the decorative patterns was accentuated, as in the rosette bowl.

At the end of the 10th century, Turkish tribes from Central Asia, Muslim converts known as the *Seljuks*, seized power in Iran and Mesopotamia. They gradually advanced to Syria and Anatolia, taking over from the Byzantines.

In order to counter Fatimid influence, the Seljuks multiplied the number of mosques and religious schools; construction was primarily in brick and stucco. The design of their mosques differed from the Omayyad's, with large vaulted halls closed on three sides. One example is the Zaware Mosque.

Ceramics excelled during this period. Examples include the large lion and rabbit bowls and the parrot bowl. The glazed and lustered dragon ewer and the hunter's bowl are reminiscent of miniature art. The bronzes of Khorassan were made in a variety of forms: vases, lamps, trays. They were cast, chiselled, and perforated. An example is the falcon incense burner. Objects made of brass were widespread. Increasingly, they were inlaid with silver and red copper. Several techniques often were associated, such as in the duck candle holder.

In Anatolia (Turkey) as in Iran, the Seljuks developed traditional stone architecture with large-scale reliefs on the outer walls. Blue, turquoise, and black were the dominant colors for interior decoration.

After their capture of Jerusalem in 1099, the *European crusaders* founded principalities in Syria and Palestine and threatened Egypt. The Muslims were long in riposting. In the middle of the 11th century, first Turkish and later Kurdish armies forced the crusaders to retreat. Jerusalem was retaken.

The most celebrated hero of this Holy War, Saladin, seized power in Egypt and declared the Fatimids heretics. He united Egypt with Syria under the *Ayyubid* dynasty. Citadels were built in Cairo, Aleppo, and elsewhere, and fortresses defended strategic zones in the Sinai and along the Euphrates. New schools and universities were constructed—sober, chiselled stone edifices displaying the first polychrome, geometric patterns. Enamelled glass and metalwork were imaginative, for example the pearl goblet and the potsherd of the lutist. Metal objects inlaid with fine silver wire in the form of arabesques were produced in numerous workshops. The Barbarini vase and the Damascene pitcher of al-Mawsili are illustrations.

In 1250 the *Mamelukes*, military guards and slaves of the Ayyubid rulers, took power in Egypt. They also extended their rule to Syria and the holy places of Arabia. The last strongholds of the crusaders fell; the capitulation of Akka in 1291 put an end to their occupation.

The Mamelukes reigned over the Near East for more than two and a half centuries. Exchanges between East and West flourished. Artists and architecture thrived. An elegant Arabic script, called cursive, with elongated letters was the fashion (see the Yemenite Sultan's platter). Heraldic bearings were elaborate, as seen on the mosque lamp with lotus motif. Large enamelled lamps were characteristic of Mameluke art, as exemplified in the St. Louis Baptistry. During the 14th century, the human figure was no longer represented in works of art, such as the chandelier. Korans were magnificently bound and illuminated. The folding door is an illustration of the refinement in woodworking.

During the middle of the 13th century, *Gengis Khan* and his successors swept across Asia from the Mongolian steppes of northern China. Iran and Mesopotamia succumbed to their force. After leaving a trail of ruins in their wake and laying waste Baghdad, they founded a number of dynasties of which several were destined to become brilliant civilizations: the *Yuan* of China and the *Il-Khanids* of Iran.

The Il-Khanids showed particular interest in the sciences, to wit the Maragha observatory in Iran. In architecture they adopted the Seljuk design of the mosque and emphasized the use of enamel. Blue and turquoise glazes covered the brick walls of their edifices (the cross and star wall panel and the funeral stele are examples).

The close ties between Iran and the Mongolian dynasty established in China (the Yuan) introduced the former to Far Eastern influences. Chinese motifs—the lotus flower, the dragon, tumultuous clouds and mountain scenes—gained the favor of ceramists and coppersmiths. Chinese celadon glazes date from that period.

At the end of the 14th and beginning of the 15th centuries, the Muslim empires of Asia once again were thrown into turmoil and ruin by the expeditions of *Timour Lang (Tamerlane)*. A Turkish adventurer from Samarkand, he launched several military campaigns and ravaged Iran, India, Syria, and Anatolia. Each time a city fell, Tamerlane deported its elite to Samarkand to enrich his capital. Following his death, during the reign of the Timorid princes, Samarkand, Bokhara, Herat, and Shiraz blossomed. Architecture developed along Iranian lines, as did ceramics. Manuscript arts, such as calligraphy, illuminating, bookbinding, and painting, were promoted and attained perfection. The Chinese influence can be seen in the ceramics, in particular the blue and white patterns that were popular in the 15th century.

The *Safavids* of Azerbaijan conquered Iran in the beginning of the 16th century. Their principal preoccupation was the development of cities. Town planning was introduced for Ispahan, centering around a vast royal square glorified by two sumptuous mosques, a palace, and the grand bazaar. Ceramic tiling was still the essential decorative material. Mosaics gradually were replaced by glazed painting, which was quicker and less expensive. Among the skills of the time, the illustration of manuscripts, miniature painting, and weaving all were perfected, as seen in the floral sash.

While the Arabs reached the Indus in the year 711, Islam was not really adopted in northern India until the Turks' arrival in the 11th century. A series of dynasties called variously *Turkish Muslim, Turco-Persian,* or *Afghan,* centering around the city of Delhi, retained power from the 13th to the 16th century. During this period monumental mausoleums were erected. In 1526 Babor, of Turkish Mongol origin, conquered part of northern India and founded the *Great Mogol* dynasty. His son, Akbar, was wise enough to rally the Indian rajas during his reign.

The Mogols maintained the delicate balance between local tradition and Persian imports. While the architectural norms remained Persian, the materials used were the red stone and white marble of India. For one of the most prestigious monuments of all time, the Taj Mahal was constructed of white marble with semiprecious stone slab inlays.

Many exquisite objects attest to the luxury of the governing class. Weapons handles in ivory and jade were incrusted with precious stones, like the horsehead dagger. Miniature painting was influenced strongly by local tradition, yielding lively, colorful, realistic, and often intimate work.

The last great wave of Islamic expansion occurred in Turkey with the creation of the *Ottoman* dynasty. After unifying Anatolia, the Ottomans conquered the Balkans and Constantinople (1453). Renamed Istanbul, the latter became the capital of a vast empire encompassing the territory of three continents. It spanned from Hungary to the Caucasian Mountains in the East, and included most of North Africa.

Ottoman art immediately displayed originality. Colorful and exquisite, their palace arts culminated in the 16th-century architecture of Sinan. Sinan's main preoccupation was with size and light. The mosques incorporated pyramidal volumes under enormous cupolas. His elongated minarets were copied throughout the empire.

The extreme centralization of the regime affected Ottoman art. The same themes, forms, and materials were found from one end of Ottoman territory to the other. Floral motifs—the tulip, jasmin, carnation, rose, poppy, as well as the long lace-edged leaf—were privileged. Ceramic tiling was produced in abundance to cover the floors and walls of the mosques and palaces. Platters, bowls, pitchers, lamps, like the vase in the form of a mosque lamp, often were outsized. Gradually new colors, turquoise, lavender, pale green, were introduced, as seen in the peacock plate. Red appeared in the middle of the 16th century, followed by yellow, as on the panel with the niche.

Egypt

The first signs of pharaonic civilization appeared in about 3200 B.C. However, it is known that Egyptians of the fourth millennium B.C. already believed in life after death and possessed well-made objects in stone, terra cotta, ivory, and schist.

The Old Kingdom covers the years 2700–2200 B.C. and represents the glorious period of the great pyramids of Gizeh and Sakkara. Documents discovered at Memphis reveal a highly structured society governed by a king. The seated scribe dates from this period.

The Middle Kingdom (2060–1786 B.C.) began with the rule of Monuhotep the Great, the unifying pharaoh. The kings of the 11th and 12th dynasties embellished the sanctuaries of the god Montu. The royal statues of that era are remarkable, as was the gold and silver jewelry. Science and literature were celebrated. Precious information about daily life has been gleaned from small-scale sculpture found in the tombs that depict everyday occurrences.

Wars of liberation waged against the Hyksos, invaders from the

Near East who ruled over Egypt for 150 years, gave birth to the New Kingdom (1575–1070 B.C.). The kings of the 18th dynasty built a veritable empire from Sudan to Syria. Cultural contacts and material wealth multiplied, contributing to the refinement of society and an explosion of artistic and architectural achievement. Amenhotep IV-Akhenaten created a new religion and a new capital. The Ramses dynasties, while returning to the classic religion, added prestigious monuments to the old sanctuaries.

At the end of the second millennium, Egypt was caught up in the turmoil affecting the entire Mediterranean basin. The kings moved north, leaving the south in the hands of a powerful clergy.

The political break-up of the country was accentuated by the annexation of Egypt by Sudan during the 25th dynasty. The Assyrians put an end to that empire in 664 B.C. Kings from the city of Saïs in the delta then undertook the reorganization of the country and established the Saïte dynasty (664–525 B.C.). The country was finally integrated into the Persian Empire from 342 to 332 B.C. Alexander the Great took over from the Persians, placing one of his generals, Ptolemy, in power. The Greek pharaohs governed for three centuries. In 30 B.C. the last ptolemaic sovereign, Cleopatra VII, was overthrown by Octavius and Egypt entered the realm of Rome for several centuries.

Sesostris III

On the right bank of the Nile, three miles from Karnak, is Medamud, the city of the god Montu, who was worshiped during the Middle Kingdom (1990–1780 B.C.). King Sesostris III of the 12th dynasty honored this ancestor with ostentation: he placed a series of twelve statues of himself in his funeral temple.

At the Louvre are two of the larger-than-life statutes in front of a stone door lintel. In accordance with tradition, the king is seated. A classic headdress is worn, the belt of his pleated loin cloth is inscribed with his name. The personage is the same, but not the faces; he is pictured at different ages, once young, once old. In one of the wall display cases, a fragment of a mask of

Sesostris III, part of the same series, places the sovereign at a median age. All were carved at the same time. There is no other example of a similar display during the Middle Kingdom.

It was Sesostris III who brought Lower Nubia into Egyptian territory after four military campaigns. He erected a series of huge fortresses along the Nile Valley up to the second cataract. Elsewhere in Nubia, border steles were planted to mark the limits of the kingdom. On the one exhibited, Sesostris III exalts himself without making reference to the gods, which is most unusual in ancient Egypt: "I have added to my legacy" and "that which my heart projects, my arm achieves."

Nakhti's tomb

Among some twenty-one tombs excavated by French archaeologists at the beginning of the century at Assiut in Middle Egypt, Nakhti's tomb (Middle Kingdom) was the largest. Egyptian antiquities policy up until the Second World War was to split the archaeological finds with the country in charge of the excavations. Half of Nakhti's tomb is exhibited at the Louvre, the other half in Cairo.

The tomb was composed of a chapel and a vault. Contrary to later custom, everyday articles were not deposited in the tomb. Rather, its furnishings were reduced models, generally carved in stuccoed wood and painted in bright colors. In the chapel were two niches, each containing a full-sized statue. In front of the statues were piles of food, pottery, a table for offerings, a boat, and carriers of offerings.

Off the chapel were four vaults or wells. Two contained one sarcophagus each, one contained two, and one the skeleton of a child. Whether there were family ties is not known.

The narrow well was amply furnished. The mummy lay on its left side, its head held in place by a wooden support. Canes, scepters, weapons, alabaster, terra cotta and wooden vases all were crammed alongside. Sandals awaited at the mummy's feet, as well as a pitcher and a basin. On the body were two necklaces, one of faience and one of silver balls, and bracelets adorned the forearms and ankles.

In addition to the two large statues, there were eight reductions of different sizes, all carved in different woods.

Amenhotep III

Amenhotep or Amenophis III was only ten years old when he sat on the throne in the year 1403 B.C. He was the descendant of a dynasty of warriors that had carved out a giant empire extending from the fourth cataract in the south to Syria in the north. Amenhotep III succeeded in maintaining these frontiers, essentially through marriage to princesses of his allies. It was a cosmopolitan era. The empire was prosperous and the king was not required to make a show of military strength.

The events that marked his rule were inscribed on the inside of a series of stone and enamelled scarabees. His marriage to Tiy, who interestingly enough was not of royal lineage, was celebrated. His other marriages were noted as well. One of the inscriptions reads: "In the tenth year of His Majesty and the great royal wife Tiy, marvels were brought to His Majesty: the daughter of King Sutarna of Naharina, Kilukhepa, and the first women of his harem, in all 327 ladies."

Amenhotep III had an immense temple built for himself on the right bank of the Nile. The pylon on the facade of the Karnak temple was the largest ever made. He founded the great temple of Luxor along the river as the secondary residence of his god and seat of the new year's festivities. Another temple was erected for Amon at Soleb in Nubia. These were gigantic enterprises rapidly executed. One of the scarabees informs us that he dug a twenty-five acre lake for Tiy in only fifteen days! He also had hundreds of statues of the dangerous lion-goddess Sekhmet carved in order to gain her protection for himself and his sanctuary.

The style of statuary tended toward round, sensual forms, such as those found in the Ramose temple at Luxor, or the lovely Louvre statues of Tuy, Nay, and the scribe Nebmertuf. Toilet articles were particularly delicate. The famous rouge spoons and the swimmer's spoon are very finely chiseled. Many objects, like the kohl pot, display real innovation.

Amarnian art

King Amenhotep IV-Akhenaten, who reigned from 1365 to 1349 B.C., was a revolutionary figure who broke with the age-old Egyptian cults. He founded a new, official religion and a new city at Tell el-Amarna to serve his god, Aton.

Since dogma had changed, divine dialogue also was modified. Henceforth, pharaoh and his god were no longer transcribed in a symmetrical composition, facing each other ready to embrace or exchange gifts. Rather, at Amarna, Aton the sun god is represented for what he is: sun in the sky, his rays extending to little hands shining upon the royal family. With the pharaoh accompanied by his entire family in religious figurations, emphasis was placed on his intimacy and his prosperity, suggesting that these attributes were the requisites of happiness for one and all. Official sculptors invented: Queen Nefertiti was seated on the king's lap, parents played with their children. Embraces, caresses, and present-giving were emphasized as never before. Vast crowd scenes with the king and family on their way to Aton's temple were engraved on the walls of courtesans' tombs. Perspective is absent but the scenes are no less lively.

Official art, as in the past, was inspired by the most royal personage who defined the canons of beauty. Heads and necks were elongated; shoulders, legs, and arms were slender; stomachs protruded. All of this was in sharp contrast to the virile, square silhouettes of preceding eras. These portrayals were perhaps a more realistic representation of the king himself. Nevertheless, former conventions prevailed in drawing—profiles only—and in statuary—front view and balance. A perceptible move toward realism, grace, and a lifelike quality can be observed.

For Egyptians, for whom there could be no salvation outside the time-proven norms, deviation could not be taken lightly. The king had to call on new people for many of the tasks to be accomplished in the building of the new city and its sanctuaries.

The sculptor Thutmes emphasized the realist trend. The famous bust of Nefertiti (Berlin Museum) is the best-known example. The king's bust on exhibit here, and a smaller one of a princess that was executed in Thutmes's studio, are probably also his work.

Amarnian art flourished and gave rise to new techniques, especially in glassmaking and faience. A good example are the multicolored glass necklaces imitating the petals of fresh flowers. The mixture of materials also was practiced, as seen in wood statues with faience headdresses and walls covered with tiles or faience inlays. Jewelry and furniture were more elaborate: gilt was tinted rose and ivory was painted (note the young prince in the garden). The tomb of the next king, Tutankhamen, who after a brief period of worshiping Aton reinstated the old gods and their cult, has revealed a multitude of richly decorated court objects.

The architects of Amarna also innovated. Temples became vast open-air courts for Aton to rest and restore himself. Even the door lintels were separated in the middle to let light through so that the king would remain constantly in contact with his god's rays.

An excellent example of the revolutionary aspects of Amenhotep IV's reign was the replacement of the old dead language in written texts. The spoken language became the new written one.

The epic of Ramses at Quadech

Here are excerpts of the epic poem, written on papyrus, of which a fragment is on display.

Here begins the story of the exploits of the King of Upper and Lower Egypt . . . Ramses . . . accomplished in the country of the Hittites, in Syria. . . .

The lamentable king of the Hittites had just assembled all around him all the foreign countries up to the banks of the sea. . . . None of the distant countries had been forgotten and their leaders were there, each one with his army, and their chariots were numerous. There were so many that they covered the mountains and the valleys like a mass of locusts. He had spent all his country's gold and silver, divesting it of its goods, in order to give them to all the foreign countries, to drag them with him into war.

This lamentable king of the Hittites and the numerous allies kept in hiding, ready for battle, in the northeast of Quadech, while His Majesty was isolated with his aides-de-camp. Amon's army was on the march far behind him. . . . Ptah's army was south of the city of Irenam and Seth's army was on the way. . . . The allied troops . . . surged forth from the south side of Quadech and attacked the center of Re's army which, on the march, was unawares and not ready for combat: soldiers and chariots of His Majesty gave way. . . .

The news was announced to His Majesty and His Majesty rose up like his father, god Montu, took his weapons in hand and donned his armor. His Majesty launched forth at a gallop and alone, without anyone at all, entered into the melee of the dirty Hittites, then he turned to look behind him and realized that he was surrounded by 2500 chariots which barred the way out. . . .

Then His Majesty said: "What has happened, my father Amon, can a father forget his son? . . . Have I not always acted in accordance with your words, without transgressing the instructions you have given me? . . . Have I not built many monuments for you? . . . I have presented you with all my goods. . . . Is misfortune going to befall the person who conformed to your desires? I appealed to you, my father Amon, when I was in the numerous melee and I did not know what to do when all the countries were leagued against me and I was alone without anyone, when my army had abandoned me, when none of my cavaliers were preoccupied with me when I called out to them. . . .

"Yes, I addressed my prayer from the very depths of the foreign countries and my voice was propelled to Thebes and I saw that Amon came at my beckoning, that he reached out his hand and I was happy. He encouraged me, saying: 'Do not fear, I am with you, I, your father, and my hand, support you. I am more useful than hundreds of thousands of men. I am the lord of victory who takes pleasure in triumph.' And I felt my heart full of audacity and joy, everything I undertook succeeded, I was like Montu. I sped my arrows to the right, I took hold of the enemy to the left, I was like Seth in action amongst them. I realized that the 2500 cavaliers amongst whom I was, were nothing more in the face of my horses than a load incapable of fighting, paralyzed by terror, with arms too weak to pull on their bows, too discouraged to lance their javelins. I pushed them into the water like crocodiles, and they fell one on the other and I massacred them at will.

"Then my army came to congratulate me, my princes came to celebrate my strength, my cavalry to exalt my glory, saying, ' . . . you have broken the back of the Hittite country forever'."

His Majesty said to his troops, his princes, his cavalry: " . . . It is in war that one gains glory and it is the former heros who are admired. . . . Are you proud to have abandoned me alone in the fray?"

Then the lamentable king of the Hittites sent his messenger carrying a letter addressed to the great name of His Majesty: " . . . The country of Egypt and the Hittite country belong to you, your subjects are at your feet. It is Re, your august father, who gave them to you. . . . Peace is more useful than war. Give us breath."

Individual statues in the temples

Not just anyone could place his statue in a temple. This favor was accorded to high dignitaries and to those who had performed exceptional services. After many generations the temples were filled with big and little statues—although they never were bigger than life, as only kings and gods had this privilege.

To serve any purpose, the statues of commoners had to be inscribed with the characteristics of the deceased's identity. Also, offerings had to be renewed regularly if one was to continue to survive in the world beyond. Actually, it was sufficient to remind passers-by of the contents of the funeral repast, the reading of which was enough to provide a whiff. Some promised the reader assistance in this world and the next. The more eminent personages, like the cupbearer, or Iymeron and Peftauneith, recounted their life's deeds in order to impress upon the priests of the temple the need to read the formula for the funeral repast:

O Temple of Montu, conserve this statue of the cupbearer of King Manakhtef inside the courtyard of the feasts so that he may breathe the perfume of the myrrh and the incense, that he may gather off the floor of the courtyard the water poured on the altar, that he may nourish himself from the remains of the divine offerings presented by the priests, that he may contemplate the morning solar disk in the house in which one spends eternity. . . .

The temple

The only point in common of all Egyptian temples is that a god's temple is his home, his palace on earth, the reproduction here below of the horizon where, like the sun, he sets and rises. Plans and size vary much more than those of Greek temples or Catholic churches. Whether humble or grandiose, all of these residences were two-part, just as those of the wealthy and the royal. There was one confined space in which the gods lived (through their representation in statuary), and an open space to allow contact between the gods and men.

The king was also a god, even though he did not possess all the attributes. He, too, had his temples in which royalty was celebrated during his lifetime, a place where his memory would be externalized for "millions of years." They could be built next to his tomb or separate from it.

King Amenhotep III built an immense "million years" temple for the god Amon at Thebes, of which the only remains are the Memnon colossi, statues of the king that stood at the entrance. Fifty feet high, each statue was carved from a solid block of crystalline sandstone. The lion-headed goddesses on display at the Louvre were part of the same temple.

The temple is a creation of the pharaoh for his god. It is this offering that will bring him health, prosperity, power, and eternal rule over Egypt and other lands. A king without a temple was, therefore, not a king. Time was of the essence and organization was the key. The enormous temple built by Ramses III at Medinet Habu was finished in the fifth year of his reign.

Delighted with the king's generosity, the gods had to return the compliment and multiply the promises of rewards. Inscribed on the temple of Tutankhamen dedicated to the goddess Mout are Mout's words:

> Beloved son of my belly, master of two lands, Tutankhamen, I, your mother who created your beauty, I brought you up when you were a child and I am going to spread your fear among the nine arcs (enemy countries), your respect among the Nubians . . . as reward for this beautiful monument which you have made for me.

Book of the Dead

> He who will have learned this book on earth or who will have had it written on his sepulchre will emerge any day he wishes and he will return to his tomb without obstacle; he will be given bread, beer and meat from the altar of Re; he will receive a plot in the rush fields and he will flourish as he did on earth.

The conditions of "learning," however, were not all that simple. One chapter had to be written with myrrh on a strip of linen tied around the neck on the deceased's burial day; another recited on an image of the deceased drawn on the sun boat. The best guarantee for eternal survival was to have a copy made on a long papyrus scroll and placed alongside the mummy.

Other than hymns to the gods, the book was composed of formulae to provide the corpse with the means to make his wishes come true. There were formulae for emerging during daylight; for eliminating the crocodiles, snakes, and other nasty creatures beyond; for transforming oneself into a pigeon, god, or nenuphar; for possessing a field of rushes; for enjoying the company of the gods; and so on.

The simplest of these books was written in narrow cursive script. The more expensive editions were illustrated. Despite the fact that the order of the formulae and the program of illustrations were rigidly fixed, the artist always managed to introduce a personal note so that no two scrolls were identical.

The mastaba

The mastaba was an oblong structure with a flat roof and sloping sides built over the opening of a burial pit or mummy chamber. The structure itself was used as a mortuary chapel, a meeting place between the world of the living and the dead. There usually were several rooms decorated with reliefs or paintings, sometimes statues. Both the gods and the deceased were absent from the representations.

Only the king could grant permission to enter the burial ground surrounding his pyramid. Depending upon the degree of esteem, he also could provide furnishings for the mastaba. Other expenses were paid by the beneficiary or his descendants.

Seeing Akhhetep's mastaba provides us with a vision of daily life during the first Egyptian civilization. To the left, textiles are being delivered. We take part in their accounting and their payment in jewelry. Money as such did not exist. To the right, we witness the installation of Akhhetep's statues. The lower illustrations are of the slaughter of meat to be served on this occasion. Inside the chapel, to the right, is a narrow panel entirely devoted to a feast and its preparation. Food was the essential preoccupation, necessary if the deceased was to live out eternal old age—the definition of death for Egyptians of the Old Kingdom.

He who worked for a master, be it for the king or another, received a pension and ate at his table. Should he himself have subordinates, he would continue in the hereafter to protect them by bequeathing part of his worldly goods or lands in exchange for food in eternity. He would even constitute and pay for a sort of foundation, presided over by priests, to perpetuate his cult for all time and recite the formulae that would provide him with sustenance forever. In this way wealth was redistributed and huge fortunes were not amassed. Akhhetep was not a large landowner. Farms in Egypt—except for the king's holdings—covered no more than four or five acres.

Navigation was also a central theme in most mastabas. Whether by sail or oar, the aim was to cross the Nile or reach the burial ground or to return from an inspection tour of one's properties. Some scenes evoke the voyage to the place of the gods. This was not a mystical undertaking; its purpose was to partake of the victuals available on the table of one's benefactor.

Ramses II

Ramses II was the archetype of the pharaoh. He reigned for sixty-seven years and brought peace and prosperity to his kingdom. He promoted literature and was a fervent supporter of Thot, the god of the scribes, to whom he devoted many scarabees. He was the pharaoh who probably built the greatest number of edifices; he also had the habit of scraping the name of his predecessors from monuments and replacing it with his own in order to gain the favor of the gods.

Ramses's capital, founded in Piramses in the north, was opulent. The site is no more than ruins today; however, many of its monuments were reemployed by his successors and can be found in nearby Tanis. In Abydos he finished his father's temple and then built a magnificent sculpted one for himself. At Thebes (Luxor) he added on to the temple erected by Amenhotep III and placed in front of its entrance two obelisks, one of which now sits in Place de la Concorde in Paris. He also enriched Karnak with several monuments, including his tomb.

However, it was in Nubia that he extended himself in the construction of the Abu-Simbel monument. The face is adorned with four colossal, sixty-five-foot-high statues, carved from the rock ledge. The two statues of Ramses are flanked by two of his wife, Nefertari.

Greece

Prehellenic art as well as that of archaic Greece was influenced heavily by the more-advanced civilizations to the east. Minoan Crete blossomed in the first half of the second millennium, followed by the Mycenaeans of Argolis. After their disappearance, Greek art adopted geometric patterns, particularly in Attica (as in the woman's head in marble).

A great wave of motifs from the Orient was to overtake Greece in the 8th century B.C. Large statuary first appeared during the 7th century B.C. Little by little it evolved toward anatomical realism, with more freedom of the reliefs; subjects were less marked by religious tradition.

At the same time painted urns and bronze and terra cotta statuary were produced in a number of centers. Corinth excelled in small ceramic oil bottles; Attica, borrowing the black-silhouette technique from Corinth, became the market leader.

At the end of the 7th century B.C., the abusive rule of a class of aristocrats provoked an economic and political crisis. The tyrant Pisistratus seized power. While many cities suffered under his rule, Athens profited from his preoccupation with his own personal glory and flourished both culturally and economically. Constructions on the Acropolis, transcription of the *Iliad* and the *Odyssey*, and export of quantities of the black-silhouetted urns left a mark on succeeding civilizations. Prosperity enabled Athens to establish the democracy that would "labor for the greatest number and not a minority," in the words of 5th century B.C. historian Thucydides.

In the aftermath of the Median wars with Iran, decisive changes took place in Greek art. Shapes were no longer conventional but approached realism. Then, with the defeat of Athens by Sparta during the Peloponnesian Wars, new values gripped society: the individual, as opposed to the group, was central. Art reflected this change. The female body was revealed under light draperies; faces wearing melancholic expressions appeared; statuary emphasized the athlete, not the gods.

The Core of Samos

During the 6th century B.C., the Isle of Samos off the Ionian coast (Turkey) was the home of architects, sculptors, and intellectuals of which Pythagoras was one. The landowners were wealthy and most probably constituted the clientele for much of the art found in the Hera sanctuary on Samos. The cult of Hera, Zeus's wife, goes back to the 10th century B.C. The sanctuary was the site of a popular pilgrimage as well as an annual celebration.

The first life-size *core* (Greek for young girl) in the Louvre is both simple and suggestive of the body under the *chiton* or tunic. The statue was perhaps part of a group of female figures.

The *chiton*, part of the Ionian coast costume, consisted of two large rectangles of linen sewn on the sides and hooked together at the shoulders; it was drawn tight with a belt around the waist. Over the tunic a *himation* or loose mantle of wool was worn crosswise on the body. It usually was held in place on one shoulder only; it also could be draped around both shoulders. A veil of varying length covered the hair and head and was held in place by a diadem or cap.

The cavalier Rampin head

This head was taken from the Acropolis in Athens in 1877 by Monsieur Rampin and later bequeathed to the Louvre. In 1936 Humfry Payne, a British archaeologist, observed that the head fitted the torso of a statue conserved at the Acropolis Museum. The marble head at the Louvre is now attached to a plaster copy of the original body. Here, too, it is possible that the statue was part of a group. It dates from about 550 B.C.

The Miletus torso

The Miletus torso has raised many questions and led to numerous studies. First of all, is it an original (Greek) or a replica (Roman)? Second, to what period should it be attributed and to which school or sculptor?

The torso was discovered in 1872 in Asia Minor (Turkey) during an expedition financed by the Rothschild brothers. It is believed to be an original.

The Ionian coast of Asia Minor was occupied by the Greeks during the second millennium. Miletus was one of the flourishing cities of that archaic period. It was destroyed in 494 B.C. following its revolt against Persian ruler Darius. Reconstructed in 479 B.C., Miletus once again thrived, even under the later

Roman occupation. Its theatre, which seated 15,000 spectators, was the largest of ancient times.

Stylistically, the torso is classified as an advanced form of the 6th century *couros* (Greek for young man) statues of the Ionian coast. After comparisons with two known works of the sculptor Pythagorus, specialists are inclined to attribute the Miletus torso to him.

Sculpture of the Parthenon

The Acropolis of Athens was already, in the second millennium, the most sacred quarter of the city. During the 6th century B.C., a temple in honor of Athena was constructed there under the tyrant Pisistratus. It was destroyed in 480 B.C. during the Persian invasion; however, Pericles, who ruled from 464 to 429 B.C., decided to lift Athena from her ruins. The result was the Parthenon, designed by architects Ictinos and Callicratus. The effigy of Athena was the work of sculptor Phidias.

Other sculptors arrived in Athens from all over the country to contribute to the embellishment of the Parthenon. Practically nothing remains on the edifice; the statues that glorified it are today in Athens at the Acropolis Museum, in London at the British Museum, and at the Louvre.

Different themes were illustrated on all sides of the edifice. On the south side is depicted the battle of the centaurs—mythical half-horse/half-man creatures—against the Lapiths, descendants of Apollo. The Louvre conserves one of the metope of this side that portrays the capture of a Lapithaean woman by a centaur.

An ionic frieze runs the length of all four sides of the Parthenon at the top. It represents the Great Panatheneans preparing for and participating in a ceremonial procession destined to present a woven tunic to Athena. Two fragments of the frieze can be seen at the Louvre: a cavalier's head and a plaque of the frieze from the east side of the building known as the Ergastines plaque. The Ergastines were the young girls chosen to weave the sacred tunic (*peplos* in Greek) for the goddess. The long tunic had, in the 5th century B.C., supplanted the more elaborate costumes of the archaic period. On the frieze the Ergastines advance with the *peplos* and offerings. In a moment the animals will be sacrificed; one of the attendants is ready with a knife.

Etruria

With the exception of the Greek colonies of the south, Etruscan society was the most remarkable of all pre-Roman Italy. Beginning in the 8th century B.C., Etruria, which never actually unified, made great strides forward politically, economically, and culturally. Hammered bronzes, followed by filigree work and granulations, and jewelry in the Near Eastern style, were produced.

Etruria reached its apogee between 675 and 475 B.C. Contacts with Greece were intense. Greek artists settled in Etruria and executed high quality work, especially in the domain of funeral painting. Grecian urns were imported in quantity. The Etruscans also developed a type of ceramics called *bucchero* and were skillful in working with bronze and terra cotta. After the creation of the Roman Empire, Etruria fell into oblivion; even its literature has totally disappeared.

The sarcophagus of Cerveteri

The sarcophagus of Cerveteri was constructed sometime between 530 and 510 B.C. and is an outstanding example of archaic Etruscan art. Little is known of the couple except that which can be deduced from the quality of the work; they certainly belonged to the upper crust of a society that had close ties with Greece and the Near East. In the Ionian world of Asia Minor of the 6th century B.C., the custom of feasting half-reclined on a couch was centuries old. It was transmitted to Greece and to Etruria with one slight difference: a Greek woman would have been seated on a stool next to the couch.

The details of the sarcophagus, its three-dimensional artistic qualities, and the attitudes of the couple, are proof of the serenity with which they envisaged their voyage through eternity.

Replicas and originals

By the early part of the 5th century B.C., Greek sculptors had acquired perfect knowledge of the human body. From then on they would attempt to infuse that body with life. This required bending the body and freeing the arms and legs without suggesting imbalance. The discus thrower is an accomplished example. Bronze was more suitable for this new expressionism than marble. Any pose can be translated into bronze, whereas marble runs the risk of tipping and breaking.

According to the ancient texts, bronze statues were everywhere in the Greek cities and sanctuaries. Few have survived, essentially because bronze can be melted down, recast, and reemployed in statuary or weapons or plates. Our knowledge of the Greek statues in bronze has been transmitted through Roman replicas.

In the 3rd and 2nd centuries B.C., the Romans attacked Greece. Syracuse fell, then Corinth. Booty in the form of statuary was transported to Rome. Grecian art became the fashion; the wealthy and the powerful were avid collectors. Sculptors' studios sprang up everywhere. The Greek pieces were copied or adapted and adorned palaces, villas, and gardens. It is these replicas (mostly of marble) that have been handed down to us.

The manufacture of Attic urns

Despite general opinion, expressed by the ancient Greeks themselves, the Athenian potters neither invented pottery nor the potter's wheel. The latter came into existence in the fourth millennium in the Near East and from there made its way around the Mediterranean. However, the quality of Grecian clay and the skill of the potters was such that Athens produced, over several centuries, ceramics unsurpassed in the Hellenic world.

Since the Greeks considered ceramics to be a craft, not art, little was written concerning the techniques themselves. The rich red-orange color was due to the high proportion of iron oxide present in the clay. A sort of dark brown cream was applied to obtain the black background of the design. The cream was actually the same clay as that of the body of the urn, but it had been decanted in a mixture of water and potassium. In the beginning the personages were silhouetted on the black urn with a sharp instrument. In about 530 B.C. this process was reversed and the field surrounding the personages was covered with the dark clay cream. Details of clothing and body were drawn in black with a fine brush or quill. A brownish color was used for the hair and certain details like muscle structure.

Once the designs were completed, the piece was lustered with a fine cloth and then fired. This was done in three stages. In the first stage the opening of the kiln's vents would bring out the red-orange color all over. In the second stage the vents were closed. Green wood was added to the fire and allowed to smoke. The smoke, in contact with the oxygen of the iron oxide, provoked the blackening of the urn. The "creamed" portions vitrified. During the third and last stage, the temperature was lowered and air allowed to circulate and penetrate the porous clay, thus reintroducing the red-orange color there where vitrification had not taken place.

Shapes and uses of Grecian urns

Urns for transporting liquids: A two-handled urn called *amphora* was used to transport and stock liquids. The pan-athenaic amphora, filled with oil, was the prize awarded to the winner of gymnastic competitions during the Attic Panathenaea Festival. The *pelike* was similar to the amphora but squatter. The *hydria* had three handles: one on each side to lift it and one in the back to pour its contents. This pitcher was used to carry water from the fountain.

Urns for stocking liquids: The *dinos* rested on a stand. The *crater* and the *stamnos* were large open urns in which wine was held for banquets. The wine in craters was diluted with water.

Pitchers for dipping and pouring: The *oinochoe*, the *olpus*, and the *kyathos*, all one-handled pitchers, served to transfer wine from the crater to drinking cups.

Drinking cups: The *cantharus* was a wide-mouthed cup with two handles rising above the brim. The *skyphos* and the *kylix* were the most popular drinking cups.

Toilet urns: the *aryballus*, the *alabaster*, and the *lecythus* were vases containing perfumed oils with which athletes and women cleansed their bodies. The neck of the vase was narrow to let pass only a few drops at a time. The flat rim of the neck could be used to apply the liquid. A vase with a cover, called a *pyxis*, served as a container for powder and rouge and even jewelry.

Ritual urns: The *labis gamikos* was offered to the bride during the marriage ceremony. The *lutrophorus* was used to transport water for the nuptial bath or to bathe a corpse.

Rome

The fall of the Roman kings in 510 B.C. led to the creation of a republic. For the next two hundred years, patricians and plebians struggled for position. Finally, in 300 B.C., plebians were admitted to the magistracy. Simultaneously, Rome undertook the conquest of the rest of Italy, and completed it in 272 B.C.

The three Punic Wars (264–146 B.C.) brought the downfall of Carthage and the capture of Corinth (Greece). Rome became the master of Asia Minor, Syria, Judea, Spain, and Gaul during the second and first centuries B.C. However, the struggle for power within the empire was to dominate and weaken Rome. Finally, in the year 31 B.C., Octavius, nephew and adopted son of Caesar, defeated Mark Anthony at Actium. As Augustus, Emperor of Rome, he exercised almost total power while maintaining a pretense of democratic institutions. His rule was one of peace and prosperity. He founded the Julio-Claudian dynasty, which reigned from 27 B.C. to 69 A.D.

At the end of the third century A.D. the military triumphed, marking the beginning of the pretorian regimes. Under Constantine (306–337 A.D.) Christianity became the religion of the empire. Decadence followed with the splitting of the empire into two parts: the Eastern and the Western Roman Empires. The

Eastern Empire survived until 1453; the Western agonized and disappeared in 476 A.D.

Augustus

The four effigies of Augustus on display depict him at different ages and in different roles. Augustus at Cos, dated 27 to 20 B.C., is the emperor at forty, a private person, patron of literature and art.

The large statue of Augustus at Velletri is composed of the head of a forty-year-old man and a body dressed in the robes of Hadrian's time. Another bust, called simply Augustus, is a later version of a thinner, more bitter man who has suffered the loss of his two grandchildren, Caius and Lucius Caesar.

Augustus of Cerveteri, larger than life, is adorned with the civil crown granted to him by the Senate in 27 B.C. Deified after his death, he is represented here at the height of manhood.

Art objects

The art of the period following the split in the Roman Empire in the 4th century A.D. is known as Bas-Empire or Low-Empire; it was essentially a revival of Greco-Roman traditions with the gradual introduction of Christian values (for example, the ivory plaque of Christ's miracles). Byzantine art of the Eastern Empire was the direct successor of the Christian Bas-Empire. See Saint Demetrios, cloisonné on gold.

Medieval French art also was a direct heir of the Bas-Empire. The Carolingians' fascination with the classic imperial Greco-Roman model resulted, under Charlemagne, in a renaissance of techniques long since fallen by the way: engraving on ivory and bronze castings (see the equestrian statue of Charlemagne). Jewelry, already a major art form, achieved perfection. Enamel work and cloisonné marked the 11th and 12th centuries. Examples include the Maestricht box-binding and St. Henry's reliquary.

Enamel work remained a leading art during the Gothic period

and benefitted from new Italian techniques at the end of the 13th century. In the 15th century, painting on enamel developed considerably, as seen in Jean Fouquet's self-portrait. Jewelry achieved a high level of beauty and elegance during this period. However, Gothic art was perhaps best perceived in the ivories of which the Louvre possesses an outstanding collection.

The Italian Renaissance (15th–16th centuries) is represented with glassware, small bronzes, and especially faience; certain pieces are from Faenza itself. See the *Isabelle d'Este* plate by Urbino.

The 16th century French Renaissance was influenced greatly by Italian art and artists, many of whom spent long periods of time working in France. In the latter part of the 16th century, the Fontainebleau School conferred new standing on French art. Jewelry was indicative of the luxury surrounding the court. Painting on enamel on a copper base became the specialty of Limoges. Ceramics contained the Italian heritage in Rouen and traditional themes in the provinces. See the altar step by La Bastie d'Urfé, the rustic *figulines* of Bernard Palissy, Charles IX's shield, and the September tapestry.

During the first half of the 17th century, Parisian artists came into their own thanks in great measure to Henri IV, who distributed housing and studios in the Louvre to artists and craftsmen. Tapestry, cabinetmaking, ceramics, and the jeweler's arts flourished. A taste for naturalist motifs was translated into large floral patterns.

Louis XIV's prestige necessitated promotion of the arts. In 1667 he founded the Royal Manufacture of Furniture of the Crown at Gobelins (Paris), which produced all that the royal décor required: tapestries, furniture, silver objects, and marble mosaics. Royal carpets were woven at the Manufacture de la Savonnerie. André-Charles Boulle was the leading cabinetmaker of the time. Royal demands were on such a scale that they determined the style of art in general; vegetal motifs were the great vogue. Numerous objects from this period attest to its splendor: the Nef vase, the *Arrival in Africa* tapestry, Boulle's armoire, Marie Licwinska's chocolate pot, the Naiade porcelain, the writing table of Marie-Antoinette, the *Love and Psyche* tapestry, and so forth.

Napoleon also encouraged the arts, and a remarkable harmonious style was implanted in the beginning of the 19th century. Furniture with bronze finishings adopted more severe lines; bronzes, porcelain, and jewelry were to the taste of the court and were produced en masse. See the bracelets of the Duchess of Angoulême, the tobacco box of the king, and Queen Marie-Amélie's Chinese breakfast set.

Sculpture

Romanesque France

Romanesque sculpture was essentially religious and destined to adorn the abbeys and sanctuaries visited by pilgrims, among them Conques, Autun, Vezelay, Toulouse, and St. Gilles. See *Christ in his Descent from the Cross*, the *Virgin and Child* from Auvergne (12th century).

Gothic France

In the 13th century, in the region around Paris, a new art form called Gothic was born. Its development paralleled that of the urban centers. The Louvre abounds in sculpture of the 14th century. Despite the plague and the 100 Years War, royalty consolidated power and patronized the arts. Two contradictory styles—naturalism and stylization—emerged. In the 15th century, the war over, art forms tainted with a new humanism appeared in the Loire Valley, Languedoc, and Burgundy, to wit St. John of Calvary, the tomb of Philippe Pot, and the *Virgin and Child*.

Renaissance France

Gothic forms disappeared gradually. Contact with the Italian Renaissance was made during the 16th century; a number of Italian sculptors were commissioned to execute major projects, such as Louis XII's tomb in St. Denis and the Fontainebleau Chateau. Jean Goujon would exhibit fluid new lines, Germain Pilon would elongate women's bodies and provide expressive force for the religious Reform movement. Henri IV's coronation was to mark the renewal of Mannerist art with sculptors Biard, Francqueville, and Jacquet. See Goujon's *Nymph and Genie* and Pilon's *Virgin in Anguish.*

17th-century France

New art forms appeared in the 1640s dominated by Simon Guillain, Jacques Sarazin, and the Anguier brothers. Nascent Baroque, allied with a taste for ancient art, gave birth to classic, balanced, intellectual forms in French sculpture. The enormous projects undertaken by Louis XIV—Versailles, the Louvre, the Invalides, Marly—provided ample work. This work was restricted, however, by the canons of the court painters. Only Puget in Provence escaped the court atmosphere and created bold, passionate forms. His influence would lead to *Rocaille* (Rococo), the French version of Baroque. Observe Anguier's *Force*, Puget's *Mion of Croton*, and Jean Arnaud or Regnaud's *Magnificent Buildings of Versailles.*

18th-century France

Rococo reached its culmination under Louis XV. Intense dynamism characterized the Marly horses, while painting and small amateur statuary were charming and attractive. In 1750 a return to nature and antique art was to be found in the works of Bouchardon, Pigalle, and even Falconet. In 1770, a veritable neoclassic style blossomed with the statues commissioned for the future museum at the Louvre. Houdon, who best typified the period, Pajou, Clodion, and Julien tended toward simplicity of volume and deep sensuality. Small statuary expressed sentiment and individuality. See Pigalle's *Mercury Attaching His Heels*, Falconet's *The Bather*, Clodion's *Nymphs*, Houdon's *Diana the Huntress*, Chaudet's *Love*, and Jehan Duseigneur's *Roland Furious.*

Italy

Thirteenth-century Italian sculpture is represented in several works of Pisan, Florentine, and Neapolitan art. In the 14th century, Pisan wood statuary was monumental (see *The Annunciation*). Fifteenth-century sculpture provided a humanist dimension, as seen in *The Beautiful Florentine, Scipion Rattier,* and Donatello's *Virgin and Child.* Michelangelo best expressed the art of the period in *Slaves.* The Mannerist art movement, inspired by the master, would lead to anti-naturalism, which emphasized the anguish of a troubled era. Italian Baroque is represented by Bernini and Canova.

Germany and Austria

With the exception of the Bavarian *Christ on the Cross* (12th century), the Louvre's Germanic sculpture is all 15th and 16th century.

At the beginning of the 15th century the *beau style,* soft and refined, reigned (Salzburg's *Virgin and Child,* for example). The more mystic *Master in the Rimini Stable* represents a subtle mixture of delicacy and harshness.

Late Gothic is amply illustrated: the Issenheim *Virgin,* the *Carriage, Christ in Prayer,* and the famous *Magdalen* of Gregor Erhart.

Low countries

Gothic art dominated in the Low Countries, sometimes picturesque, more often strong and angular. Northern Mannerism is represented by Adrien de Vries' *Mercury and Psyche.*

Painting

The Louvre conserves some 6000 paintings by European masters dating from the 13th to the middle of the 19th century. The French collection is overwhelming.

Few paintings exist from before 1420. The portrait of Jean II Le Bon is a rare painting on wood and also the first known independent portrait, as opposed to portraits in group scenes.

The leading French painter of the 15th century, Jean Fouquet, introduced a new style in portrait painting with life-size effigies presented waist up and not quite full face, like the portrait of Charles VII.

Enguerrand Quarton celebrated the theme of the Pietà (pity, compassion) in *The Villeneuve-lès-Avignon Pietà*. In the last years of the century, Jean Hey, trained in Flanders, became a court painter of talent; see his *A Donor and St. Mary Magdalen* and *Suzanne of Bourbon*.

The epitome of 16th century art was the first Fontainebleau School. François I invited a number of artists to participate in the decoration of the chateau at Fontainebleau. They were of different nationalities; however, the decisive talents were three Italians: Rosso, Primatice, dell'Abate. Their styles, called International Mannerist art, were to dominate French art. Compare Andrea del Sarto's *Charity* and the Fontainebleau School's *Charity*. Jean Cousin's *Eva Prima Pandora* was typical of the court art of the period: refined and allegorical, epic or mythological. The elongation of the body was probably directly inspired by Cellini's *Nymph of Fontainebleau*.

The 16th century also is known for portrait painting as well as for drawings in chalk or sanguine. The trend toward veracity of expression is portrayed by the Italians, da Vinci and Solario, and the northern schools, Joos Van Cleve and Holbein. François Clouet well expressed this tendency in his portraits of *François Ier* and *Pierre Quthe Apothecary*. Corneille de Lyon's portraits of *Clément Marot* and *Pierre Aymeric* are other examples of this type of 16th-century French portrait.

The other trend was more directly rooted in the Fontainebleau School. Here mythology and history tended toward the idealization of the figure, suggesting, through allegory, the character or function of the individual, ofttimes infused with political or erotic symbolism. Observe *Gabrielle d'Estrées and One of Her Sisters*.

In the last years of the 16th century, Henri IV set in motion a series of artistic and architectural projects at Fontainebleau, the

Louvre, the Tuileries, and St. Germain-en-Laye. The second Fontainebleau School elaborated a new style that would continue into the 17th century under Marie de Médicis. The majority of the painters of this period were French, a few were Flemish. Italianism, however, had left its mark and the Mannerist art of Michelangelo continued to exercise a decisive influence throughout the second half of the 17th century. The themes were Romanesque. The style leaned toward accentuated perspective and volumes, abrupt contrasts of light and dark, and the use of strong yet smooth colors. See Toussaint Dubreuil's *Angelica and Medor* and Martin Freminet's *Marriage of Cana*.

The other overriding Italian influence of the end of the 16th and beginning of the 17th century was that of Caravaggio. Turning his back on tradition and aiming at authenticity, even his religious works were treated as scenes from everyday life. The theme of the *fortune teller* would be repeated by several of the major French painters of the 17th century. See those by Valentin de Boulogne, Nicolas Regnier and, of course, Caravaggio.

The most perfect representation of Caravaggio's precepts is to be found in Georges de la Tour's work. Whether he actually visited Italy is not known. His repertory was limited to deeply moving religious painting. It can be separated into two categories: those reflecting natural light and those illuminated by the light of a single candle *(St. Joseph the Carpenter, The Terff Magdalen)*.

The 17th century featured Baroque art *par excellence*. The essential difference between Baroque and the Classicism that preceded it was its pictorial quality. Classicism in art had delineated objects and forms, whereas in Baroque a visual whole is presented. This is a softer art, blending and harmonious. In the 17th century Simon Vouet translated Italian Baroque for France. Vouet's painting was lyric, light, and spacious, as shown in *Allegory of Wealth*. Among his students, note Eustache Le Sueur's *A Gathering of Friends* and *Clio, Euterpe and Thalia*. Among his rivals, see Jacques Blanchard's *Venus and the Three Graces Surprised by a Mortal*. The most celebrated French painter of the 17th century was Nicolas Poussin, who remained a classicist. Except for a short period from 1640 to 1642, he spent all of his adult life in Italy. His themes were ancient history *(The Rape of the Sabines)*, mythology *(Echo and Narcissus)*, the Old Testament *(St. John the Baptist Baptizing the People)*, philosophy *(Shepherds of Arcadia)*, and the New Testament *(The Judgment of Solomon)*. Poussin especially is admired for his paintings of the Holy Family, two of which the Louvre exhibits.

Classic landscape painting also was one of Poussin's great accomplishments, especially toward the end of his life. With Claude Gellée, better known as Claude Lorrain or The Lorrain, the vision of the landscape was based not on realistic perception but on an ideal representation of nature as portrayed in antiquity or in the fable. See The Lorrain's *Ulysses Returns Chryseis to Her Father* and *Ocean Harbor at Sunset*, and Nicolas Poussin's *Summer* and *Winter*.

Poussin and The Lorrain, both painting in Rome but filling orders for the French bourgeoisie, made themselves felt on the Parisian scene, as did the arrival of the Flemish and other northerners, who were naturalists in their approach. Laurent de La Hyre's biblical and mythological themes were presented with small figures against a large luminous background of nature. See *Laban Searching Jacob's Baggage for the Stolen Idols.*

The prosperity of Parisian society under Louis XIII led to a spate of building and opened the way to sculptors and painters. Interiors were lavish. Simon Vouet, Eustache Le Sueur, Pierre Patel, Henri Mauperché, François Perrier, and others received commissions for the interior decoration of many of the great town houses, the best known being the Hôtel Lambert at the eastern tip of the Ile St. Louis, now owned by the Rothschilds. The Hôtel Lambert paintings were purchased by Louis XVI in 1776 and now are conserved at the Louvre. See Eustache Le Sueur's *Three Muses: Melpomene, Erato and Polyhymnia* and François Perrier's *Aeneas and His Companions Fighting the Harpies.*

Philippe de Champaigne arrived in Paris from Brussels in 1621 and remained there for the rest of his life. He allied the

Flemish art of landscape painting, of studied concern for the details of clothing and complexion, with the fresher colors and more symmetrical compositions of the southern masters. See his *The Miracles of the Penitent St. Mary* as well as *Portrait of a Man* and the very famous *The Ex-voto of 1662*, which is the portrait of the artist's daughter, paralyzed, awaiting the miracle of the use of her legs.

The Brothers Le Nain also figure among the great names of French 17th century painting. They were three: Louis, Antoine, and Mathieu; however, they simply signed their work Le Nain. They have been categorized as painters of history, which is to say authors of mythological or religious compositions. Their celebrity certainly is due to their representations of peasant life. In their naturalism they willingly ignored antique statuary and turned their backs on the worldly elegance of the Fontainebleau School. See *The Peasant Family, The Forge,* and *The Haywain.* A deep knowledge of the peasant's world is evinced, not to be seen again until the 19th century with Millet and Corot.

Still-life painting experienced a certain vogue during the 17th century, introduced by the Flemish artists who settled around St. Germain-des-Près. The austere quality of much of this work is attributed to Protestant influences. See Lubin Baugin's *Still Life of the Chessboard* and Louis Moillon's *Bowl of Cherries, Plums and Melon.* Another major theme for the still life was called vanity; the term designated a group of objects representative of the wealth of nature and human activity juxtaposed with others symbolizing the triumph of death. This genre was favored by the religious fervor of the Counter-Reformation. See the anonymous work titled *Vanity.*

The foundation, in 1648, of the Royal Academy of Painting and Sculpture by some of the greatest artists of the 17th century—Bourdon, Perrier, Le Sueur, La Hyre, Le Brun—was to contribute immensely to the enrichment of the décor of Parisian churches. See La Hyre's *Apparition of Jesus before the Three Marys.*

It was from this period that the *Mays* of Notre Dame date.

These were paintings offered annually to the cathedral by the corporation of silversmiths and goldsmiths. Each year's gift was displayed on the first of May. Dispersed during the revolution, some ten canvases hang once again in the chapels of Notre Dame. The Louvre also possesses eight of them, including Eustache Le Sueur's *Predication of St. Paul at Ephesus.*

The most powerful man of the arts in the second half of the 17th century was Charles Le Brun. A student of Vouet in Paris and Poussin in Rome, his portraits were to develop as stage settings for his personages surrounded by the luxury of their functions. See *Chancellor Séguier.* Called into Louis XIV's service, he became the king's "First Painter" and was to play a leading role thereafter in the elaboration of French Classicism at Versailles. Appointed lifetime chancellor of the Royal Academy of Painting and Sculpture, director of the Royal Manufacture at the Gobelins, and entrusted with the direction of all paintings for the royal houses and the guardianship of His Majesty's collection, some referred to Le Brun as the Dictator. See his portrait by Nicolas de Largillierre. See also Le Brun's own work: *The Adoration of the Shepherds* and *The Virgin of the Grapes.*

Charles Le Brun is perhaps best known for his epic paintings of the *History of Alexander.* Poorly exhibited in his own time, they now are displayed at the Louvre as Le Brun would have wished. His purpose may well have been to rival the Raphaelian frescoes of the Vatican, and perhaps the work of Leonardo and Michelangelo—such was his concern with posterity.

Jean Jouvenet of Rouen devoted himself exclusively to religious art. At the end of the century, artists were divided between those emphasizing the strength and warmth of color, à la Rubens, and those for whom the quality of the drawing was paramount, such as Poussin. Jouvenet espoused the Rubens style. See *The Descent from the Cross.*

French painting of the early 18th century was long considered uninteresting. A re-evaluation of that period reveals, however, both Hyacinthe Rigaud, for her sumptuosity and solemnity, and Jean Antoine Watteau, for his sensitive and alluring elegance.

See Rigaud's *Louis XIV, King of France* and *Portrait of the Artist's Mother from Two Different Angles* and Watteau's *The Pilgrimage to Cythera* and *Gilles.*

Unfortunately, neither Louis XV nor Louis XVI were particularly interested in art. Some of the greatest painters of the middle of the 18th century—Watteau, Lancret, Chardin, Boucher, Fragonard, Van Loo, Vernet, Soubleyras, and Greuze—were all but ignored by the royal commissioners. The Louvre's collection is either the result of bequests or purchases made during the 19th century.

Boucher's style is Rococo, as seen in *Vulcan Presenting Venus with Arms for Aeneas, Diana Bathing,* and *The Afternoon Meal.*

Chardin continued in the tradition of the Dutch painters while adding his own appreciation of rich color. See his *Portrait of the Artist Jacques André Joseph Aved, The Diligent Mother, The Buffet,* and *Still Life with Jar of Olives.*

Fragonard abandoned any pretense of mythological themology and, upon his return from Italy, painted the lovely, rounded nudes for which he is famous. See *The Bathers, The Bolt,* as well as *The Storm.*

Greuze was to develop a taste for pathos and for modern dress. See *The Punished Son* and *The Village Bride.*

The neoclassical period of French painting (from the end of the 18th to the beginning of the 19th century) is richly represented in the Louvre's collections. Jacques-Louis David was the decisive figure of the era, bursting upon the world of art with a new plasticity yet utilizing classic themes. See *The Oath of the Horatii,* the painting that marked a turning point in art. Realism combined with valor, richness of color, and simplification of form. Among the many examples of David's works are *The Sabine Women, Madame Récamier,* and *The Consecration of the Emperor Napoleon.*

One of David's students, Antoine-Jean Gros, devoted huge canvases to the Napoleonic epic. See *Napoleon Bonaparte on the Battlefield of Eylau* and *Bonaparte Visiting the Plague-stricken at Jaffa.* This latter work foreshadowed the Romanticism of the 19th century: naturalism in corporal attitudes, nuance of color, and the appeal of the Orient.

The main exponent of Romantic art was Eugene Delacroix. His *Liberty Guiding the People* is considered to be one of the most outstanding paintings of the 19th century. It was purchased by Louis-Philippe at the beginning of his reign and quickly was hidden from the sight of the public for fear of its revolutionary message. See also Delacroix's *The Women of Algiers*, *The Jewish Wedding*, and *Still Life with a Lobster*.

Another prime example of Romanticism is Théodore Géricault's *The Raft of the Medusa*. For the first time an artist was to treat a current event in a work of art. When it was presented at the 1819 Salon, it created a sensation and was qualified as "scandalous."

The theme of the Orient that exercised such fascination in the 19th century was a favorite of Jean Auguste Dominique Ingres. See his *The Turkish Bath* and *The Grand Odalisque*. Théodore Chassériau's *The Toilet of Esther* is in a similar vein.

Hubert Robert's passion for ruins is wonderfully rendered in *The Gard Bridge*. Robert also painted many views, both as it was and as it should be, of the Grand Gallery of the Louvre. When he painted his 1796 version of the ideal museum gallery, the only light came from side windows.

While many canvases by Ingres, Delacroix, Chasseriau, and Corot are now to be found at the Orsay Museum of 19th century art, several major works of each remain at the Louvre. Corot's *Memories of Mortefontaine*, *Woman in Blue*, and *The Marissel Church* clearly illustrate the transition between the 19th-century romanticists and 20th-century impressionists.

Italy

Italian primitives—masters prior to Leonardo da Vinci and Raphael—are present at the Louvre. See Cimabue's *The Madonna and Child in Majesty Surrounded by Angels*, Giotto's *St. Francis of Assisi Receiving the Stigmata*, Bellini's *The*

Madonna and Child Adored by Lionello d'Este, Pisanello's *Ginerva d'Este,* Fra Angelico's *Crowning of the Virgin,* Piero della Francesca's *Portrait of Sigismond Malatesta,* and Uccello's *The Battle of San Romano.*

Giotto was the first western painter to provide his figures with space and consistency. Fra Angelico introduced perspective. Piero della Francesca and Pisanello were initiators of the independent portrait in Italy in a style known as International Gothic.

Sandro Botticelli is present with a magnificent fresco painted, probably in 1483, which represents the refined humanism of the time: *Venus and the Graces Offering Gifts to a Young Girl.*

The Louvre's collection of 16th-century Italian High Renaissance painting is incomparable outside Italy. In addition to the *Mona Lisa,* works of Leonardo da Vinci include *Madonna of the Rocks, The Beautiful Ironsmith, St. John the Baptist,* and *Virgin and Child with St. Anne.* The latter is one of the last, unfinished works of Leonardo, in which he put into practice his studies of perspective and expressed the full depth of his feeling for harmony and balance.

Raphael's *The Virgin and Child with St. John the Baptist* dates from the painter's Florentine period, during which he studied Leonardo, Michelangelo, and Fra Bartolomeo. The portrait of *Balthasar Castiglione* by Raphael is revealing of the deep friendship of the two men. Andrea del Sarto's *Charity,* painted in France in 1518, was to serve as model for the Fontainebleau School. It represents Florentine Classicism on the advent of Mannerist art. Correggio's *Venus, Satyr and Cupid* displayed new luminosity and served as forerunner of that of the 18th century.

Titian's masterpiece, *The Entombment,* is typical of the Venetian Grand Manner. Here he intensifies the dramatic quality with use of waning light. His *Concert in the Country* belongs to an earlier period.

The monumental *Marriage at Cana* by Veronese was painted in 1562–1563 for the decoration of the refectory at the Benedictine Abbey on the Island of San Giorgio Maggiore in Venice.

Among the musicians are portraits of Titian, Bassano, Tintoretto, and Veronese himself in white. The restoration of this sumptuous canvas is interestingly described.

Tintoretto's *Paradise* is the sketch in the master's hand for one of the walls of the Great Council Room of the Ducal Palace of Venice. More than the finished studio work, it highlights the painter's vibrancy and rhythmical perception in the Mannerist tradition.

Caravaggio's *Death of the Virgin*, painted for the Santa Maria della Scala Church in Rome, was refused for the very reasons he was to influence a whole generation of European artists: realism, the introduction in his religious compositions of the humbler members of society. Note the use of light and dark that also was characteristic of his technique.

See also Guido Reni's *Deianira and the Centaur Nessus*, Pannini's amazing *Gallery of Views of Antique Rome*, and Guardi's *Scenes of Venice between Sea and Sky*, worthy of the impressionists.

Spain

The Louvre's collection of Spanish art, though limited in number, is representative.

In International Gothic style, Bernardo Martorell, the Catalonian painter of the first half of the 15th century, is present with his masterpiece *Judgment of St. George.* His successor was Jaime Huguet; see *Flagellation of Christ.* El Greco's 16th-century Mannerist training in Italy is recognizable in *Christ on the Cross Adored by Donors.*

Francisco de Zurbaran, whose work covered the first half of the 17th century, was the privileged interpreter of the spirituality of the Golden Age. See his *The Lying-in-state of St. Bonaventura.* Jusepe de Ribera's realism is best translated in *The Club-footed Boy;* Murillo's realism is seen in *The Young Beggar.*

The brilliant portrait of the *Marquesa de la Solana* by Francisco Goya y Lucientes is both elegant and profound in its psychology of a woman to be struck by illness.

Germany

Again a collection of few but remarkable canvases. The Cologne School of the 15th century is on show with the Master of the Holy Family's *Altarpiece of the Seven Joys of Mary* and the Master of St. Bartholomew's *Descent from the Cross.*

Albrecht Dürer's self-portrait dates from 1493, when he was twenty-two. Dürer's contemporary, Lucas Cranach, reveals his allegorical style in *Venus.* See also his portrait presumed to be *Magdalena Luther,* Martin Luther's daughter.

Hans Holbein, in his portraits of *Erasmus* and of *Nicholas Kratzer,* displays meticulous virtuosity and objectivity.

Early 19th-century painter Caspar David Friedrich, with *The Tree of Crows,* reflects on death, a major theme in German Romanticism.

Flanders and Holland

The Louvre possesses 1200 canvases of Flemish and Dutch art, covering from the 15th to the 20th century. Those after 1850 have been transferred to the Orsay Museum.

The first of the Dutch masters, Jan van Eyck (15th century), conferred intense spirituality on his *Madonna of Chancellor Rolin.* Roger van der Weyden's *Braque Family* bears the stamp of Fra Angelico through its rigorous symmetry.

Quentin Metsys's *The Banker and His Wife* probably was inspired by van Eyck; notice the mirror reflecting a reader. Memling's work is well represented. See *The Portrait of an Old Woman.*

The major painter of Antwerp in the middle of the 16th century was Frans Floris. See *The Sacrifice of Christ Protecting Humanity.*

The sole canvas of Pieter Bruegel the Elder, *The Beggars,* has been the object of diverse interpretations as to its meaning, whatever its power.

From 1622 to 1625 Peter Paul Rubens, the master of Baroque art, accomplished the extraordinary feat of producing twenty-four immense paintings of the tumultuous life of Marie de Médicis, some 2700 square feet of canvas, which now cover the walls of a single room at the end of the Grand Gallery. Rubens also is here with other exuberant works. His portrait of his wife and child, *Helena Fourment with a Carriage*, is a high point of humanist art.

Anthony Van Dyck was a student of Rubens. He developed his own original style, subtler in color and more tormented in expression. His *Venus Asking Vulcan for Arms for Aeneas* literally walks out of the frame into our midst. His portrait of *Charles I of England out Hunting* was to serve as model for English portrait painting until the 19th century.

Ruben's rival and successor, Jacob Jordaens of Antwerp, expressed the epitome of Baroque art. See his *Christ Driving the Merchants from the Temple*, full of dynamism, richness of tone, freshness of light, and plastic plenitude.

Frans Hals's *The Gypsy Girl* recalls Caravaggio—the choice of popular subjects to which Hals adds his own vitality and spontaneity.

Rembrandt (1606–1669) was little known and scarcely appreciated in France during his lifetime. According to an art critic of the time, his technique "often seems nothing but a rough sketch." A few years after the master's death, the *Portrait of the Artist at His Easel* entered the king's collection. Others were to follow, including *The Supper at Emmaus* and the extraordinary *Bathsheba*.

Jacob Ruisdael's *The Ray of Sunlight* is perhaps the synthesis of Dutch landscape painting. The only Vermeer in the Louvre's collection are the moving canvases of *The Lacemaker* and *The Astronomer*.

Great Britain

Paintings by the English artists of the 18th century, the golden age of the portrait, are few but expert. See Thomas Gainsborough's *Conversation in a Park* and the striking portrait of *Lady Alston,* and Joshua Reynolds's *Master Hare.*

Landscape painting was to follow. The quintessential artist was Turner, whose romanticism is so well expressed in *Landscape with a River and a Bay in the Background* (1845), the unfinished work of an aging artist.

•

CHAPTER 8

The Orsay Museum, the Invalides, the Stately Mansions of the Left Bank

Yes, the Orsay was a railroad station. Adjoining it was a luxury hotel. Designed by architect Victor Laloux, it was inaugurated on July 14, 1900. It incorporated the main architectural highlights of the time: glass between steel girders dissimulated behind a classic Napoleon III stone facade.

In the 1930s the station became obsolete; trains were then too long for the short platforms, which could not be extended. The *Gare d'Orsay* was abandoned and used only occasionally for one

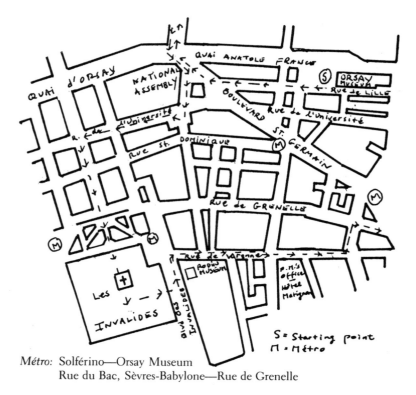

Métro: Solférino—Orsay Museum
Rue du Bac, Sèvres-Babylone—Rue de Grenelle

Bus: 24, 63, 68, 69, 73, 84, 94

Orsay Museum: 1 Rue de Bellechasse
10 A.M.–6 P.M.
Thursdays until 9:45 P.M.
Closed Mondays
English cassettes

National Assembly: Quai d'Orsay
3 P.M. days Assembly is in session
Passport required

Army Museum and Hôtel des Invalides, Quai d'Orsay
Emperor's Tomb: 10 A.M.–5 P.M. every day

Rodin Museum: 77 Rue de Varenne
10 A.M.–5 P.M.
Closed Mondays

Time: All day

thing or another: a center for returning prisoners in 1945, a shelter for the destitute and derelict during the bitter winters of the early 1950s, the scene of Orson Welles's film *The Trial*. More recently, it was transformed into a theatre for the Madeleine Renaud/Jean-Louis Barrault company and housed the Drouot auctioneers.

In 1970 its demolition was authorized in order to make way for a giant deluxe hotel. The hue and cry this news produced swayed President Georges Pompidou, who had the buildings classified as "historic monuments." A museum devoted to art of the second half of the 19th century then was projected and an international competition organized. The difficult task of turning the railroad station and hotel into a museum palace, of providing proper lighting and exposure, and of utilizing the huge hall to the fullest while not overwhelming visitors with its size was entrusted to Italian architect Ms. Gae Aulenti.

The museum covers the period from the Revolution of 1848—the overthrow of King Louis-Philippe—to the First World War in its variety of expression. In addition to painting and sculpture, photography (born in 1839), furniture design, objects of art, and architectural models are honored.

It is impossible to enumerate the marvels on show within the Orsay's walls. Sculpture is presented with great originality in the center aisle. On the ground floor, Daumier enjoys, at long last, full display. Major works of Millet (*The Angelus* and *Gleaners*) and of Courbet are on one side; Delacroix and Ingres are on the other. Also on the left is a wealth of impressionism prior to 1870: Sisley, Monet, Whistler, Pissaro, Jongkind, and Renoir. See Manet's famous *Déjeuner sur l'herbe* or *Bathing*, and Fantin-Latour's *A Batignolles Studio*. Nascent photography is displayed here as well.

On the upper level are the former *Jeu de Paume* collections of impressionists and neo-impressionists: Monet, Toulouse-Lautrec, Gauguin, Signac, Seurat, Cézanne, Van Gogh, Pissarro, Degas, and Renoir.

On the median level, riverside, *art nouveau* furniture by

Charpentier and Gallé is featured. Inside the towers you'll find Guimard. To the right is *art nouveau* of Vienna (Moser is a must), Glasgow, Chicago, Maillol's sculpture, Bonnard (*In a Boat* is breathtaking) and Vuillard post-1900. Following is the new art of cinematography. Do not miss the former hotel drawing room with its striking, eclectic pieces of art and furniture.

There is a good restaurant and tearoom, handsomely decorated and moderately priced, on the mezzanine. Upstairs is a welcome coffee shop. From the deck there is a clear view of Right-Bank Paris as far off as Sacré Coeur.

On leaving the Orsay, observe the row of bronze statues of the continents to the left. Take the Rue de Lille to the right and note, in passing, the quadrangle of the *Légion d'Honneur Museum* with its formal and somewhat pompous column attire.

At numbers 91 and 93 are two attractive hotels. *Hotel Solférino* rates two stars, and charges 336 francs for a large double bed, 373 for two single beds. *Hotel Résidence Orsay*, also two stars, and just as quiet, costs 290 francs for two.

At number 80 is the *Ministry of Commerce and Handcrafts*. This is the neighborhood par excellence of official buildings and embassies. They are, in general, conversions of the stately 18th-century mansions.

Turn right on Boulevard St. Germain and go one block to the National Assembly.

National Assembly

For a first look at the French parliament building you might advance to the middle of the Concord Bridge, where you also will be able to take in (to the left and right) the Grand Palace, the Alexander III Bridge, and the Louvre. Straight ahead are the Place de la Concorde and the Madeleine Church with peristyle.

The Assembly or Chamber of Deputies was originally the Bourbon Palace, which it sometimes still is called. The columns were added during Napoleon's reign—shades of Rome—and match those of the newer church across the bridge. Actually, this is a false front, for we are at the back of the Palace.

The Duchess of Bourbon was one of eight natural children of Louis XIV and Madame de Montespan. (All were finally recognized and legitimized.) A young widow, the duchess built both the Bourbon Palace and the Hôtel de Lassay. They were built side by side, the former for herself; the latter, smaller, for her young lover, the Count of Lassay. Why it was called "palace" is not clear since it was no more royal than many other private residences of the time. Perhaps the reason lies in the Duchess's personality. Strong-willed, with biting wit, she was a social grandee.

Later in the 18th century, the Duchess's grandson made lavish transformations on the two estates and lived the sumptuous life in a dying regime. On Bastille Day 1789, this Prince of Condé and family slipped stealthily out of Paris and France to Turin. The palace, newly named *House of the Revolution*, first became a prison and then a warehouse. In 1789 the property played host to the people's representatives for the first time. Thereafter, on and off, it was to be the seat of the National Assembly. The present hemicycle was built in 1831. The adjoining Hôtel de Lassay became the residence of the Speaker of the House shortly afterward.

Visitors are welcome in the hemicycle at 3 P.M. on days the assembly is in session. The entrance is just to the right of the columned facade as you face it. Be there at 2:45 at the latest and have your passport in hand.

Now skirt the building to the right (if you are facing the bridge). Take rue Aristide-Briand and come around to the *Place du Palais Bourbon*, which is in fact the front entrance to the assembly. In the middle of the square a statue represents The Law. In a word, the square is elegant, a choice place to inhabit. Take a swing around, beginning on the left. *Le Bourbon* has a pleasant sidewalk dining area that is moderately expensive. In the courtyard of number 3 is *Monsieur Renard's workshop*. He is one of the few remaining craftsmen of handmade leather goods in

Paris. Ring the bell. At number 5 is *Vogue's photographic studio*. The offices of *Condé Nast Publications*, publishers of *Vogue*, are across the square at number 4.

Just at the beginning of the Rue de Bourgogne, at the south end of the square, are two good addresses: *Le Bourgogne*, for their fixed-price menu (130 francs at this reading), and the adjoining three-star hotel. The *Rollet-Pradier Bakery* across the street is both snack and tea room. They have a luncheon menu, with prices around 60 francs.

As you leave the Place du Palais Bourbon, take a quick look at the assembly's pretentious quadrangle. Compare it with the lovely courtyard of the *Hôtel de Lassay*, 128 Rue de l'Université. Note, across the street, number 91, with two cherubs holding the house number in hand for eternity.

Keep on Rue de l'Université until you arrive at the Invalides.

Invalides

From the middle of the esplanade, you will have the Alexander III bridge and the Grand and Petit Palais to your right, all three built for the 1900 International Exhibition. To the left is the Invalides, comprising a hospital and a home for old soldiers, the Army Museum, two churches (one gilt-domed), and Napoleon's Tomb.

With the first breath of warm weather, the esplanade is overrun by students and office workers. Divesting themselves of shirts, trousers, or skirts, they stretch out and soak up the sun. There also are benches in the shade.

Look first at the wide facade, its splendid portal, and the perfect dome that tops the cake. This is one of the architectural masterpieces of Paris: the Hôtel des Invalides. The project owes its being to Louis XIV, the main buildings to architect Libéral Bruant, the domed church to Jules Hardouin-Mansart.

In the 17th century permanent armies were small; wars were fought with mercenaries. The time of glory past, regiments were dispersed and the men, deprived of their pay, swelled the ranks of the destitute. King Louis XIV attempted to form permanent units of the mercenaries and constructed military barracks for them. In addition, out of a sense of charity and recognition of deeds past, he solicited donations for the Invalides project. It would include a hospital, a hospice, a church, and become something of a lay brothers' cloister or monastery for former mercenaries. Those who left the institution were fitted out, in addition to a small amount of money, with a suit of clothes and linen. For some men this bounty was reason enough to enter the ranks of the Hôtel des Invalides. In the beginning the community spirit prevailed. The men organized workshops and supplied the city with objects and clothing of all sorts. It thrived for some years, reaching a high of 4000 residents. Then it slowly declined. Today there are 600 patients and residents; most of the living quarters are occupied by the museum.

On either side of the portal are the emblems of the Sun King, Louis XIV: the *fleur-de-lis*. They were chipped away after the French Revolution but since have been replaced.

The cannons on the lawn also have a story to tell. The first of them implanted there in the 17th century sounded off to commemorate the great moments of the Sun King: victories in battle, royal births, and distinguished visitors. Others now adorn the front approach, among them Prussian, Spanish, Ottoman, Austrian, Russian, Algerian, Chinese, and Indochinese cannons taken in battle. In the 19th century Louis-Philippe renewed the tradition and salvos thundered again until 1853.

Go through the gates into the quadrangle. Forget its present austere aspect and try to imagine the military on ceremony here, with mounted cavaliers, flags, banners, ribbons, feathers, and braid. The quadrangle resounds with the sounds of the clarion, martial music, hoofs on the cobblestones, the grand ladies and illustrious personages in the stands along the side, ripples of applause.

On your left is an entrance to the Army Museum, which houses relics and remembrances from the paleolithic to the atomic. On the ground floor are French as well as Japanese,

Indian, and Turkish arms and armor. On the second floor are uniforms and arms, objects and documents from the two World Wars, a museum of plans, reliefs and reduced models, as well as a replica of the room in which the prisoner Napoleon lived on Saint Helena.

The flags and banners of the flag room originally hung in the crypt of the church. During the Napoleonic Wars they were taken as trophies from the Germans at the Battle of Austerlitz in 1805. After the fall of Paris in 1940, the Germans took them home. At the end of World War II, the French reclaimed them. As you observe them today they are not mere flags, but symbols of power and sovereignty.

After the museum you might visit Napoleon's Tomb in the exquisitely proportioned, domed church built at the end of the 17th century by Jules Hardouin-Mansart. Napoleon's remains are enclosed in six caskets. The outer one is of oak. Napoleon died at Saint Helena in 1821; his burial in this church took place on December 15, 1840. The coffin was placed on a monumental float drawn by twenty horses in full parade dress. These were accompanied by soldiers, delegations, and veterans of the former Emperor's Grand Army. They descended the Champs-Elysées, crossed the Concord Bridge, and followed the river to the esplanade, which was bordered with great statues of France's most illustrious leaders. Despite the winter cold, 600,000 people lined the streets. In 1861 the six caskets were placed in the red sarcophagus atop the green granite pedestal that you see today. It seems that Napoleon was buried with his boots on, and that they were torn along the seams of the soles. When his tomb was opened in 1840 for its transfer to Paris, his toenails had grown through his socks!

Before leaving the church we should recall some of the noteworthy events of more recent times. It was here that Lieutenant Colonel Dreyfus was decorated with the *Légion d'honneur* in 1906. Hitler knelt in front of Napoleon's tomb in 1940. It was he who ordered the transfer of Napoleon's son to his side.

In 1945 General Montgomery received the *Légion d'honneur* in this place; Churchill received it in 1947.

There is a second "soldier's" church behind the domed Saint Louis. At one time they were adjoined; now there is a glass separation.

As you leave the church, turn left and pass through the hospital-hospice area. The pensioners living here are the more necessitous cases.

Leave the premises through the side gate. Cross over the Boulevard des Invalides and turn left. Your first right will be the Rue de Varenne. On the corner, at number 77, is the Rodin Museum.

Rodin Museum

The Thinker is among the rose bushes to your right. The *Bourgeois de Calais* is to your left.

But let us visit the museum itself first. The building, called the Hôtel de Biron, dates from 1731. Taken over by the church in 1820, it became a boarding school for young girls. In 1908 certain master artists were granted permission to work here: Rainer Maria Rilke, Isadora Duncan, Matisse, and Rodin. In 1910 the French government bought the building and authorized Rodin to remain on the condition that he will his sculpture to the State.

Rodin's most celebrated works are on display. In the middle room, ground floor, are *The Secret* and *The Cathedral* (Hands); both are pure marvels. Also displayed is *Iris, the Gods' Messenger.*

To the right is the Camille Claudel room. A number of examples of her genius are here. *Abandon* (1888), the green onyx *The Gossipers* (1895), her superb portrait of Rodin (1888), *Jeanne a Child, The Waltz* (1893) and the portraits of Camille by Rodin are featured. Camille Claudel and Rodin were lovers for some fifteen years. When he left her for others, she was so totally bereft that she forsook her art completely. In 1913, her brother, well-known French writer Paul Claudel, had her interned for the last thirty years of her life. Camille died in total abandon in a hideous asylum in the south of France. Her story, little known until a recent biography brought it to public notice, was absolute tragedy.

In the far left and far right rooms are a number of busts by Rodin of especially graceful women. *Young Woman with Hat*, for example.

Upstairs is the Balzac room, with heads and studies of his body. There also are several great Van Goghs and a Renoir. Note *The American Athlete, Man and His Thought,* and *The Good Genie.*

In the *Bourgeois de Calais* room is a colossal head of Jean d'Aire. Then busts of some of the distinguished men of Rodin's time: Victor Hugo, Georges Clemenceau, and George Bernard Shaw.

Visit the gardens. If the weather is amenable, stop for tea at the far end.

On leaving the Rodin Museum, turn right. This general area is called the Faubourg St. Germain. Its construction in the 18th century precipitated the decline of the Marais further east, on the other side of the Seine. There were some 150 private mansions at the time. The general architectural pattern was a first formal courtyard behind the street wall and gate. The horse-drawn carriages entered here to leave their passengers at the main door. At the back of the town house is the formal garden as at the Rodin Museum.

In the Rue de Varennes there are a number of pleasant sights for the eyes: at number 51 is the *Cité de Varenne*; at number 48 is a sweet courtyard; at number 46 another agreeable courtyard with a false brick front and a handsome staircase.

Number 42, *La Cour de Varenne,* is an interesting antique dealer specializing in 19th-century paintings and art objects.

Across the way, number 57 is the Prime Minister's Office, the *Hôtel Matignon.* On weekdays you can glimpse something of French officialdom coming and going.

Turn left at the end of the street and right into the Rue de Grenelle. At number 63 is *Dalloyau*, one of the best pastry shops and caterers in Paris, maybe in the world! Number 61 will soon become the *Maillol Museum* of sculpture. Number 57 is a very special fountain.

Along the way

Restaurants
Arpège
Le Bistrot d'Orsay
Le Bourbon
Le Bourgogne
Chez Muriel et Isabelle
Le Divellec
Nara
Orsay Museum restaurant
La Petite Chaise
Le Télégraphe

Tea, Snacks, Ice Cream, Pastry
Dalloyeau
Rollet-Pradier

Hotels
Hôtel Bellechasse
Hôtel Bersolys St. Germain
Hôtel Duc du St. Simon
Hôtel Elysées-Maubourg
Hôtel Résidence Orsay
Hôtel Solférino
Hôtel de Suède
Hôtel de Varenne

CHAPTER 9

Place Vendôme, Place de la Concorde to the Arch of Triumph

While our aim is to visit the Place Vendôme, we cannot decently by-pass the *Opera* without a glance when slipping into the Rue de la Paix.

Built during the Second Empire (Napoleon III) by architect Charles Garnier, the Paris Opera is a pastiche of several classic architectural styles. Inaugurated in 1875, it has had its supporters and its detractors. For Claude Debussy, "it will always resemble a railway station; once inside, it can be mistaken for a Turkish bath."

While the stage can accommodate 450 players at a time, the hall seats only 2200 spectators. Needless to say, ticket lines are long and form early.

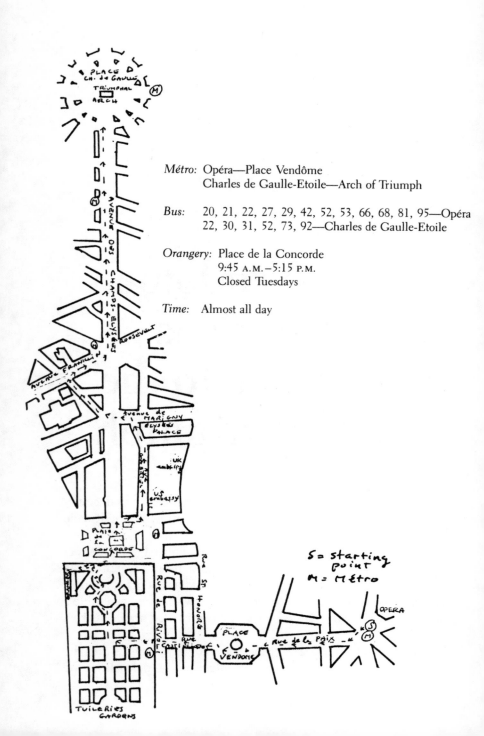

Métro: Opéra—Place Vendôme
Charles de Gaulle-Etoile—Arch of Triumph

Bus: 20, 21, 22, 27, 29, 42, 52, 53, 66, 68, 81, 95—Opéra
22, 30, 31, 52, 73, 92—Charles de Gaulle-Etoile

Orangery: Place de la Concorde
9:45 A.M.–5:15 P.M.
Closed Tuesdays

Time: Almost all day

The Opera's ballet troupe, composed of 160 dancers, until recently was directed by Rudolf Nureyev.

Enter the Rue de la Paix—an attractive street, although not as exclusive as in times past. On your right are jewelers Dunhill, Mellerio, and Cartier; on your left are Poiray and Boucheron. Also on your left are Burma's gaudy imitations. The wide street is a proper introduction to the Place Vendôme.

Place Vendôme

The Place Vendôme was intended as an administrative center to balance the Place des Vosges in the eastern part of the city. The original plan was a rectangular square open on one side like a theatre stage. The facades of the buildings were constructed in 1686 and stood, empty behind, like rows of empty upright shells. Twelve years later few of the plots had been sold and in 1699 Louis XIV had the facades dismantled and commissioned a new project.

The new square was octagonal. In its center was a statue of Louis XIV sporting Roman garb and a Renaissance wig. The land around the place was high-priced and would be acquired almost exclusively by wealthy financiers.

The Sun King's statue was overturned following the revolution. In 1803 it was replaced by a column brewed from the metal of 1200 captured Austrian and Russian cannons. A first statue of Napoleon in a Roman toga survived until the end of the emperor's rule in 1814. It was replaced by a large *fleur-de-lis*. In 1833 the emperor was back, depicted as "the little corporal," with his right hand inside his redingote and a tricorn on his noggin.

A third Napoleon, again in Roman imperial attire, was to find his way to the top during nephew Napoleon III's reign. The spiral column recounts the grandiose feats of the 1805 military campaign.

During the Paris Commune, on May 16, 1871, painter Gustave Courbet was authorized to flatten the column. Felled like a tree onto a bed of firewood, sand, and dung, Napoleon's deeds and statue were reduced to smithereens before a cheering crowd. A few days later, the commune was routed and Courbet summoned to pay for the monument's reconstruction; he was ruined, totally disheartened, and died soon after.

On the west side of the Place Vendôme is the Hotel Ritz, which was built in 1705 and turned into a hotel in 1898 by César Ritz. It was the most luxurious hotel in Paris. Eleanor and Franklin Roosevelt stopped here in 1919 when FDR attended the Peace Conference as U.S. secretary of the navy.

The hotel was requisitioned from August 1944 to the summer of 1945 for high-ranking officers and important guests, among whom was Fred Astaire, on a USO tour. He recalled that there was neither heat nor hot water.

One day in 1956, Ernest Hemingway stopped in for a drink. The baggage captain, recognizing him, asked him to remove trunks he had left in the storage room in 1927! In them he found lost notes that became the basis for A *Moveable Feast*.

On the east side of the Place Vendôme are some of the world's top jewelers: Van Cleef and Arpels, Chaumet, and Buccellati.

As you leave the Place Vendôme, you come to Rue St. Honoré, the fashionable shopping street which, to the right, becomes Faubourg St. Honoré and is lined with the ready-to-wear shops of the top couture houses.

Cross over Rue St. Honoré and continue on Rue Castiglione past the Intercontinental Hotel (with an attractive bar) to the Rue de Rivoli. Shop after shop along this street is filled with gifts and souvenirs for tourists. There also are two excellent English bookstores: Galignani's at 224 and W. H. Smith's at 248.

On the other side of the Rue de Rivoli, enter the *Tuileries Gardens*, a very French representation of a garden or park.

The Tuileries were designed and created by the garden architect Le Nôtre in 1664 and became a model for the French garden. Their central promenade is an important link in the perspective which, beginning at the Louvre, includes the Carrousel Arch, the Luxor obelisk and the Triumphal Arch of the Champs-Elysées. There is something very soothing about the trees in their alignment and precise pruning, the filtering of light, the absence of grass or bushes, and the benches.

Above the Place de la Concorde and to the right are two pavilions, the *Orangery* and the *Jeu de Paume*. The latter formerly housed the Louvre's collection of impressionists, now at the Orsay. The Orangery, on your left, is permanently occupied by the very imposing Walter Guillaume collection as well as by Monet's famous water-lily murals on the lower level. Among the Guillaume collection are several outstanding works by Picasso, numerous Renoir (including *Children at the Piano* and a series of the nude Gabrielle), fourteen Cézanne, several Modigliani, Derain, Monet, and others. The 144 pieces represent the collection amassed by Domenica Walter and her two husbands, Paul Guillaume and Jean Walter.

Below the Orangery is the *Place de la Concorde*.

Place de la Concorde

The idea of a square on a plot of ground that was once marshland derived from a group of city aldermen anxious to gain the favor of Louis XV, who, astride a magnificent stallion, would throne over Louis XV Square.

Gabriel designed the octagonal place and the handsome buildings on the right. The first is the Ministry of the Navy, the second the Automobile Club of France and the luxurious Hôtel de Crillon. On either side of these, separated by narrow streets, are the American Embassy (far side) and the American Consulate on Rue St. Florentin.

The Place de la Concorde has witnessed many an episode in French history. In 1770 a fireworks display was organized to celebrate the marriage of the future Louis XVI and Marie Antoinette of Austria. It was a grand occasion until the crowd panicked and 103 people were trampled to death.

In 1783 throngs of Parisians crowded into the square to see the first Montgolfière climb skyward from the Champ de Mars. Among those present was Benjamin Franklin, who noted that "all eyes were gratified with seeing it rise majestically from among the trees. . . ." He added:

> Could it (the hot-air balloon) not convince sovereigns of the folly of war . . . Where is the prince who can afford to cover his country with troops for its defense as that 10,000 men descending from the clouds might not in many places do an infinite deal of mischief before a force could be brought together to repel them?

In 1792 the equestrian statue of Louis XV was felled and the following year the guillotine was set up on the square for the execution of Louis XVI. The national "razor blade" decapitated another 1343 victims, including Marie Antoinette, Madame du Barry, Danton, and Robespierre before it was removed in 1795. Hopefully, the square was renamed Place de la Concorde.

On October 25, 1836, before 200,000 people, King Louis Philippe presided at the inauguration of the Luxor obelisk, a more neutral symbolism than the statues of kings. The Egyptian sovereign Mohamed Ali had, in 1830, offered the three Luxor obelisks to France. A boat was constructed especially for their transport. The first (and only) obelisk to make the voyage was surrounded by a wooden casing and overturned. On December 25, 1831, it was aboard ship. It was impossible, however, to lift anchor until the summer of 1832 floods of the Nile would buoy it up from the riverbed.

Tugged by the steamship *Sphinx*, the obelisk arrived in Toulon on May 11, 1833, and in Paris on December 23 of that year. A new pedestal of granite, twelve feet high and five feet wide, had been prepared and, on October 24, 1836, the obelisk was raised onto its base.

Parisians had launched into passionate debate as to the most suitable spot to plant the monument. Simulacres were fashioned and criticism was rife. Few were satisfied. Baron Haussmann declared in his *Mémoires* that the placing of the obelisk at the Concorde was one of the regrets of his existence. Pamphleteer Pétrus Borel decried the project: "Can you not leave to each latitude, to each zone its glory and its ornaments? Each thing has value only in its proper place, on its own native soil and under its own skies. . . ."

For the next thirty years, numerous festivities were organized around the obelisk, which was decorated in a thousand and one ways.

Two majestic fountains were erected on the square, one symbolizing the seas and the other the rivers. The female figures around the square represent eight great cities of France.

Although the 19th-century lampposts no longer sparkle with the flicker of gas lighting, the Place de la Concorde also is well worth a visit after dark.

At the entrance to the *Champs-Elysées* are two exciting marble statues by Coustou. These are the *Numidian Horses being Mastered by Africans* (called the Marly horses because they were delivered from Marly Castle, one of Louis XIV's chateaus near Versailles, destroyed during the French Revolution.)

Before taking another step, view the Avenue of the Elysian Fields in its total span, ever so slightly inclined upwards. The French call it "the most beautiful avenue in the world."

We shall, however, leave the Champs-Elysées and turn right and then left, passing in front of the American Embassy on Avenue Gabriel. It was once the home of famous epicurean Grimod de la Reynière. On your left are a theatre and the fashionable restaurant *Ledoyen*. In the 18th century, it was a modest country inn where you could obtain a glass of milk fresh from the cows grazing outside.

Further along on your right are the gardens of the British Embassy and then the Elysées Palace, the residence of the President of France. Entrances to both are on the Rue du Faubourg St. Honoré, which runs parallel. Should you wish to have a glimpse, take the Avenue de Marigny to your right; otherwise, turn left on Marigny. An open-air stamp market for sales and exchanges holds sway here on Thursdays, Saturdays, Sundays, and holidays from 10 A.M. until sunset.

On the opposite side of the Champs-Elysées are, left and

right, the Petit and Grand Palais, halls built for the 1900 International Exhibition. The glass-roofed steel and stone structures are now permanent edifices on the Parisian scene and the site of exhaustive temporary exhibits, often very complete retrospectives. Check to see what is going on now. The same Grand Palais, entering from Avenue Franklin Roosevelt, is Discovery Palace, a scientific, hands-on museum for children and planetarium.

The flower arrangements at the Round Point are better and better as the years go by. Nearby are several 19th-century buildings. The other Second Empire homes, dance halls, and cabarets disappeared long ago. The avenue is now criss-crossed with a vast array of chic shops, honky tonks, movie houses, shopping galleries, tourist agencies, banks, fast-food hangouts, and sidewalk cafés. Among the latter is *Fouquet's*, one of the rare old landmarks left on the Champs Elysées, frequented by politicos and the press. Fouquet's is good for a drink and for lunch or dinner, but is expensive.

At the top of the avenue is the *Arc de Triomphe* (Arch of Triumph). Although the place surrounding the arch has been rebaptized Place Charles de Gaulle, for Parisians it remains *l'Etoile* (or star) with its twelve points or thoroughfares.

It was Napoleon Bonaparte who ordered the construction of a triumphal arch in honor of the Grand Army. Work began in 1806 but proved more costly and more complicated than anticipated. When the new Empress Marie-Louise made her formal entrance into Paris in 1810, a mock arch of painted canvas mounted on scaffolding saved appearances.

With the overthrow of Napoleon, the project was abandoned for thirty years and completed, under Louis Philippe, in 1836. Napoleon's body, transferred from St. Helena to the Invalides in 1840, passed under it. The victorious Allied Armies passed under it as well on July 14, 1919, as did the people of Paris to acclaim de Gaulle on August 26, 1944.

On November 11, 1920, an unknown soldier was laid to rest under the arch. Three years later, the flame of remembrance was kindled for the first time. Every evening at 6 P.M., it is relumed in the course of a brief public ceremony. From the top of the arch, there is an excellent panoramic view of the quarter, the Champs-Elysées, and the new arch at the Défense.

Along the way

Restaurants
L'Alsace
Carré des Feuillants
Le Céladon
La Couronne
Elysées-Lenôtre
Espadon-Hôtel Ritz
La Fermette Marbeuf 1900
Hippopotamus
Ledoyen
L'Obélisque-Hôtel de Crillon

Tea, Snacks, Ice Cream, Pastry
La Boutique à Sandwiches
Chicago Pizza Pie Factory
Flora Danica

Beer, Wine Bars, Cafés
Bar-Hôtel Intercontinental
Bar du Sommelier
Café de la Paix
Espadon-Hôtel Ritz
Fouquet's
Kitty O'Shea's

Hotels
Hôtel Atala
Hôtel Balzac

Hôtel de Crillon
Family Hotel
Hôtel Intercontinental
Hôtel Ritz
Hôtel St. Romain
Résidence St. James and Albany

CHAPTER 10

On a Rainy Day: Arcades and Galleries, Old and Renewed

At one time there were over one hundred glass-vaulted arcades in Paris; all were built between 1800 and 1860. Philip, Duke of Orleans, was their innovator. In 1786 he put up a wooden arcade around the Royal Palace Gardens in the center of the city. The ensemble comprised 120 units, which he rented out as shops, gambling halls, and cafés. As you can see, the aristocracy of the time was not adverse to turning a quick franc, be it at the expense of royal properties.

The arcades that followed, from 1800 on, served a dual purpose. As breakthroughs in an impossibly congested city, they enabled people to move from one place to another. They also

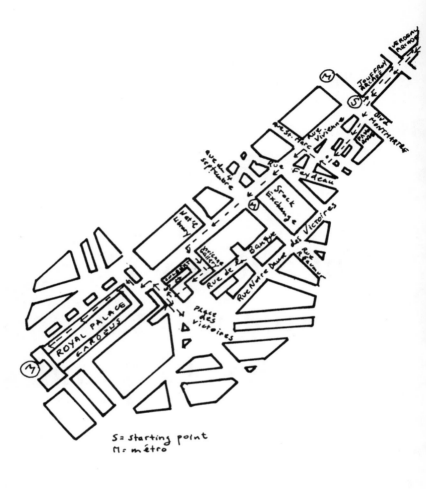

S= starting point
M= métro

Métro: Richelieu-Drouot, Rue Montmartre—Passage Jouffroy
Louvre, Palais Royal

Bus: 20, 39, 48, 67, 74, 85—Passage Jouffroy
21, 27, 39, 48, 67, 72, 81, 95—Louvre, Palais Royal

Arcades: Closed on Sundays
Many shops also closed on Mondays

Louvre des Antiquaires: 2 Place du Palais Royal
11 A.M.–7 P.M.
Closed Mondays

Time: Half to full day

provided Paris with its only clean, modern, permanent shops. Hitherto, tradesmen conducted their business from the roadbeds. According to a police report, some 30,000 were on the streets with their wares in the 1830s.

The arcades generally were situated near railway stations or theatres, in places where masses of people went to and fro daily. They could best be described as a contemporary adaptation of the middle-Eastern bazaar. The style, simple and functional, referred to as neoclassical, is noted for iron supports and vaulted glass roofs. Gas lighting was introduced in 1817. Their reputations varied—many catered to the shadier side of theatre and café life.

In the second half of the 19th century, Baron Haussmann razed whole sectors of the city to put through broad avenues and boulevards. As the city gained breathing space, the arcades were no longer vital. The department store was to fulfill their function.

The arcades fell into disuse and disrepair. Some were destroyed, others housed poorer artisans or specialized businesses such as philatelists or vendors of military decorations.

One hundred years later, a number of arcades are being renovated and resuscitated. Art and ecology have combined in evoking the daguerreotype image of Paris where browsing is a virtue and small is beautiful. In the 1970s the arcades were classified as "historical monuments," the equivalent of a state guarantee against destruction or further emasculation.

Passage Jouffroy

Alongside the Grévin Wax Museum at 10 Boulevard Montmartre is the entrance to the Jouffroy Arcade. Inside, on the right, is the *Hôtel Ronceray*. On the left is a real *Indian emporium* brimming over with clothes, carpets, handcrafts, and jewelry. Further along, on the right, is an *antique shop* with a large collection of canes next door to a modern *cane and um-*

brella shop. La Tour des Délices, a tempting oriental tea shop, is next in line.

Directly in front of us is the *Hôtel Chopin*, a two-star establishment with rooms priced from 210 to 400 francs. In addition to a lovely mahogany facade and an entryway of comfortable English leather furniture, the Chopin boasts very quiet rooms and is a bit old-fashioned.

As we turn the corner from the Hôtel Chopin, we run straight into a vast *secondhand book store*. A salesperson sits perched on a high stool in the passageway to collect for purchases. More often than not, he or she superbly ignores the clientele, head immersed in a novel.

Continue out through the back of the arcade, across the street, and enter Passage Verdeau.

Passage Verdeau

On your left is a *café* with several old *baby-foots*, France's equivalent of early pinball machines. Baby-foot is a bar game par excellence. Two or four can play at a time; give it a try. This may be your only chance, for these are among the last ones.

On your right, *Buret*, at number 6, specializes in old comic books, children's adventure stories, and original designs of thriller book covers (upstairs).

At number 8 is *Bonheur des Dames*, a charming gift and needlework shop with knickknacks for the house and kids and Christmas stockings.

There are old prints and books at numbers 10 and 11. *Ghislaine Maillard*, at number 11, sells very affordable decorative prints from 50 francs up.

Sophie Marcellin, opposite on the right, is another interesting print shop. The Verdeau Arcade dealers compete with those of the Left Bank by offering better prices.

La Comedia bookshop specializes in the world of entertainment. At *Photo Verdeau* (numbers 14–16), a secondhand and antique camera shop, specialists will recognize the Dubroni, developed in 1860 and forerunner of the Polaroid, as well as the ontoscope and the polyscope. Everything is in working order. Old silent films and Pathé newsreels also are on sale here.

Next door is an old post card and map store.

For lunch you have the choice of *Martin-Malburet*, a charming two-story restaurant, or *Les Menus Plaisirs*. At the latter, number 18, everything is homemade. Specialties of southwestern France are prepared daily by the cook and owner. Try the aligot pie (potatoes and cantal cheese), the spinach and goat cheese pie, or the super chocolate cake or light cheesecake. Pie (tourte), salad, and dessert cost 50 francs at this writing.

Now go back through the two arcades to where we started. Cross Boulevard Montmartre. Directly opposite is the entrance to Passage des Panoramas.

Passage des Panoramas

The Panoramas Arcade is the oldest existing passageway, or group of passageways. Built in 1800 to house "circular" or "panorama" paintings, it was imagined and commissioned by none other than Robert Fulton of submarine and steamship fame. Fulton had brought the idea from England, where it had acquired a tremendous vogue.

A static forerunner of slides and the moving picture, the paintings were tagged "endless" and covered the walls of two specially built towers at the entrance to the arcade. They told, in dramatic pictorial form, stories such as the burning of Moscow or the evacuation of Toulon harbor by the British, or produced a panoramic view of Paris as seen from the top of the Tuileries. The artist, Pierre Prévost, painted a total of eighteen panoramas before the towers were taken down in 1831. There was an entry fee for this first "o-rama" with which Fulton was to subsidize his experiments.

Here reigns a village-like atmosphere; many storekeepers still live upstairs over their shops. Between noon and 2 P.M., there is a great deal of friendly bustle. The restaurants and luncheonettes are crowded; in warmer weather some spill over into the passageway itself.

The choice of food is varied: the *Wagon Restaurant* has pizza and Italian specialties; a *crêpe and ice cream parlor* is across the way. *L'Arbre à Cannelle* (Cinnamon Tree), at number 57, is both restaurant at lunch time and an afternoon tea shop. Against an authentic Napoleon III 19th-century décor, you can order wholesome salads or apple crumble with *crème fraîche*. Just around the corner is the *An Lôc*, an inexpensive, spic-and-span Vietnamese restaurant.

At number 20, *Perry Brothers*, run by Welshman Alan Perry, serves truly international fare in an elegant setting. Brownies, muffins, *et al.* are on sale in the shop at the side entrance to the restaurant.

At the *Croquenote*, number 22, you can dine to music. Eric Zimmermann nightly plays and sings French hits of the 1950s and 1960s (Jacques Brel, Georges Brassens, Félix Leclerc, Léo Ferré). Get reservations ahead of time.

Philatelists abound at the Panoramas at numbers 9, 11, 15, 16, 17, and 48.

On leaving the arcade, be it on Rue St. Marc or Rue Feydeau, go right and then take your first left to Rue Vivienne. Stay on this street, and go past the Stock Exchange (Bourse) and Club Med's general headquarters until you arrive (on your left) at the back entrance of Galérie Vivienne and Galérie Colbert.

Galérie Vivienne *and* Galérie Colbert

On your left you will find *Si Tu Veux*, two children's toy shops, featuring both modern toys and 19th-century reproductions.

On your right *Jean-Paul Gaultier*, the mad designer of men's and women's fashions, has his shop. Films of his fashion shows flash on the walls of the arcade.

Go up the steps on the right and take a moment to be daunted by the rotunda of elegance, completely renovated by the National Library, which owns the arcade.

Back down the steps and past the toy shops, you will find a well-stocked *secondhand bookseller,* perhaps the oldest in Paris.

Along Galérie Vivienne are many interesting and inventive fashion shops: *Camille Blin, (Ixi:z), Yuki Torii, Christian Astuguevieille, Catherine Vernoux* for sweaters and skirts, and to the left at that corner, *Moholy-Nagy* for shirts and ties.

Casa Lopez has very tasteful carpeting and needlepoint as well as needlepoint kits. (English is spoken there.)

Just opposite is A *Priorité Thé,* an American-owned restaurant and tea shop that serves scrumptious pecan pie and brownies by Peggy.

Around the corner and to the left is Martine Moisan's *Galérie Satirique,* at numbers 6 and 8, where there is always some amazing piece of sculpture or painting to discover. Martine runs weekend art classes with Paris as her open-air workshop (see chapter 24).

Head back to the main passageway again. Go past an attractive *fabrics shop* that also sells lovely large, printed wool scarves to *LeGrand Filles et Fils,* wine merchants. Their cellar numbers over 50,000 bottles. They ship all over the world.

Out you go now, into the street, and immediately to the right. Reenter the Galérie Colbert, where you have a *post card and greeting card shop* with a small selection of art books. In the passageway on the right is a *gallery* for temporary shows, often of photography or posters, that always is worthwhile. You are now at the south end of the Colbert Arcade and can see the rotunda from a distance.

Now go back out to the street behind you (Rue des Petits-Champs) where, if you like, a side trip to the *Place des Victoires* would be in order. It is to the left a few yards.

The Place des Victoires is another example of a royal square designed as background for a statue of the ruling monarch, in this case Louis XIV.

The statue was commissioned and paid for by the Duke de la Feuillade; the square was designed by Jules Hardouin-Mansart and the elegant residences were bought and occupied by rich financiers. De la Feuillade was gratified by the king's appreciation and a sum of money. However, the money was insufficient to cover his debts, and he went into bankruptcy.

The statue was melted down in 1792. The present statue of Louis XIV is by sculptor Bosio (1822).

The shops surrounding the square—*Thierry Mugler, Stéphane Kélian, Junko Shimada, Chevillon, Kenzo,* and so on—are chic and trendy.

To continue our tour, return to the Rue des Petits-Champs. Next, head to number 5, the inviting shop of designer *Jean-Charles de Castelbajac.*

Take Rue Vivienne to the left for the few feet that remain and enter the Royal Palace Gardens.

Royal Palace Gardens

In the short Galérie Perron is a mini-antique shop with a "no bargaining" sign.

Exit Perron to your right. On your right is the *Restaurant Grand Véfour,* with one of the most exquisite décors of the 19th century—Restoration ceilings and Second Empire allegoric paintings. Grand Véfour is very good and very expensive (two hats from Gault Millau).

Now to our left is the long *Galérie Montpensier,* which borders the gardens lengthwise. These arcades are not the original Duke of Orleans constructions, which were burned down during the Paris Commune of 1871, but a reconstruction.

The Royal Palace Gardens today breathe calm and non-chalance. We might be in the provinces—a far cry from the agitation and debauchery that characterized them in the 19th century. It seems that in 1815, after Napoleon's defeat, the Russians and Prussians lost the entire pouch of war damages paid by France in the gambling dens of the Royal Palace.

The prohibition of gambling in 1838 by Louis Philippe marked the end of an era. It was only after World War II that the Gardens' anonymity was broken as Jean Cocteau moved into the

Montpensier Arcade and the novelist Colette set up across the way at 94 Beaujolais.

From 1786 until 1914 the small toy cannon on the grass went off every day at noontime when the sun, reflected through a magnifying glass, was hot enough to ignite its charge.

As you go down the Montpensier side, your first temptation will be the sidewalk and garden terrace of the *Muscade*, which serves tasty homemade tarts. The outside tables are shaded by elegant white garden parasols.

Check out the hand-painted, gilt-edged, dishware for a king at the *Manufacture de Palais Royal*; African artifacts and jewelry from *Ivana Dimitrie*; and tin soldiers at *Drapeaux de France*.

Raymonde Duval (numbers 32–33) has a nice choice of classic paintings by good if not too well-known artists of the end of the 19th and beginning of the 20th centuries. You'll receive a warm welcome.

At *Didier Ludot's* (numbers 23–24) an extensive secondhand bag collection features alligator from the 1930s. *Dugrenot* (number 18), a pleasant antique dealer with a mixture of Oriental and European pieces, was founded in 1856. If you have left your military or civilian decorations behind, A *Marie Stuart* and *Bacqueville*, will make you feel at home. At the end of the arcade on your right is a well-stocked pipe shop.

Out to the right is the entrance to the *Théatre français*, featuring French classical theatre.

Here at the south end of the gardens we are face to face with another world: the bar columns of Buren—a vast, recent sculpture particularly appreciated by young roller skaters and skateboard enthusiasts most afternoons. The building at this end of the garden was the Royal Palace, in which the child Louis XIV was raised before moving to the Louvre. It now houses the State Council and the Constitutional Court, the French equivalent to the U.S. Supreme Court.

We should note before leaving that it was here in 1823 that John Howard Payne wrote *Home Sweet Home* while living at 156 Galérie des Valois.

"Mid pleasures and palaces
Though we may roam . . ."
On leaving the Royal Palace Gardens, turn left on Rue St.
Honoré. On the far side of the Palais Royal Square is the *Louvre
des Antiquaires*, a swank mall of antique dealers only. This
former department store, *The Louvre*, has been converted into a
three-level marketplace for everything from military or naval art
and reduced models to 18th-century Limoges, 19th-century automats, ancient Chinese ivory figurines, Gallé lamps and vases
by Poiret, art déco, rare stamps, Oriental carpets, Louis-Philippe
armchairs, and so on. There is no antique mart anywhere in the
world as complete or as eye-smashing.

Along the way

Restaurants
An Lôc
L'Arbre à Cannelle
Le Croquenote
Restaurant Grand Véfour
Martin-Malburet
La Muscade
Perry Brothers
Wagon Restaurant

Tea, Snacks, Ice Cream, Pastry
A Priorité Thé
Les Menus Plaisirs
La Tour des Délices (Oriental pastry)

Beer, Wine Bars, Cafés
Aux Bons Crus
Willi's Wine Bar

CHAPTER 11

Montmartre and Its Artists

The history of Montmartre begins with a legend: St. Denis was decapitated on the *Butte* in 250 A.D. for his Christian beliefs. He then tucked his lost head under his arm and footed it to the place now named St. Denis.

The Romans, masters of Paris for 500 years at the beginning of our era, left two temples on Montmartre hill, one dedicated to Mars and the other to Mercury. Therein resides the dilemma: is Montmartre the Mount of Mars or the Mount of the Martyr St. Denis? The question remains largely unanswered, although most specialists lean toward the latter.

What is certain is that a Benedictine convent was founded on the butte in the 12th century. In fact, the nuns of Montmartre earned such a reputation that during the annual street procession of the monks of St. Denis, the nuns and abbesses were quarantined. Henry IV took as his mistress the seventeen-year-old abbess, Claude de Beauvillier, during his siege of Paris in 1590. At the time of the French Revolution, the last abbess, Louise de

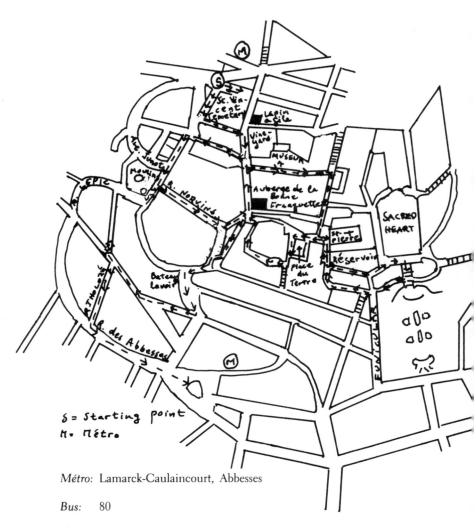

δ = Starting point
M = Métro

Métro: Lamarck-Caulaincourt, Abbesses

Bus: 80

St. Vincent's Cemetery: Rue Lucien Gaulard
8:30 A.M.–5:30 P.M.
Sundays 9 A.M.

Museum of Montmartre: 12 Rue Cortot
2:30 P.M.–6 P.M.
Sundays 11 A.M.–6 P.M.
Closed Mondays.

Time: All day

Montmorency, a royalist conspirator, went to the guillotine and the convent itself was razed.

Until just over one hundred years ago, Montmartre hill was littered with gypsum or chalk quarries, some dating from Roman times. In 1830 ten veins were still being exploited down mine shafts; there were eighteen open sky quarries and thirty ovens for the confection of plaster of Paris. The underground mines were closed by decree in 1860 when Montmartre was incorporated into Paris.

At that time it was still a country village adorned with vineyards and windmills. The latter first appeared in the 13th century. Today only two remain: the Moulin de la Galette and the Radet. La Galette still was grinding wheat in 1883. Underneath it was a dance hall.

Parisians were fond of excursions to Montmartre. They loved to drink its wine and dance in the barns and gardens. Artists and writers were drawn here as well. First came Gérard de Nerval, Murger, Heine, and then the great generation of 1871–1914, painters and poets. The Moulin Rouge opened its doors in 1889 with stars like Yvette Guilbert, Valentin le Désossé, Jane Avril, and La Goulue, silhouettes of which were passed on to us by Toulouse-Lautrec and Steinlen posters. Literary and artistic life centered around the Lapin Agile and the Billiards en Bois cafés, and the Bateau Lavoir artists' studios.

Today, we shall weave a spider's web on Montmartre hill, circling it until we reach top center. We shall meet bottomside, at métro Lamarck-Caulaincourt or at the number 80 bus stop and set out for St. Vincent's Cemetery.

St. Vincent's Cemetery

Mount the steps called Rue de la Fontaine-du-But, cross over Rue Caulaincourt, and take Rue Lucien Gaulard to the left. Crammed in between the low apartment buildings is an astonishing hillside cemetery, varying in shades of grey marble and pink granite and intermixed with delicate acacias. One of the first pink granite gravestones as you enter is that of Arthur Honegger, 1892–1955, and his wife. I leaned on their rose tablet to note impressions. Next to it Jeanne and René Dumesnil are immortalized in stone aloft and away.

A little higher up and to the left, Paulo of the Lapin Agile café (Paul Gérard 1895–1977) is just down the alley from Maurice and Lucie Utrillo against the far wall. Rose granite was used here, too, but without the same purity of line. The painter Steinlen is curled up under a cypress tree in the upper left-hand corner.

Fresh flowers and plants lie at the foot of many graves; others are flowered with permanent ceramic decorations, roses, pansies, and forget-me-nots. A few are mantled entirely in ivy. Near the entrance a list of the famous people buried here is posted. No plots are available!

On leaving Rue Lucien Gaulard, turn left and take Rue St. Vincent, which skirts the upper part of the cemetery. Walk on the right-hand side of the street along the upper railing. Expect total enchantment. You are approaching the café *Au Lapin Agile* and the *vineyard* of Montmartre; hovering high above are the Sacré Coeur mamelons. At the corner are some park benches.

The Lapin Agile has changed very little since the days of its fame, when it was glorified for all time in the paintings of the impressionists. It is a small country inn covered with vine and announced by two acacias, open every evening except Monday from 9 P.M. to 2 A.M. Ninety francs buys you the show and one drink. Wit has certainly evolved since the time of the charismatic Aristide Bruant, actor and one-time owner. Among the clientele at the turn of the century were Apollinaire, Picasso, Max Jacob, Vlaminck, as well as a host of small-time crooks.

Take the Rue des Saules to the right, past the vineyard. A harvest festival takes place in the fall. Bottles of Montmartre red are auctioned off yearly at prices totally unrelated to the quality (poor) of the wine.

At the corner of the Rue de l'Abreuvoir, which we shall take to the right, is a charming *pink-hued restaurant* with a 69-franc menu, including onion soup. The house next door boasts a sundial with the inscription "When you ring, I shall sing." We continue down this country lane to the corner of the Rue Girardon. The *manor house* here was once the home of 19th-century writer Gérard de Nerval and later became a dance hall. On the right of the Allée des Brouillards are some very pleasant homes.

Up the hill on the Rue Girardon we arrive at Avenue Junot. Across the street to the right of the cinema are entrances to the most-elegant artists' studios in the quarter. The Moulin de la Galette of impressionist renown also is here. Unfortunately, the gates are firmly locked.

We shall continue one more small block to the end of Rue Girardon, where it joins Rue Lepic. There is the other remaining Montmartre windmill, the Radet, atop the *Da Graziano Restaurant* of Italian specialties. The décor is most inviting and the food reputable. It is expensive, except for the fixed-price menu.

Backtrack to the corner of Rue Girardon and Marcel Aymé Place where we shall turn right into the Rue Norvins. The man in sculpture advancing from the far wall is writer Marcel Aymé himself. Up the street on the left, turn in at number 24. This is an *artist colony* owned by the City of Paris. A number of studios to the back are reserved for short stays by artists from different parts of the world.

Just to the left at the corner with Rue des Saules is the *Auberge de la Bonne Franquette*. The garden of this inn served as Van Gogh's model for his famous painting *La Guinguette*, exhibited at the Orsay.

Continue down the Rue des Saules to the Rue Cortot, where we shall turn right. Number 12 was home to Suzanne Valadon and son Utrillo, Raoul Dufy, and Renoir. It is now the entrance to the *Museum of Montmartre*, which is located down the garden path and through the arbor. It is the oldest house on the butte and belonged to actor Claude la Roze de Rosimond, a Molièrian adept who followed so closely in the footsteps of his master that he met death, in 1686, on stage, as had Molière.

The museum retraces the history of Montmartre. Among the exhibits are the original painting of the Lapin Agile (in the bar), the zinc counter of the Café de l'Abreuvoir (so pillared by Utril-

lo), a maquette of the Bateau Lavoir studios, mementos, paintings, and so forth.

Continue up Rue Cortot to the water tower and turn right in
the Rue Mont Cénis. At number 6 is *Jean Decker's gallery,* where
he exhibits his own fine, medium-priced work and organizes
shows of general interest.

Cross over at the end of the street for a visit of St. Peter's
Church.

St. Peter's Church

The church is all that remains of the Benedictine Abbey that
once covered the butte. Dating from 1147, St. Peter's of
Montmartre also can claim to be the oldest church of the city. It
contains four marble columns said to date from the Roman
temple dedicated to Mars (in the choir and along the inside of the
facade). St. Peter's has been completely cleaned and renovated. It
is classified as early Gothic, but vestiges of Romanesque capitals
also have survived. It is harmonious in design, long and narrow.
The stained glass windows dating from 1955 add a happy note of
brightness to the simple, familiar lines.

A telegraph pole was affixed to the church tower for many
years. Thanks to the new invention, Napoleon's victories were
honored in Paris minutes after the battles of Strasburg and Lille
(1792).

We may either leave St. Peter's to the right and take the Rue
Chevalier de la Barre, right again, to the small public park from
which a glimpse of the backside of the Sacred Heart can be
gleaned, or we can leave the old church to the left and come
straight to the facade of the white heap.

From St. Peter's purity to Sacré Coeur may be a stone's throw
in space, but the two structures are in fact worlds apart.

Sacré Coeur Basilica

Coming into Paris from Roissy Airport, the first monument

the visitor espies is the Sacré Coeur, aloft on its Oriental carpet over the city. After the dull ride into the city, the church with its five white mamelons pointing skyward jolts one into recognition.

The Basilica was placed atop Montmartre hill following the Paris Commune of 1871. After Paris's fall to the Prussians, the people of Montmartre rose to save their quarter from the invaders. The inhabitants amassed 171 cannons at the Place du Tertre and prepared to face the Prussian army. It was, however, Napoleon III's army which advanced on the butte to seize the cannons. Two generals were taken prisoner and killed by the crowd. Throughout the city, people then rose against the regime. Defeat in the hands of the Prussians had been humiliating. At the time France was the second world power (after England), and that war had been fought on the slimmest of pretexts: essentially, Napoleon III had wanted to flex his muscles.

The result was the Paris Commune, a revolutionary government that remained in power for a little more than two months. It was brutally dismantled in house-to-house fighting that left 30,000 dead.

Since the commune had originated in Montmartre, the succeeding "loyalist" parliament was not about to extend pardon. On the contrary, a national subscription was voted to pay for the construction of the Sacred Heart Basilica as a monument of atonement for the quarter's "transgression." Criticism of the project was vociferous. Emile Zola wrote of it: "One cannot imagine a more ridiculous and meaningless project. Paris, our grand Paris, crowned, dominated by a temple built for the glorification of absurdity."

The building was begun in 1876, completed in 1910, and finally consecrated in 1919. Since 1878, men and women relay one another twenty-four hours a day to pray in expiation of the "sins of humanity."

Sacré Coeur was designed to reign supreme, despite difficulties with the supporting pillars that had to be sunk to a depth of 125 feet; the hill was spongy with the holes left by the mine shafts of yesteryear. The goal was to impress: the Savoyard bell weighs almost 40,000 pounds; it is one of the largest ever cast and literally exhausted the twenty-eight horses that hauled it to the top of the butte.

The style of the church is 12th-century Byzantine. Inside, it is big without a dimension of greatness. There are souvenir shops on either side of the transept.

At the foot of the Basilica lies the City of Paris.

When leaving the terrace, take the first street to the right and then first left to the Place du Tertre.

Place du Tertre

When Montmartre was a village outside the city's walls, this was its square. Its houses were rustic, its pavements cobbled and irregular.

Today every square centimeter is valued and occupied. The center is for tables and parasols of the restaurants across the road; the outer limits on the northern half are covered by artists and their wares; the southern half is the haven of the portraitists and silhouettists. They can be classed from bad to fairly good. It is a matter of taste and pocketbook, and it is fun.

On the south side of the place, *Patachou*, the former nightclub singer, has opened a magnificent restaurant, café, and pastry shop with a terrace commanding the most perfect view of Paris.

You can walk through Patachou's to the pastry shop and leave the Place du Tertre there. Go past the Wax Museum, which is an amusing stop if you still have the strength, and skirt around until you reach Rue Norvins again. Go left at Clement Square and right at Rue Ravignan until you come to Emile Goudeau Square. In the middle under the foliage is a Wallace fountain, of which there are several in Montmartre. Sir Richard Wallace, 19th-century English philanthropist, endowed Paris with 100 similar-styled fountains now spread throughout the city.

On the right is the reconstruction of the artists' studios, the *Bateau Lavoir*. It was here that Picasso painted his celebrated *Desmoiselles d'Avignon*, considered to be the beginnings of cubism. At the time, he and Max Jacob shared a bed, one occupying it by day and the other at night. The original structure burned down in 1970, but has been duplicated and now has room for twenty-five artists.

Before leaving Montmartre, take Rue Ravignan to the right at the bottom end of the place. Continue on Rue Durantin. At the corner of Rue Tholozé, you will finally get a look at the now-sequestered *Moulin de la Galette*. Do you remember Renoir's extraordinary painting of the Moulin's dance hall, now hanging at the Orsay? Van Gogh and Willette also contributed to the Moulin's immortalization. It was the rage in its day.

Go to the left on Rue Tholozé and left again at the Rue des Abbesses to the Place des Abbesses. There you will find a fine Guimard turn-of-the-century métro entrance.

Along the way

Restaurants
A. Beauvilliers
L'Assommoir
Le Bateau Lavoir
Au Clair de la Lune
La Cremaillère
Da Graziano Restaurant
Grain de Folie
Patachou
A la Pomponnette
Le Taroudant
Au Virage Lepic

Tea, Snacks, Ice Cream, Pastry
L'Epicerie de la Butte
Le Moule à Gâteaux
Patachou
Le Téléphone

Beer, Wine Bars, Cafés
Auberge de la Bonne Franquette
Au Lapin Agile
Le Tire-Bouchon

Hotels
Hôtel Caulaincourt
Hôtel du Coeur de la Butte
La Résidence Montmartre
Tim Hôtel

CHAPTER 12

From the Eiffel Tower to the Trocadero and Its Museums

The Eiffel Tower was built for the Universal Exhibition of 1889. It was a temporary structure, the expression of the triumph of the industrial age. Its success was so great, however, that it remained and became the symbol of Paris.

During its construction from January 1887 to May 1889, Parisians flocked to the site on weekends to measure progress. It was then the tallest man-made structure in the world. With its TV and radio transmitter and antennae, it now rises 1263 feet off the ground. Its original antenna served both radio and telegraph. In 1916 it became the terminal for the first trans-Atlantic telephone linkup. On the top platform is an aircraft meteorological

Métro: Ecole Militaire, Bir-Hakeim, Trocadéro, Iéna

Bus: 42, 69, 82, 87—Eiffel Tower
          22, 30, 32, 63—Trocadéro
          32, 63, 82—Iéna

Eiffel Tower: Champ-de-Mars
                  10 A.M.–11 P.M. every day

Chaillot Palace fountains: afternoons and evenings

Naval Museum: West Wing, Chaillot Palace
                  10 A.M.–6 P.M.
                  Closed Tuesdays.

Museum of Man: West wing, Chaillot Palace
                  9:45 A.M.–5:15 P.M.
                  Closed Tuesdays and holidays.

Museum of French Monuments: East wing, Chaillot Palace
                  9 A.M.–6 P.M.
                  Closed Tuesdays.

Cinema Museum: East wing, Chaillot Palace
                  Guided visits at 10 and 11 A.M., 2, 3, and 4 P.M.
                  Closed Tuesdays and holidays.

Aquarium: East end garden entrance, Chaillot Palace
                  10 A.M.–5:30 P.M. every day

Guimet Museum: Place d'Iéna
                  9:45 A.M.–5:10 P.M.
                  Closed Tuesdays and holidays.

Children's Museum: East wing, Tokyo Palace
                  Temporary exhibits:
                  10 A.M.–5:40 P.M.
                  Closed Mondays and holidays.

Museum of Modern Art: Tokyo Palace
                  11 Avenue du Président Wilson
                  10 A.M.–5:40 P.M.
                  Closed Mondays and holidays.

Museum of Fashion and Costume: Galliera Palace,
                              1 Avenue Pierre Ier de Serbie
                              10 A.M.–5:40 P.M.
                              Closed Mondays.

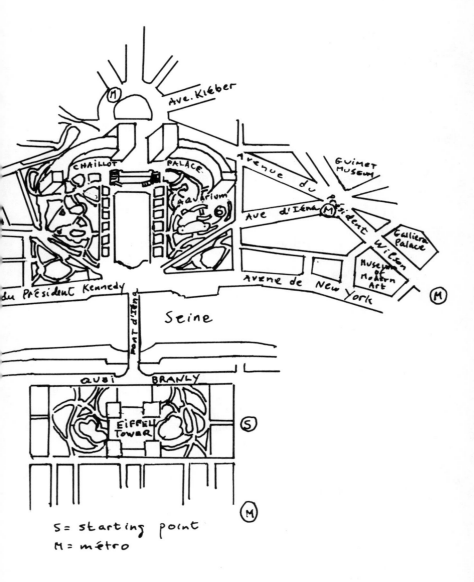

S = starting point
M = métro

and navigation station fitted with a revolving beacon. Two-and-one-half million rivets hold the steel latticework together.

There are three floors. From the third, at 900 feet, you can see forty miles away on a clear day. The best time to attempt the view is about one hour before dusk. The restaurant on the first platform is pleasant and medium-priced. The *Jules Verne*, on the second platform, is a gastronomic and visual delight, although expensive.

The tower was the brainstorm of two engineers, Koechkin and Nouguier, who worked in Eiffel's office. They entered and won the international competition for the design of an 1181-foot iron structure for the Universal Exhibition of 1889. Once the success of the tower seemed certain, the initially skeptical Eiffel became its chief proponent and the principal beneficiary of the excitement its construction generated. Everyone—from Queen Victoria to Thomas Edison to Mahatma Gandhi—visited the Eiffel Tower.

In 1986 the lighting was modified. Rather than spotlights from the grounds to the Tower, it is now lit from within with sodium lamps. The effect is jewellike, a devastating fairy scepter over the tops of the city.

Trocadero—Chaillot Palace

Cross the Iéna Bridge over the Seine to the gardens and fountains of the Chaillot Palace. On this site Catherine de Médicis built a country home in the 16th century. In the 17th century Henrietta of England, wife of Louis XIV's brother, turned the estate into a convent to which many a past favorite of the court retreated.

Napoleon I razed the convent, built the Iéna Bridge, and made plans for a very grand palace for his son, King of Rome. The empire collapsed before construction began. In 1937 the present palace was built in the pre-war style for the Paris exhibition of that year.

The twin pavilions separated by a portico are lined with a

series of wan gilt statues. There is a magnificent view of the Eiffel Tower and gardens from here. The fountains surge outward with force during afternoons and evenings; the lighting is effective. On weekends skateboards and roller skaters play to the crowds. Vendors, dancers, and mimes are in attendance as well.

The number of museums catering to the most varied interests is considerable. There is much to see at the Chaillot Palace, next door at the Tokyo Palace, and across the street from the latter at the Guimet Museum and the Galliera Palace.

The *Naval Museum* in the west wing of Chaillot Palace displays French sea power and shipping throughout the centuries. Life-size and scale models of naval and merchant ships and fishing and pleasure boats are featured. Among the models is Columbus's *Santa Maria*.

The *Museum of Man* in the west wing of the Chaillot Palace tells the story of the human race through prehistory, anthropology, and ethnology. Many everyday objects are presented in mock displays of natural habitats.

The *Museum of French Monuments* in Chaillot Palace's east wing contains reproductions of French monumental art, sculpture, and murals. The exhibits are grouped by region, school, and period. Romanesque and Gothic frescos have been reproduced on life-size architectural replicas of domes and bits of walls of Chartres, Notre Dame, and so on placed at eye level!

The *Cinema Museum* in the east wing of Chaillot Palace has posters, authentic costumes, film décors, the reconstitution of a French movie set, and displays of some of the industry's predecessors—magic lanterns, shadow plays, Edison's kinetoscope, and so on.

The *Aquarium* at the east end garden entrance of Chaillot Palace contains the principal species of freshwater fish from the rivers of France.

The *Guimet Museum* at Place d'Iéna is devoted to Asian art. Exceptional pieces from Cambodia, Vietnam, India, Tibet, China, and other lands are displayed, including an unequalled collection of ceramics.

The *Museum of Modern Art*, down the hill on the right side of

President Wilson Avenue, has 20th-century paintings not removed to the Pompidou Center. Included is Dufy's fabulous mural *Fairy Electricity*, 180 feet long and thirty feet high. Temporary exhibits also are organized here.

The *Children's Museum* in the east wing of Tokyo Palace has very inventive and didactic temporary exhibits.

The *Museum of Fashion and Costume* at Galliera Palace is just across the way from the Museum of Modern Art. Built in the 1880s in Italian Renaissance style, it possesses a collection of 400 complete costumes that trace the history of male and female dress from 1750 to the present day.

Along the way

Restaurants
L'Ancien Trocadéro
La Belle France
Le Bourdonnais
Chez Ribe
Conservatoire Rachmaninov
Le Florence
Le Parisien
Jules Verne
Le Western (The Hilton)

Tea, Snacks, Ice Cream, Pastry
Carette
Gérard Beaufort

Beer, Wine Bars, Cafés
Le Bar Suffren (The Hilton)
Cocktail Corner (The Hilton)

Hotels
Le Hilton
Résidence Bouquet de Longchamp

CHAPTER 13

How to Survive in Paris with No Knowledge of French

Are you tired of struggling with foreign tongues? Has the effort of ordering food from French menus, of having to make yourself understood from dawn to dusk, worn you down? Are you panting to relax in the vernacular and bask in total English? Nothing is simpler in Paris. Try this formula for a day.

Begin your morning with the *International Herald Tribune*, the only English-language daily published in Paris and the first truly international newspaper. Jointly owned by the *New York Times* and the *Washington Post*, its news originates from those two establishments, is edited and supplemented in its Paris offices, and then is printed simultaneously in Paris and ten other cities around the world. This unique enterprise, begun in 1887 by the former *New York Herald*, was the first European news-paper to introduce linotype, the first to use radio transmissions to send and receive news, and the first to employ the automobile and then air carriers to distribute newspapers. As you pick up your copy of the *Herald*—as the French vendors call it (not "the Trib" as is familiar to New Yorkers)—160,000 other copies are being distributed worldwide in such far-flung places as Singa-pore, Hong Kong, London, and Amsterdam.

For a real English breakfast, you might stop at *The Pacific and East Company—British Colonies*. If it happens to be Sunday, how about brunch at *American Legion headquarters* on Rue Pierre Charron? or at the *Cotton Flag* on rue Richelieu? If you happen to be near the Ile St. Louis, try brunch at *Les Fous de l'Ile*. Or simply head for *Marks and Spencer*, where everything you may require to confect your own version of breakfast can be purchased at its freshest and most desirable.

Did you want to get in some shopping? The major department stores (*Printemps, Galéries Lafayette, Bon Marché,* and so on) all have English-speaking employees to guide you from floor to floor. The deluxe food market *Fauchon's* in-house interpreter is Cristo, out of New York.

If it is your day for perfume shopping, *Catherine* on rue Castiglione will serve you in fluent English and also ship to the United States. The chic shops on Rue St. Honoré all have English-speaking personnel, as do all the perfume and cosmetics discount stores (*Michel Swiss, Raoul et Curly,* and so on).

For lunch there is great variety: *Joe Allen's* if you are dying for spare ribs, *Mother Earth* for salads and hamburgers, smoked salmon or Irish stew at the *Ferme Irlandaise*, fish and chips at *Hamilton's*, or deli sandwiches at *Jo Goldenberg's*. If nothing on this list makes your mouth water, there is always a McDonald's down the street.

Now, what about an afternoon at the *Louvre*, the *Orsay Museum*, *Picasso's* magnificent collection, or one of the extensive one-man shows of the famous at the *Grand* or *Petit Palais*? For a nominal charge, all major museums offer a walkman guide with English-speaking cassette.

On the other hand, you could take in an English or American film. A large number of movie theatres on both sides of the river show nondubbed films in English (with French subtitles). Look for the term "V.O.", meaning "original version." Even the French want their Bogart straight.

Just a little something before going back to the hotel? How about tea and lemon tarts at *Fanny's Tea* on wistfully charming Place Dauphine; or at the *Tea Caddy* in a lovely little street alongside one of the oldest churches in Paris, St. Julien-le-Pauvre, just around the corner from *Shakespeare and Co.*, where you can pick up some reading material for the return trip? Don't forget A *Priorité Thé*, where you can try Peggy's homemade apple pie or cheesecake in one of the most elegant covered passageways imaginable, Galérie Vivienne, just off Place des Victoires.

How about ice cream at *Häagen-Dazs*, Place Victor-Hugo, or *Baskin and Robbins* on Rue du Four? The recipes are authentically American, albeit concocted in Europe.

Did you say back to the hotel for a shower and change?

If you're planning to head back out, I would suggest *Willi's Wine Bar* for a starter. Universally recognized as having the best selection of wines at any bar in Paris, let Englishman Mark Williamson guide your choice. The food also is recommended; they have good desserts.

Several Parisian bars are landmarks for the Anglo-American community. If bar-hopping is one of your favorite pastimes, try *Harry's Bar*. Harry's is the seat of Bar Flies International, founded in 1924, which now claims over 100,000 members spread through some twenty "traps." Another not-to-be-forgotten bar is the *Closerie des Lilas*, where each table sports a brass plaque dedicated to the Hemingways and Fitzgeralds for whom the Closerie's sidewalk and greenery were more home than home. Here, you can forget the food.

From the bar at *Joe Allen's* you will know you never left New York. The chief barman at the *Espadon Bar* of the *Hotel Ritz* is

Michel Bigot, president of the International Bartenders Association. If your preferred drink is not among the sixty-odd cocktails on the bar list, just ask for it. Very few mixtures have escaped his science. A pianist is on hand for cocktail hour. *Flann O'Brien's* bar just off the Chatelet is also a heartwarming establishment, known to every Irishman from Paris to Killarny. Very British is the *Regency Bar* at the Hotel Prince-de-Galles-Mariott.

And now for food. May I suggest *Haynes*, in Paris since 1947, making it the first American restaurant in the French capital and serving true soul food: southern fried chicken, black-eyed peas, yams, and homemade apple pie. You'll find real Tex-Mex food at the *Rio Grande.*

Marshal's Bar and Grill on Avenue Franklin-Roosevelt is good for caesar salads, hamburgers, and New York steaks. The *Western* at the *Hilton* also is known for its steaks, flown in daily from the U.S. as well as from Aberdeen.

If you are game for entertainment, an English-language theatre raises its curtain at 8:30 P.M. in the Latin Quarter: *Galérie 55*, at 55 Rue de Seine.

You can catch country music at *Cactus Charly's*, 68 Rue de Ponthieu, and jazz at the *Patio Bar* of the *Hotel Méridien*. At *La Calavados*, Joe Turner takes his place at the piano at midnight, as he has every night except Sunday for the past twenty-five years. At the *Montana Bar* in St. Germain–des–Près, excellent modern jazz pianist René Urtrager officiates from 10 P.M. until 2 A.M.

Among the jazz and rock clubs of the city, *Gibus* has played host to practically every rock star from Birmingham or Nashville to come through Paris. The leader of the new- and old-time jazz concerts is the *New Morning* (which seats 400). There's authentic U.S. jazz every night at *Le Petit Opportun.* Get there early for a good seat. The show begins at 11 P.M.

You can dance to be-bop at the *Slow Club.* You can try your skating skills on roller skates at *La Main Jaune* from 10 P.M. to dawn Fridays and Saturday.

If, however, it is your 1950 Olds or your 1952 Thunderbird that brings back sweet memories, you can check out the best in vintage American automobiles belonging to French amateurs, there to parade and trade every Friday night after 10 on the Tuileries garden-side of the Place de la Concorde.

The Pacific and East Company-British Colonies, 40 Rue Vieille-du-Temple, 4th arrondissement, 4272-4096. Métro: St. Paul. See chapter 5, itinerary 1.

American Legion headquarters: see chapter 20 under inexpensive, 7th arrondissement. American Pershing Hall.

Cotton Flag, 45 Rue de Richelieu, 1st arrondissement, 4296-9058. Métro: Pyramides. Closed Sundays and Monday evenings. Real cheesecake, ribs, and grilled salmon steaks.

Les Fous de l'Ile: see chapters 3 and 21, 4th arrondissement.

Marks and Spencer, 35 Boulevard Haussmann, 9th arrondissement, 4742-4291. 9:30 A.M.–6:30 P.M. Métro: Havre-Caumartin. The well-known British department store has an excellent food market.

Printemps, 64 Boulevard Haussmann, 9th arrondissement, 4282-5000. 10 A.M.–7 P.M. Métro: Havre-Caumartin. Elegant, very complete department store.

Galéries Lafaytte, 40 Boulevard Haussmann, 9th arrondissement, 4282-3456. 9:30 A.M.–6:30 P.M. Métro: Havre-Caumartin. The top Parisian department store.

Bon Marché, 38 Rue de Sèvres, 7th arrondissement, 4260–3345. 9:30 A.M.–6:30 P.M. Métro: Sèvres-Babylone. The only large department store on the Left Bank.

Fauchon: see chapter 21, 8th arrondissement.

Catherine: see chapter 17.

Michel Swiss: see chapter 17.

Raoul et Curly: see chapter 17.

Joe Allen: see chapter 20 under expensive, 1st arrondissement.

Mother Earth, 66 Rue des Lombards, 4th arrondissement, 4236–9013. Métro: Châtelet. Brunch on Sundays, live rock on Friday and Saturday evenings.

Ferme Irlandaise, 30 Place du Marché St. Honoré, 1st arrondissement, 4296-0299. Métro: Pyramides. Closed Sundays.

Hamilton's Fish and Chips, 51 Rue de Lappe, 11th arrondissement, 4806-7792. Métro: Bastille.

Jo Goldenberg: see chapter 20 under moderate, 4th arrondissement.

Fanny Tea: see chapter 21, 1st arrondissement.

Tea Caddy: see chapters 3 and 21, 5th arrondissement.

Shakespeare and Co.: see chapters 2 and 3.

A *Priorité Thé:* see chapters 10 and 21, 2nd arrondissement.

Häagen-Dazs, Place Victor-Hugo, 16th arrondissement. Métro: Victor-Hugo.

Baskin and Robbins: see chapter 21, 6th arrondissement.

Willi's Wine Bar: see chapter 18, 1st arrondissement.

Harry's Bar: see chapter 19, 2nd arrondissement.

Closerie des Lilas: see chapter 19, 6th arrondissement.

Espadon-Hemingway Bar, Hotel Ritz: see chapters 9 and 28, 1st arrondissement.

Flann O'Brien's: see chapter 19, 1st arrondissement.

Regency Bar, Hotel Prince-de-Galles-Marriott: see chapter 19, 8th arrondissement.

Haynes, 3 Rue Clauzel, 9th arrondiseement, 4878-4063. Métro: St. Georges.

Rio Grande, 24 Rue Aubry-le-Boucher, 4th arrondissement, 4272-6349. Métro: Les Halles, Châtelet.

Marshal's Bar et Grill: see chapter 20 under expensive, 8th arrondissement.

Western, Hotel Hilton, 18 Avenue de Suffren, 15th arrondissement, 4273-9200. Métro: Bir-Hakeim.

Galérie 55: see chapters 4, 22, and 25.

Cactus Charly: see chapter 20 under expensive, 8th arrondissement.

Lionel Hampton-Patio Bar, Hotel Meridien: see chapter 19, 17th arrondissement.

Le Calavados: see chapter 22.

Montana Bar: see chapter 22.

Gibus: see chapter 22.

New Morning: see chapter 22.

Le Petit Opportun: see chapter 22.

Slow Club, 130 Rue de Rivoli, 1st arrondissement, 4233-8430. 9:30 P.M.–2:30 A.M. (–4 A.M. Saturdays). Closed Sundays and Mondays. Métro: Châtelet. Live music. 50 francs on Tuesdays, Wednesdays and Thursdays, 62 francs on Fridays and Saturdays.

La Main Jaune: see chapters 22, 23, and 25.

CHAPTER 14

Excursions

Giverny

If you want to climb onto a pink cloud and tremble with visual ecstasy, you must make the trip to Giverny, the home and gardens of Claude Monet from 1883 to 1926.

Here swampland was transformed by the hand of the artist into a fairyland of flower gardens, moist country paths and lily ponds under a Japanese bridge. To the pink brick and green-shuttered, rambling country house with the grey slate roof, Monet added three studios, the last and largest being the one in which he painted the famous water-lily murals that cover the walls in the circular room under the Orangery in Paris. With his eyesight failing in his later years—he was eighty-six when he died—his works enlarged in scale.

Claude Monet's home is now as it was upon his death in 1926. We may wander from room to room and admire his extensive collection of Japanese prints as they line the walls; we may touch his old wood furniture. The sunken living room with the worn couch and armchairs await the arrival of the master after a stroll around the lily pond. The table is set for eight in the bright yellow and green dining room.

Following the Second World War, the property was reduced to a truly sad state. The gardens were gone, the pond was overrun with weeds, the house and studios were musty with disuse and in need of total renovation. It was thanks to Lila Acheson Wallace of *Reader's Digest* that this estate has regained its past glory. As in the days when Monet received his friends Clemenceau, Cézanne, Renoir, Manet, Sisley, and Pissaro, the old house is once again dressed for the gentle life.

Claude Monet Museum: Open from April 1st to October 31st
Closed Mondays.

   House: 10 A.M.–12 noon and 2–6 P.M.

   Gardens: 10 A.M.–6 P.M.

Train: From St. Lazare Station to Vernon, 2½ miles away.
45-minute trip. Trains at frequent intervals. Sunday schedule differs. For exact train information, call 4582-5050.

Round trip train fare is 94 francs (roughly $15).

Buses meet certain trains.
Bicycles for hire at railway station.
Taxis available at station, approximately $10.

Tourist buses: Excursions certain afternoons operated by:

Paris Vision, 214 Rue de Rivoli, métro Tuileries or Palais Royal, Tel. 4260-3125

Cityrama, 4 Place des Pyramides, métro Tuileries or Palais Royal, Tel. 4260-3014

Price 250 francs (roughly $40 at present exchange rate). Includes museum entry fee of 30 francs ($5). Departure 2 P.M.

Road: Take Autoroute de l'Ouest (Western Parkway) towards Rouen. Get off Parkway at Bonnières.

Time: Half to full day

The Grand Arch

The Grand Arch at the *Défense* represents the finishing touch on the long, straight-line perspective departing from the Louvre Palace.

The arch was conceived by Danish architect Johan Otto von Spreckelsen. It posed serious construction problems, the principal one being how to plant the giant structure on a site overlying a two-lane parkway, three rapid underground transit lines, part of a mall's parking lot, a corner of the local train station, and a series of freight tracks. Only two parallel strips of land, roughly 260 feet apart, could be considered *terra firma*; they would bear the weight aboard twelve concrete piles, each supporting from 25,000 to 27,000 tons of structure. There, too, lies the explanation for the fact that the arch is slightly off center.

The simplicity or severity of the design is broken by a canvas "cloud mass" flown from cables hooked into the sides of the arch. At night, color is projected on the walls in geometric design. These techniques provide tone to an otherwise silent cube. For cube it is: 360 by 360 by 360 feet. Carrara marble— grey on the outside of the arch and white on the inside—conceals the concrete interior.

The arch is located at the exact point of entry or, as the case may be, exit, where in 1871 the defenses of the capital waged their ultimate battle against the Prussians and succumbed.

The construction of a modern quarter began in 1962 with the CNIT trapeze destined to house trade fairs and congresses. At the time the tent structure sat alone amid mud-soaked, undulating vacant lots and squishy car parks. Today, some 50,000 people live in the modern apartment buildings in the area. Many more come and go to work here. Three hundred to 400 national and multinational corporations operate from the forty-odd towers of the Défense and carry the names of their sponsors-funders: Esso, Mobil, BP, Rhone Poulenc, IBM, Elf, Winterthur, and so on.

The thirty-five story arch was inaugurated with pomp during the July 1989 bicentennial celebrations; the circumstance was the annual meeting of heads of state of the world's most-developed nations. The two massive sides are office-spaced, harboring, among others, ministries and official bodies. Conference rooms and temporary exhibit halls occupy the area at the top and bottom of the cube.

Fountain ballet concerts are held daily on the esplanade. For an impressive view of Paris, tempt fate on the outside elevators in a ride to the top. Available from 9 A.M. to 5 P.M., the cost is 30 francs.

An evening visit also is time well spent in the light of the Grand Arch.

RER: Défense

Fountain concerts: 12 to 2 P.M. and 8:45 to 9:30 P.M. weekdays; plus 4:30 to 6:30 P.M. Tuesdays, Thursdays, Fridays; 3 P.M. only, Saturdays and Sundays.

Terrace Grand Arch: 9 A.M.–5 P.M.

Time: Half day

The Palace of Versailles

Versailles is the palace of palaces. It represents the epitome of French art and French power. It has been the envy of kings and would-be monarchs, and copied the world over.

Actually Versailles was the result partially of a king's sentimentality and partially of his cupidity. On this site Louis XIII had built a small, rose brick and stone hunting lodge in 1631. His son, Louis XIV, who sat on the throne of France from the age of five, had fond memories of his father's country chateau. In 1661, at his majority, he decided to enlarge it.

The most exquisite castle of France had just been completed at Vaux-le-Vicomte for Fouquet, Louis XIV's finance minister. The king would have a finer palace than Fouquet. He commissioned the same architect, Louis Le Vau; the same painter-decorator,

Charles Le Brun; and the same landscape architect, Le Nôtre.
Jules Hardouin-Mansart took over from Le Vau upon his death.

Construction lasted for fifty years. Thirty-seven thousand
acres of marshland had to be drained. A river had to be diverted
to feed the 1400 fountains. One hundred fifty thousand plants
were bedded and 100 statues ordered for the gardens alone.
Thirty-five thousand workers still were employed on the site
when the king and his court went into residence in 1682.

The court numbered 20,000. This figure included 9000 soldiers billeted in the town and 5000 servants in an annex. One
thousand noble men and women and their 4000 servants were
housed at the palace. Louis XIV overlorded this personal establishment, keeping an eye on all, creating rivalries, settling dis-
putes, indulging in favors, maneuvering on his society
chessboard. When he died in 1715, the court returned to Paris.

In 1722 Louis XV went back to Versailles. Louis XVI and
Marie Antoinette lived there until 1789. As the symbol of monar-
chial absolutism, Versailles was marked for spoliation. Its furniture was auctioned; its works of art transferred to the Louvre;
even its destruction was envisaged.

The palace was saved during the rule of Louis-Philippe, who
contributed personally to its renovation in order that it become a
museum "to the glories of France." A large donation from John
D. Rockefeller, following the Second World War, provided the
means for its restoration.

Versailles is tremendous in both size and imagery. It should be
visited several times, for there is much to see: the palace itself and
its state rooms, chapel, royal apartments, opera, the Grand
Trianon, the Petit Trianon, and the gardens.

RER: C-5 line from Left Bank

Rail: From Montparnasse or Saint Lazare railway stations

Bus: 171 from the Pont de Sèvres

Palace: 9:45 A.M.–5 P.M.
　　　　Closed Mondays and public holidays.

Grand Trianon: 9:45 A.M.–12 P.M. and 2–5 P.M.
　　　　Closed Mondays and public holidays.

Petit Trianon: 2–5 P.M.
　　　　Closed Mondays and public holidays.

Gardens: From sunrise to sunset.

Fountains: Show from June to September, Sundays at 3:30 P.M.

Sound and light shows: July, August, September—certain Saturdays. Time
　　　　varies. Call 3950-3622.

Chapel: Mass first Sunday of month at 5:30 P.M.

Time: All day

Boat Rides

Batobus: New boat service on the Seine in central Paris. Five
　　　　embarkation points along the quays: Bourdonnais (near
　　　　Eiffel Tower); Solférino (near Orsay Museum); Quai
　　　　Malaquais (near School of Beaux-Arts); Quai de Mon-
　　　　tébello (across from Nôtre-Dame, Left Bank); Quai de
　　　　l'Hôtel de Ville (near City Hall). Cost is 30 francs.

*Boat rides
on the Seine:* Although Parisians call all the sightseeing boats
　　　　bateaux-mouches, there are actually a number of
　　　　companies operating excursions on the Seine.
　　　　Most organize luncheon and dinner excursions in
　　　　addition to normal rides of approximately one
　　　　hour. Hotels and travel agencies can provide de-
　　　　tails.

For your information:

Bateaux-Mouches operate from Alma Bridge, Right Bank (métro Alma-Marceau). Tel. 4225-9610 and 4225-2255.

Bateaux Parisiens operate from Iéna Bridge, Left Bank (métro Trocadéro and cross over) and from Nôtre-Dame (métro Saint-Michel). Tel. 4705-5000.

Bateaux Vedettes du Pont Neuf operate from Pont Neuf-New Bridge (métro Pont Neuf or Louvre). Tel. 4633-9838.

St. Martin Canal: Three hours. Departure from Bassin de la Villette, Quai de la Loire (métro Jean-Jaurès) or Port de l'Arsenal, across from 50 Boulevard de la Bastille (métro Bastille).

Excursions operated by:

Canauxrama—Tel. 4239-1500
Paris Canal—Tel. 4240-9697

Cruise from Orsay Museum to Villette Park:

Three hours. Departure from Quai Anatole-France (métro Chambre des Députés). Tel. 4240-9697.

CHAPTER 15

Markets, Markets, Markets

Flea markets

Are they what they used to be? Definitely not. The days when vacant lots were littered with genuine bric-a-brac and with castaway U.S. Army clothing and equipment are gone. Gone, too, are the engraved crystal and handblown glasses from the beginning of the century available for a few sous; as are authentic flapper duds, lace-edged or embroidered undergarments, and linens for a couple of francs.

But there are still the *puces*, minus the fleas, and there are still finds to be had. At St. Ouen-Clignancourt, there are now nine markets, over 3000 stands, ten miles of sidewalk, and 150,000 visitors on a weekend.

Between the métro and the overhead highway are a multitude of blue-jeans vendors. The real stuff begins after the overhead. Take Rue des Rosiers on the left. Sign posts indicate the various markets. Remember, bargaining—to a point—is permitted.

Just off the corner, on Rue Jean-Henri Favre (the street parallel to the overhead highway) is *Veyrier*, a good source of old prints and books.

Biron is definitely the chicquest of the older flea markets. There are roughly 200 stands, including many run by antique dealers with elegant shops in town. Each dealer signs the "charter," a document that guarantees the authenticity of objects on display; no new things will be sold for old. Each shop has its specialty. Among others, see *Jeanne Moufflet* at number 137 for old posters and *Christine Cazenave* at 153 for old-fashioned lace and clothes.

You can stop across the way at *La Chope des Puces* for a drink or coffee and listen to a father-and-son team play Django Reinhardt tunes.

Cambo is actually an annex, a continuation of Biron.

Jules-Vallès is a real flea market. Among others, see *Pierre Jonchères* at stand 110. He is a former journalist who knows his Asian stuff. For antique dolls go to *Detave*, stand 24. *Bekka*, the king of bronze, is not to be missed.

At *Malik* are many specialists of secondhand clothes. The clothing is shipped mainly from the U.S. and Germany and sold by the pound to dealers who recycle it. Malik also has jeans. Among the best stands are *Daniel et Lily*, for small art objects and jewelry from the 1920s to the 1950s, and *Josiane* for old-fashioned clothes.

Malassis, which just opened, is an upgrade market, mainly covered, with verandas and vaulted glass roofing. There are 240 select shops, a restaurant, and an underground garage. The entrance is at 142 Rue des Rosiers, in between Vernaison and Malik. Is this the way of the *puces?*

Paul Bert has over 200 "in" stands, heteroclite but fashionable. *Olivier* (stand 232bis) for example, features vases, fixtures, and lamps of the early 1900s.

Rosiers is a small market with 30 stands and lower-class objects.

Serpette is located in a former garage, with 160 stands of good merchandise essentially from the 1920s. See *Marie-Eve Rosenthal*, stands 11 and 13, alley 4, for mirrors; *Bachelier*, stand 5, alley 6, for bistro accessories; and *François Leloup*, stand 116, alley 6, for posters.

Vernaison, last but not least, is the largest and first permanent market, founded in 1918. Hitherto, the ground played host to the ragmen of Paris for presentation of wares. There are over 300 merchants, among whom is *Nelly* at 137 for secondhand clothes with couture labels. At 141, *Janine Giovannoni* specializes in linens for the home from the 19th and early 20th centuries. *Michel Morin* at 112 has pottery, baskets, and furniture from the provinces. Stand 11, alley 1, is *Formes 7*, displaying Art Déco, glasses, and stoneware.

You can stop at *Lisette's* for lunch. There is always someone there singing Piaf and a fortune teller in the back alleyway to propel you into the future.

Métro: Porte-de-Clignancourt

Bus: 56, 85

Open: 5 A.M.–8 P.M.
         Saturdays, Sundays, and Mondays.

Beware of pickpockets on this métro line and at the Puces.

American flea market—For something more home-grown, the American Church sponsors a rummage sale on Saturday afternoons from 2 to 5 P.M. No one goes for broke: prices range from 5 to 50 francs.

Métro: Invalides, Alma-Marceau

Bus: 28, 42, 49, 63, 80, 82

American Church: 65 Quai d'Orsay
                 Tel: 4705-0799

Hours: 2–5 P.M. Saturdays.

Street Markets

The *Fabrics Market,* known to Parisians as St. Pierre's Market, is not a market in the technical sense of the word. It is a series of shops and stores spread over several small streets and in one covered market area at the foot of Sacré Coeur Church. Materials for home and dressmaking are sold at bargain prices, and everything from the finest cotton to the best silks and linens, as well as the cheaper stuff, is available.

The epicenter, and your best bet, is *Dreyfus.* They have a tremendous selection, and are at 20 Rue Pierre Picard, 4606-9225.

A word of caution: watch out for pickpockets.

Métro: Barbès-Rochechouart, Anvers

Bus: 30, 54, 85

Hours: 9:30 A.M.–6:30 P.M.
        Closed Sundays and Monday mornings.

Aligre Market, Place de l'Aligre, is the least expensive of the open-air food markets, with a mini-flea market adjunct. It is a very colorful market that caters to French and African customers, in the vernacular.

Métro: Ledru-Rollin

Bus: 61, 76, 86

Open: 8:30 A.M.–1 P.M.
         Closed Mondays.

Buci Market, Rue de Seine and Rue de Buci, is a lively market with trendy clientele. Those who cross Paris to do their Sunday morning shopping here are looking for atmosphere more than anything else. With few exceptions, the stands are owned and operated by one of the two supermarkets on Rue de Seine. There are good bread and pastry shops along Rue de Buci and *Le Fournil de Pierre* on Rue de Seine; excellent charcuterie at *L'Alsacienne,* Rue de Buci. There often is music by amateurs on Sunday mornings. See Chapter 4.

Métro: St. Germain des Près, Mabillon

Bus: 39, 48, 58, 70, 86, 87, 95, 96

Open: 8:30 A.M.–1 P.M. and 4–7:30 P.M.
          Closed Sunday afternoons and Mondays.

Mouffetard Market, Rue Mouffetard. This Roman artery makes the "Mouffe" one of the oldest streets in Paris. All up and down the hill you'll find food, food, and more food, including a large, exotic fruit and vegetable stand in the Rue de l'Arbalète. A real cornucopia, the market is at its best on weekends. At the top, Place de la Contrescarpe and the narrow streets leading into it are laden with the charm of old Paris.

Métro: Censier-Daubenton

Bus: 27, 47

Open: 8:30 A.M.–1 P.M. and 4–7:30 P.M.
          Closed Sunday afternoons and Mondays.

The *Stamp Market* at Cours Marigny is an outdoor market for amateurs who come to buy, sell, and exchange. It is located practically at the back door of the Elysées Palace, home of the French president. See Chapter 9.

Métro: Champs-Elysées-Clemenceau

Bus: 42, 52, 73, 83

Open: 10 A.M.–Sunset
Thursdays, Saturdays, Sundays, and holidays.

Flower Market, Place Louis-Lépine and Quai de Corse. The flower shops, although recently renovated, date from 1808. Wonderful, odorous cut flowers and plants are on sale. See Chapter 3.

Métro: Cité

Bus: 21, 24, 27, 85, 96

Open: 8 A.M.–7 P.M.
Closed Sundays.

Bird Market, Place Louis-Lépine and Quai de Corse. On Sundays birds displace flowers on the island square.

Métro: Cité

Bus: 21, 24, 27, 85, 96

Open: 9 A.M.–7 P.M.
Sundays only.

THE GRAND ARCH
AT THE DÉFENSE

GARNIER OPERA HOUSE

TURN-OF-THE-CENTURY
MÉTRO ENTRANCE
BY GUIMARD.

A PORTRAITIST ON THE PLACE DU TERTRE IN MONTMARTE

THE INVALIDES CHURCH

GEORGES POMPIDOU CENTER,
FRONT VIEW

GEORGES POMPIDOU CENTER

LUXEMBOURGE PALACE-THE FRENCH SENATE

MODERN STATUE AT THE FORUM DES HALLES

PLACE DES VOSGES

HÔTEL DE SULLY

THE SEINE

BARGES ON THE SEINE

THE CONCIÈRGERIE

STATUE ON ALEXANDER III BRIDGE

NOTRE DAME CATHEDRAL

Comparative Table of American, British and French Sizes:

Women's dresses

USA	8	10	12	14	16	18	20
UK	30	32	34	36	38	40	42
Fr.	38	40	42	44	46	48	50

Blouses, sweaters

USA	32	34	36	38	40	42
UK						
Fr.	38	40	42	44	46	48

Shirts

USA	14	14½	15	15½	16	16½	17	17½	18
UK									
Fr.	36	37	38	39	41	42	43	44	45

Men's suits

USA	34	36	38	40	42	44	46	48
UK								
Fr.	44	46	48	50	52	54	56	58

Women's shoes

USA	4½	5	5½	6	7	8	9	10
UK								
Fr.	35½	36	36½	37	38	39	40	41

Men's shoes

USA	7	8	9	10	11	12	13
UK							
Fr.	39½	41	42	43	44½	46	47

CHAPTER 16

Couture and Just Clothes

Paris is a shopper's mecca. There is just so much to be ogled at and to be bought.

To begin with there are a number of streets or areas where shops are concentrated. Here are the best of them.

Right Bank

Avenue des Champs-Elysées: 3 malls, numbers 26, 74, 78.

Avenue Montaigne: *haute couture* houses with ready-to-wear styles.

Forum des Halles: a mall of the top trademarks.

Place de la Madeleine, Rue Tronchet, Boulevard Haussmann: busy area of stores and department stores (Printemps, Galéries Lafayette, Marks and Spencer, Trois Quartiers).

Place des Victoires: younger designers' boutiques on the square and in the offshoots from it.

Porte Maillot: another top-labels mall.

Rue St. Honoré and Rue du Faubourg St. Honoré: very chic indeed.

Avenue Victor-Hugo: a classic shopping street.

Left Bank

Maine-Montparnasse Tower: Mall sheltering Habitat, C & A, Galéries Lafayette, and an assortment of boutiques.

Rue d'Alésia: outlet stores for major labels (Cacharel, Hecter, MicMac, etc.) between Alésia métro stop and Rue Didot.

Rue de Grenelle: one of the newer shopping streets with original boutiques. From Rue du Dragon (Sonia Rykiel) to Boulevard Raspail (Kenzo).

Rue St. Placide: a street for bargains, beginning at the Bon Marché Department Store and ending at Rue de Rennes, where, to the right, is the FNAC (books, records) and Tati, a bargain department store.

St. Germain des Près, Rue de Rennes, Rue du Four, Rue Bonaparte, Rue St. Sulpice: "in" boutiques.

Hours

Most clothing shops are open from 10 A.M. until 7 P.M. and closed on Sundays. Generally speaking, July, August, and January are sales months. Many shops begin earlier—in June for summer sales and mid-December for winter sales.

Détaxe

For purchases over 1200 French francs—roughly $200 at to-day's six to one exchange rate—you are entitled to a sales tax refund of anywhere from thirteen to twenty percent, depending on whether your purchase falls in the luxury category or not. Request a refund, called *détaxe*, whereupon you will be given a stamped envelope with some forms that you will fill out with the storekeeper. At the airport, on departure from France, this envelope should be turned in at the *détaxe* customs desk where the forms will be visaed. If the customs official returns the stamped envelope to you, drop it in the airport mailbox (keep the green copy for yourself). Upon receipt of the visaed pink slip, the shop will reimburse you—to your account in the U.S. or wherever—for the sales tax. If you leave France by train or car, give the *détaxe* envelopes to customs on the train or at the border.

For Women

Let us skip *haute couture*. If you have the means to become one of the happy few—and wish to—you probably already know the ropes. If not, just knock on the masters' doors.

We shall stumble on to their ready-to-wear shops.

Couture ready-to-wear
Azzedine Alaïa, 17 Rue du Parc Royal, 4272-1919. Métro: Chemin-Vert. The brightest and sexiest thing to happen to *la couture*.

Emmanuel Ungaro, 2 Avenue Montaigne, 4266-4570. Métro: Alma-Marceau. The less-expensive Ungaro line is called Parallèle.

Givenchy, 8 Avenue Georges V, 4723-8136. Métro: Alma-Marceau. The ready-to-wear line is called Life.

Jean-Louis Scherrer, 51 Avenue Montaigne, 4359-5539. Métro: Franklin-Roosevelt. See under discount heading.

Nina Ricci, 39 Avenue Montaigne, 4723-7888. Métro: Franklin-Roosevelt. Ready-to-wear here. Downstairs are permanent sales of *haute couture,* generally models used in fashion shows (about size 8).

Yves St. Laurent, 6 Place St. Sulpice, 4723-7271. Métro: St. Sulpice. The king of French couturiers for the last thirty years.

Creative ready-to-wear

Angelo Tarlazzi, 74 Rue des Saints-Pères, 4544-1232. Métro: Sèvres-Babylone. Bataclan is his cheaper line. See *Annexe des Créateurs* and *Fresque* under discount heading.

Anne-Marie Beretta, 24 Rue St. Sulpice, 4329-8404. Métro: Odéon. For the tall girl, well-structured clothes.

Gianni Versace, 67 Rue des Saints-Pères, 4544-0952. Métro: Sèvres-Babylone. Interesting materials.

Jean-Charles Castelbajac, 5 Rue des Petits-Champs, 4260-3733. Métro: Pyramides. Original, sporty clothes in wonderful setting.

Jean-Paul Gaultier, 6 Rue Vivienne, 4286-0505. Métro: Pyramides. Beautiful shop, mad clothes.

Kenzo, 3 Place des Victoires, 4236-8141. Métro: Bourse. Astonishing use of textures and colors.

Michel Léger, 22 Place du Marché St. Honoré, 4260-4790. Métro: Pyramides. One of the less-expensive designers.

Missoni, 43 Rue du Bac, 4548-2802. Métro: Bac. The most fabulous sweaters. Expensive.

Olivier Strelli, 55 Rue Bonaparte, 4046-0569. Métro: St. Sulpice. More moderately priced sports clothes.

Sonia Rykiel, 175 Boulevard St. Germain, 4954-6000. Métro: St. Germain-des-Prés. Her seams and long, loose look now are classic.

Thierry Mugler, 49 Avenue Montaigne, 4723-3762. Métro: Franklin-Roosevelt. Severe and flamboyant.

Valentino, 17–19 Avenue Montaigne, 4723-6461. Métro: Alma-Marceau. Two shops: one for clothes, one for the home.

Workshop—Comme les Garçons—Shirt, 4 and 15 Rue du Dragon, 4544-9440. Métro: St. Germain-des-Près, Sèvres-Babylone. Japanese designer Kawakubo.

Other ready-to-wear
A La Bonne Renommée, 26 Rue Vieille-du-Temple, 4272-0386. Métro: St. Paul. Dresses and jackets with a folk air and a bit of patchwork.

Benetton, 82 Avenue Victor-Hugo, 4227-7373. Métro: Victor-Hugo. They also have many other locations. Sweaters.

Cacharel, 74 Avenue des Champs-Elysées, 4563-2309. Métro: Franklin-Roosevelt. The same neat look. See, under discount, *Cacharel Stock*.

Eric Bompard, 28 Rue Montrosier, 4747-7656. Métro: Porte-Maillot. Cashmeres from China, silk shirts.

Et Vous, 64 Rue de Rennes. Métro: St. Germain-des-Près. The newest back-when look.

Fabrice Karel, 39 Avenue Victor-Hugo, 4500-5922. Métro: Kléber. Classic knitwear.

Fac Bazar, 38 Rue des Saints-Pères, 4548-4615. Métro: St. Germain-des-Près. Original bulky sweaters.

Hermès, 24 Rue du Faubourg St. Honoré, 4265-2160. Métro: Concorde. Oh, those scarves.

Kookaï, 15ter Rue St. Placide, 4544-0566. Métro: St. Placide. Knitwear with a flair.

Laura Ashley, 94 Rue de Rennes, 4548-4389. Métro: St. Placide. Still old England, including wedding dresses.

Marithé et François Girbaud, 38 Rue Etienne Marcel, 4233-5469. Métro: Etienne Marcel. The same pants year after year, admirably cut.

Max Mara, 265 Rue St. Honoré, 4020-0458. Métro: Concorde. Sportswear with style.

Monoprix-Uniprix, 21 Avenue de l'Opéra, 4261-7808. Métro: Pyramides. All over the city. Good quality and style for the price.

Prisunic, 109 Rue de la Boétie, 4225-2746. Métro: Franklin-Roosevelt. Many stores throughout the city. Up-to-date. Good quality and style. Reasonably priced.

Rodier, 21 Rue Danielle Casanova, 4260-0325. Métro: Pyramides. Classic knitwear, very matchable.

Shoes
Camille Unglik, 66 Rue des Saints-Pères, 4222-7877. Métro: Sèvres-Babylone. Unbeatable quality and design. My absolute favorite.

Roberto Botticelli, 1 Rue de Tournon. Métro: Odéon. Fashionable Italian shoes, medium-priced.

Robert Clergerie, 5 Rue du Cherche-Midi, 4548-7547. Métro: Sèvres-Babylone. Trendy and flat, good quality.

Stéphane Kélian, 6 Place des Victoires, 4261-6074. Métro: Bourse. Specialty is plaited leather. Well-made. Expensive.

Walter Steiger, 5 Rue de Tournon, 4633-0145. Métro: Odéon. Elegant, expensive.

Handbags and luggage

Bottega Veneta, 48 Avenue Victor-Hugo, 4501-7058. Métro: Victor-Hugo. Expensive but eternal.

Furla, 40 Rue du Dragon, 4049-0644. Métro: Sèvres-Babylone. All leather, including the imitation alligator. Good designs moderately priced.

La Peau de Porc, 240bis Boulevard St. Germain, 4548-8117. Métro: Bac. Pigskin classics from an old, reputable house.

Louis Vuitton, 97 Avenue Montaigne, 4720-4700. Métro: Franklin-Roosevelt. Just looking is an experience.

For Men

Aristote, 91 Rue de Seine, 4354-7309. Métro: Mabillon. Good choice of elegant sportswear by Cerruti, Smalto, and Pancaldi.

Barbara Bui, 13 Rue de Turbigo, 4236-4434. Métro: Etienne-Marcel. The designer's own line of shirts, pants, and jackets at acceptable prices.

Burberry's, 8 Boulevard Malesherbes, 4266-1301. Métro: Madeleine. Classic and British.

Cerruti, 27 Rue Royale, 4265-6872. Métro: Madeleine. Superbly casual—and expensive.

Charvet, 28 Place Vendôme, 4260-3070. Métro: Opéra. An institution from another era. Sober elegance, ready-to-wear, and custom-made.

Christian Aujard, 15 Rue de Tournon, 4325-6450. Métro: Odéon. Sportswear with a casual look by an excellent designer.

Ermenegildo Zegna, 10 Rue de la Paix, 4261-6761. Métro: Opéra. High-quality Italian suiting manufacturer's high-fashion clothes.

Francesco Smalto, 5 Place Victor-Hugo, 4500-4864. Métro: Victor-Hugo. Beautifully cut, classic suits and separates with style.

Motton's, 39 Rue du Cherche-Midi, 4222-2997. Métro: Sèvres-Babylone. A mixture of tweed, dandy and fun.

Shoes
Finsbury, 17 Rue des Petits-Champs, 4015-9299. Métro: Pyramides. Good selection of well-known trademarks.

J. Fénestrier, 23 Rue du Cherche-Midi, 4222-6602. Métro: Sèvres-Babylone. High quality, direct from the factory.

Michel Delauney, 6 Rue de l'Oratoire, 4260-2085. Métro: Louvre. The designer's shoes at reasonable prices.

For Children

La Châtelaine, 170 Avenue Victor-Hugo, 4727-4407. Métro: Pompe. Luxury shop for children's clothes.

Jacadi, 60 Boulevard de Courcelles, 4763-5523, and many other locations. Métro: Monceau. Adorable and medium-priced. 119 Rue d'Alésia for discounted merchandise.

Tati, 140 Rue de Rennes, 4548-6831. Métro: Montparnasse. Bargain department store. Beware of pickpockets.

Shoes

Till, Beaugrenelle Center, 5475-7617. Métro: Charles-Michel. Good quality, low prices.

Discount

Alice Landais, 5 Rue du Faubourg St. Honoré, 4265-9324. Métro: Concorde. Silk scarves, ties, and handkerchiefs. Manufacturer's prices.

Anne Lowe, 35 Avenue Matignon, 4359-9661. Métro: Miromesnil. Designer clothes.

Annexe des Créateurs, 19 Rue Godot-de-Mauroy, 4265-4640. Métro: Madeleine. Angelo Tarlazzi and a few others.

Bab's, 29 Avenue Marceau, 4720-8474. Métro: Alma-Marceau. 89bis Avenue des Ternes, 4574-0274. Métro: Porte-Maillot. Designer clothes.

Betty, 10 Place de l'Aligre, 4307-4065. Métro: Ledru-Rollin. Closed Mondays. Silk jerseys.

Cacharel Stock, 114 Rue d'Alésia, 4542-5304. Métro: Alésia.

Chercheminippes, 109–110–111 Rue du Cherche-Midi, 4222-3389. Métro: Vaneau, Falguière. Resale clothes for men, women, and children.

Courrèges, 7 Rue Turbigo, 4333-0357. Métro: Etienne-Marcel. His own label.

Dépôt des Grandes Marques, 15 Rue de la Banque, 4296-9904. Métro: Bourse. Menswear with designer labels.

Les Deux Oursons, 106 Boulevard de Grenelle, 4575-1077. Métro: La Motte-Picquet. Secondhand furs.

Didier Ludot, 22–24 Galérie Montpensier, Palais Royal, 4296-0656. Métro: Palais-Royal. Secondhand luxury leather goods, accessories, and Chanel suits.

Ellipse, 26 Rue Gustave-Courbet, 4727-3674. Métro: Pompe. A resale shop with some couture merchandise.

Fikipsi Stock, 84 Avenue d'Italie, 4589-0352. Métro: Maison-Blanche. Cacharel's cheaper line.

Fresque, 13 Rue de Tournon, 4325-4269. Métro: Odéon, Mabillon. Angelo Tarlazzi and others.

Gigi's Soldes, 30 Place du Marché St. Honoré, 4260-0898. Métro: Pyramides. Italian shoes, many with designer labels.

Goupil, 28 and 50 Boulevard St. Germain, 4354-1372. Métro: Maubert-Mutualité. Leather garments at wholesale prices.

Halle Bys, 60 Rue de Richelieu, 4296-6542. Métro: Bourse. Brand names for men, women, and children.

Lanvin-Soldes Trois, 3 Rue de Vienne. Métro: St. Lazare. Both men and women's wear, discounted.

Mendès, 65 Rue Montmartre, 4236-8332. Métro: Sentier. Jobber for Yves St. Laurent, Valentino, and others.

Miprix, 27 Boulevard Victor. Métro: Balard, Porte-de-Versailles. Designer shoes and ski clothes.

Pierre Cardin Soldes, 11 Boulevard Sébastopol, third floor. Métro: Châtelet. Returned merchandise at discount prices.

Réciproque, 95, 101 and 123 Rue de la Pompe, 4704-3028.
Métro: Pompe. Resale shop for men, women, and children.

Rodier, 11 Boulevard de la Madeleine. Métro: Madeleine.
Closed Saturdays. Rodier's own discount basement.

Scherrer Soldes, 29 Avenue Ledru-Rollin, 4628-3927. Métro:
Gare-de-Lyon. Last season's collection discounted.

Sport Cash, 2 Rue de la Bastille. Métro: Bastille. Bathing suits,
tennis and ski outfits.

Top Griffes, 1 Rue de Marivaux, 4296-4026. Métro: Richelieu-
Drouot. Shoes at a discount.

CHAPTER 17

Gifts, Souvenirs, Artifacts

Perfume

"Perfume is not just a good scent. It is a work of art." This statement by Robert Ricci, Nina's father and manager, takes on particular significance at a time when perfume is being overtaken by industrialization. Synthetics are rapidly replacing the fine natural essences extracted directly from the rose, jasmine, lemon and bergamot, lavender, cloves—the list is limitless. While synthetics themselves are cheap, synthetic perfumes—or mixtures of synthetics and natural oils—are not. With over 800 perfumes on the market today, we have made this our first rule for selection: quality products are made with natural essences.

Should you choose perfume, toilet water, or eau de cologne? Cologne is the most diluted of the three and is to be used primarily as a scented body wash. Toilet water is about halfway between the strength of perfume and the evaporative nature of cologne. Perfumes contain fixatives that make them longer lasting and should be used sparingly. The better labels include Caron, Chanel, Christian Dior, Guerlain, Houbigant, Jean Patou, Lanvin, Molyneux, Nina Ricci, Rochas, and Roger et Gallet.

There are discount shops for perfume and cosmetics everywhere in town. Count on a minimum of twenty-five percent plus the sales tax refund which is more or less fifteen percent. The prices of perfume products and cosmetics are fixed by the manufacturer; only the discount rate varies.

Most *détaxe* shops discount you at time of purchase. There are no forms or formalities to be completed at the airport, but you must have your passport in hand when buying.

Catherine, 6 Rue de Castiglione, 4260-8149. Métro: Tuileries.

Centre Franco-Américain, 49 Rue d'Aboukir, 4236-7746. Métro: Sentier.

Michel Swiss, 16 Rue de la Paix, 4261-6111. Métro: Opéra.

Raoul et Curly, 47 Avenue de l'Opéra, 4742-5010. Métro: Opéra.

Guerlain merits special mention. On the one hand, their products are fragrantly fabulous, and, on the other, they are not available in shops other than Guerlain's own. Sales tax discounts are given for purchases over 1200 French francs. (If you buy less than that amount, try the airport tax-free shops before departure.)

Guerlain Shops:
68 Avenue des Champs-Elysées, 4562-5257. Métro: Franklin-Roosevelt.

35 Rue Tronchet, 4742-5323. Métro: Havre-Caumartin.

2 Place Vendôme, 4260-6861. Métro: Tuileries.

93 Rue de Passy, 4288-4162. Métro: La Muette.

29 Rue de Sèvres, 4222-4660. Métro: Sèvres-Babylone.

Would you like to take a lesson in makeup?

Lancôme, 29 Rue du Faubourg St. Honoré, 4265-3074. Métro: Concorde. 240 francs ($40) for forty-five-minute session.

Serge-Louis Alvarez, 45 Rue St. Honoré, 4233-1052. Métro: Louvre. 150 francs ($25) for forty-five minute session.

Shu-Uemura, 276 Boulevard St. Germain, 4548-0255. Métro: St. Germain-des-Près. Japanese cosmetics. Free counseling with no obligation to buy.

Jewelry

Frenchwomen are insatiable consumers of jewelry and it abounds—from the street vendor's junk and fun to perfectly cut, exceptionally white diamonds. Intentionally, we have not placed Cartier, Van Arpels, *et al.* in our enumeration. In any event, if they are a must for you, you will find them in the hundred yards that separate the Rue de la Paix from the Rue St. Honoré. The shops listed carry, essentially, articles made in France unless otherwise stipulated.

Argana, 33 Rue Jacob, 4260-8923. Métro: St. Germain-des-Près. Very fine ethnic jewelry from North Africa and Asia.

Arthus Bertrand, 6 Place St. Germain-des-Près, 4222-1920. Métro: St. Germain-des-Près. Closed Mondays. Copies of antique jewelry from the Louvre collection in silver, vermeil, and gold. Exclusive agent of Zolatas Prestige.

L'Avant Musée, 2 Rue Brisemiche, 4887-4581. Métro: Hôtel-de-Ville. Some eighty innovators have joined together here to sell their wares. Costume and crazy jewelry from 25 francs up.

Cipango, 14 Rue de l'Echaudé, 4326-0892. Métro: Mabillon. One-of-a-kind necklaces of rough and cut semiprecious stones, coral, turquoise, and so on.

Danielle Livet, 7 Rue La Feuillade, 4703-9290. Métro: Bourse. Costume jewelry from the trendy to the outspoken.

Fabrice, 33 Rue Bonaparte, 4326-5795. Métro: St. Germain-des-Près. High-fashion contemporary jewelry. Expensive.

Isadora, 10 Rue du Près aux Clercs, 4222-8963. Métro: Bac. Reminiscent of the 1920s, bakelite designs and clean colors.

Jeanne Do, 67 Rue de Seine, 4633-4894. Métro: Mabillon. Original designs with an Art Nouveau flavor.

Maud Bled, 20 Rue Jacob, 4329-4651. Métro: St. Germain-des-Près. Nothing but authentic Art Déco. Afternoons only.

Le Parthénon, 54 Rue des Ecoles, 4354-2604. Métro: Maubert-Mutualité. Pewter and stones. Wonderful with sportswear.

Poiray, 8 Rue de la Paix, 4261-7058. Métro: Opéra. The geometrics of the 1920s transferred to jewels of today in gold.

Othello, 21 Rue des Saints-Pères, 4260-2624. Métro: Bac. Wood, leather, horn, plus bronze and silver. Contemporary designs.

La Squadra, 368 Rue St. Honoré, 4296-0972. Métro: Concorde.

Closed Saturday. Contemporary Italian designs in gold and semiprecious stones.

Troc de Bijoux, 3 Rue Coëtlogon, 4558-9354. Métro: St. Sulpice. Afternoons. Antique jewelry sold for private clients at reasonable prices.

Les Trois B, 92 Rue St. Martin, 4278-2370. Métro: Les Halles. Excellent choice of contemporary handcrafted pieces.

Household Items

We have limited ourselves to objects you hopefully can carry home.

A. *Simon*, 48 Rue Montmartre and 36 Rue Etienne-Marcel, 4233-7165. Métro: Etienne-Marcel. Two shops, supermarkets for cooking equipment and dishware.

La Carpe, 14 Rue Tronchet, 4742-7325. Métro: Madeleine. Elegant culinary and table gadgets.

Chiff-Tir, 104 Rue de Rennes, 4222-2513. Métro: St. Placide. Less-expensive linens and tablewear. Often seconds.

Cir-Roussel, 22 Rue St. Sulpice, 4326-4650. Métro: St. Sulpice. Wax manufacturer for over 350 years. You will find an amazing assortment of candles.

Dehillerin, 18–20 Rue Coquillère, 4236-5313. Métro: Les Halles. Copper pots, iron pots, and cutlery galore.

Forestier, 35 Rue Duret, 4500-0861. Métro: Argentine. A seasonal shop with verve: gifts, dishes, gadgets for the wine harvest, Halloween, April Fool's Day, or Christmas. Beautiful shop in former dairy.

Habitat, 17 Rue de l'Arrivée, Montparnasse Tower, 4538-6990. Métro: Montparnasse. Household department store of furniture and utility items from the world over. Kitchen and tableware, gadgets, and office items, all well chosen, are moderately priced.

Isler, 44 Rue Coquillère, 4233-2092. Métro: Les Halles. Knives for every purpose.

Le Jardin Moghol, 74 Rue Vieille-du-Temple, 4887-4132. Métro: St. Paul. Textile designs from the Moghol period. From India, fabrics, dressing gowns, tablecloths, baby clothes, and more.

Les Olivades, 25 Rue de l'Anonciation, 4527-0776. Métro: Passy. Fabrics from Provence printed with wood blocks of yore. Moderately priced.

Porthault, 18 Avenue Montaigne, 4720-7525. Métro: Alma-Marceau. Sheets and tableware fit for royalty. The Studio line is a little less expensive.

Quartz, 12 Rue des Quatre Vents, 4354-0300. Métro: Odéon. A house of modern glassware.

Scandia, 3 Rue de Rivoli, 4272-1299. Métro: St. Paul. Scandinavian table and kitchenware and gadgets.

Simrane, 23–25 Rue Bonaparte, 4354-9073. Métro: St. Germain-des-Près. Indian block prints for bedspreads, curtains, tablecloths, mats, and so on.

Souleïado, 78 Rue de Seine, 4354-1513. Métro: Mabillon, Odéon. Provençal fabrics, wallpaper, and clothes. Magnificent and expensive.

La Tuile à Loup, 35 Rue Daubenton, 4707-2890. Métro: Censier-Daubenton. Traditional objects from the French provinces: pottery, tiles, baskets, and wooden articles.

Toys

L'Amicale-Comptoir des Articles de Fêtes, 32 Rue des Vignoles, 4370-2100. Métro: Avron, Buzenval. Closed Mondays and August. Everything-for-a-party store.

Boutique D.A.C., 10 Rue du Cardinal-Lemoine, 4354-9951. Métro: Cardinal-Lemoine. Closed August. Marionettes, porcelain dolls, automats, and doll houses and furnishings.

Chat Perché, 54 Rue du Roi-de-Sicile, 4277-2048. Métro: St. Paul. Closed Mondays and August. All sorts of toys presented any which way.

Le Ciel est à Tout le Monde, 10 Rue Gay-Lussac, 4633-2150. Métro: Luxembourg. Closed August. Kites and anything that flies.

Jouets et Cie, 11 Boulevard de Sébastopol, 4233-6767. Métro: Châtelet. Supermarket of assorted toys and gimmicks.

La Maison de la Pelouche, 74 Rue de Seine, 4633-6021. Métro: Mabillon, Odéon. Wonderful animal world of fluff.

Le Monde en Marche, 34 Rue Dauphine, 4326-6653. Métro: Odéon. Closed Mondays and August. Tin miniatures and wooden toys.

Pain d'Epices, 29–31 Passage Jouffroy, 10 Boulevard Montmartre, 4770-8265. Métro: Richelieu-Drouot, Rue Montmartre. Miniature world. Everything for Christmas stockings and doll houses.

Si Tu Veux, 62 and 68 Galérie Vivienne, 4260-2997. Métro: Bourse. Lovely selection in two inviting shops.

Art Treasures

This is the place to talk about street vendors of art. They are to be found alongside many museums and churches and at strategic locations. Some sell artwork, others create it in the form of portraits and caricatures in front of you. It is up to you to judge the quality 'of the work and the price, which in general is negotiable.

Among the vendors there has been an infiltration of knaves selling as original paintings simple black-and-white reproductions on which someone has dabbed a bit of color or a wash. An open box of paints is often set alongside to give the impression that the individual present is a genuine artist. The price, mind you, is that of a hand-painted original. At the Place du Tertre in Montmartre, an artists association has been created for the purpose of eliminating the rogues and putting an end to this hoodwinking practice.

A wide interpretation is given here to *art*. It includes everything—from war medals to antique dolls, lithographs, old newsreels, posters, and more. These are affordable items. I have not listed art galleries. Some are pointed out along the various itineraries, in Chapter 4 in particular.

Antoinette, 7 Rue Jacob, 4326-8485. Métro: St. Germain-des-Près. Naive art plus owls and other animals sculpted in wood.

Au Petit Mayet, 10 Rue Mayet, 4567-6829. Métro: Odéon. Specialist of antique toys: Soldiers, boats, cars, trains, and so on.

Aux Soldats d'Antan, 12 Rue de l'Université, 4260-8956. Métro: Bac. Well-known specialist of antique tin soldiers, war medals, and decorations.

Ciné-Images, 68 Rue de Babylone, 4551-2750. Métro: St. François-Xavier. One of the best film poster shops, recent and less recent.

Documents, 53 Rue de Seine, 4354-5068. Métro: Odéon. Good collection of original posters from late 19th century until today. Prices run from fifty to 2500 francs ($10 to $400).

Duvelleroy, 6 Rue de La Michodière, 4742-5577. Métro: Quatre-Septembre. Fans for *grandes dames*.

Frédéric Marchand, 6 Rue Montfaucon, 4354-3282. Métro: Mabillon. Mechanical toys and games from the past.

Galérie Urubamba, 4 Rue de la Bûcherie, 4354-0824. Métro: Maubert-Mutualité. Beautiful collection of masks, feathers, turquoise and silver jewelry, and old and new handloom, work of North and South American Indians.

Garnier-Arnoul, 39 Rue de Seine, 4354-8005. Métro: Odéon, Mabillon. Photos of your favorite stars of today and yesteryear.

L'Herminette, 4 Alley Germain, Louvre des Antiquaires, 4297-2809. Métro: Louvre. Locks and old tools.

L'Ile du Démon, 13 Rue Bonaparte. Métro: St. Germain-des-Près. African artifacts and ethnic jewelry.

Madeleine Gély, 218 Boulevard St. Germain, 4222-6335. Métro: Solférino. Fabulous collection of canes and umbrellas of different eras.

La Maison de Poupée, 40 Rue de Vaugirard, 4633-7405. Métro: St. Sulpice. Antique dolls and doll clothes in a museumlike shop.

La Monnaie de Paris, 2 Rue Guenégaud. Métro: Pont-Neuf. The mint sells, to the public, special series of cast-iron and bronze medals and jewelry, made in its workshops.

Monsieur Renard, 6 Rue de l'Echaudé, 4325-7072. Métro: Mabillon. Antique dolls and mechanical toys.

Numistoria, 49 Rue Vivienne, 4233-9345. Métro: Montmartre. Bank notes, old paper (engraved stocks and bonds), and coins for collectors. Large choice.

Patrice Reboul, 6 Alley Riesener, Louvre des Antiquaires, 4297-2893. Métro: Louvre. Old war medals and reduced models of ancient headgear.

Photo Verdeau, 14–16 Passage Verdeau, 4270-5191. Métro: Le Peletier. Antique and secondhand cameras, silent films, and old newsreels.

Roger-Viollet, 6 Rue de Seine, 4354-8110. Métro: Mabillon, Odéon. Photo archives from 1850 to the present.

Prints
Prints in black and white, sanguine, or color are wonderful lifetime souvenirs or gifts. Here follows a list of excellent dealers carrying prints. Prices vary tremendously in a same shop: from 25 francs to thousands of dollars.

But let's begin with a short definition of terms. A *print* is a picture printed off a plate, block, or roll. An *etching* is a print made from an etched plate, accomplished with the use of acid on the plate. A *lithograph* is a print made off a flat stone or metal plate, on which drawing is made with greasy matter that repels water and then accepts ink. A *wood cut* is a print made on an engraved wood block.

Al'Imagerie, 9 Rue Dante, 4325-1866. Métro: Maubert-Mutualité. Very large choice of old and new posters, lithographs, and Japanese prints.

Arsène Bonafous-Murat, 15 Rue de l'Echaudé. Métro: Mabillon. Good stock of 19th- and 20th-century prints. Frequent new acquisitions. Wide range of prices.

Galérie de la Hune, 14 Rue de l'Abbaye, 4325-5406. Métro: St. Germain-des-Près. Contemporary prints by Lalanne, Kozo, Masurovsky, and Piza.

Galérie Jan et Hélène Lühl, 19 Quai Malaquais, 4260-7697. Métro: St. Germain-des-Près. Specialists in Japanese prints.

Girand, 76 Rue de Seine, 4326-0761. Métro: Odéon, Mabillon. Extensive collection of old Japanese, English, and French prints by subjects.

Ghislaine Maillard, 11 Passage Verdeau, 4246-5320. Métro: Le Peletier. Tasteful decorative prints, fifty francs ($10) and up.

Janette Ostier, 26 Place des Vosges, 4887-2857. Métro: St. Paul. Lovely little shop devoted to Japanese prints. Interesting exhibitions.

Lecomte Galérie, 17 Rue de Seine, 4326-8547. Métro: Odéon, Mabillon. Good selection of 19th-century and early 20th-century etchings and lithographs.

Louvre Museum. Métro: Palais-Royal, Louvre. Closed Tuesdays. The chalcography shop sells prints by old masters—Degas, da Vinci *et al.*—made off old plates in their possession. Reasonably priced.

Paul Prouté, 74 Rue de Seine, 4326-8980. Métro: Odéon,

Mabillon. One of the oldest and most reputable shops of prints by illustrious masters.

Sophie Marcellin, 18 Passage Verdeau, 4246-3955. Métro: Le Peletier. Another interesting print shop with reasonable prices.

Tanakya, 4 Rue St. Sulpice, 4325-7291. Métro: Odéon. Fine prints and other objects—vases, boxes, etc.—from Japan.

Odds and Sundries

Agathe Gaillard, 2 Rue du Pont-Louis-Philippe, 4277-3824. Métro: Pont-Marie. Photo gallery stocking Cartier-Bresson, Doisneau, and others. Interesting shows.

Au Chat Dormant, 13 Rue du Cherche-Midi, 4549-4863. Métro: Sèvres-Babylone. The kingdom of the cat, from post cards to cushions to ceramics.

La Banque de l'Image, 8, 9, and 13 Rue de La Cossonnerie, 4508-5356. Métro: Les Halles. Supermarket of photo posters, post cards and photos of the stars.

Boutique Chic et Choc, in hallway of Châtelet métro station leading to RER. The métro ticket that becomes stationery, pencil cases, napkins, key rings, t-shirts, and what have you.

La Chambre Claire, 14 Rue St. Sulpice, 4634-0431. Métro: St. Sulpice. Unique photography bookshop. Exhibit every Saturday of a different book of photos, with the photographer, who will inscribe his work.

Charvet, 28 Place Vendôme, 4260-3070. Métro: Opéra. Passementerie cuff links in every color. Inexpensive souvenir from high-class shop.

Le Chat Huant, 50 et 52 Rue Galande, 4329-9995. Métro:

Maubert-Mutualité. Judicious selection of handicrafts from the world over. Many small, easily transportable articles.

Denise Corbier, 3 Rue de l'Odéon, 4326-0320. Métro: Odéon. For the smoker in general and the pipe adept in particular.

Deyrolle, 46 Rue du Bac, 4222-3007. Métro: Bac. Minerals, fossils, shells, butterflies, and stuffed animals.

Dubos-Maison de la Mouche, 1 Boulevard Henri IV, 4354-6046. Métro: Sully-Morland. Everything for fly fishing. Lessons every Saturday in front of the store. Register in advance for appointment.

Dupré Octante, 39 Rue d'Artois, 4563-1011. Métro: St. Philippe-du-Roule. Good selection of press books.

Fleurs Trousselier, 73 Boulevard Haussmann, 4266-9795. Métro: St. Lazare. Gorgeous silk flowers, handmade, for your hat, buttonhole, hair, or belt.

Louvre Museum. Métro: Palais-Royal, Louvre. Closed Tuesdays. The bookshop claims to be the largest art bookshop in the world and it probably is.

Melodies' Graphiques, 10 Rue du Pont-Louis-Philippe, 4274-5768. Métro: Pont-Marie. Florentine stationery representing bookbinders' themes of flowers and birds using technique developed by this firm in the 16th century.

Montorgueil, 34–36 Rue Montorgueil, 4026-8439. Métro: Les Halles. Handmade stationery in trompe l'oeil: imitation wood, marble, and so forth.

Motillon, 83bis Rue de l'Abbé-Groult, 4828-5894. Métro: Vaugirard. Equipment for deep-sea and fly fishing, including weights by *Catherine.*

Movies 2000, 49 Rue La Rochefoucault, 4281-0265. Métro: Pigalle. Choose from slides the portrait of your favorite star or a film poster: 10 to 30 francs.

Olrik, 11 Rue Falguière, 4783-7657. Métro: Falguière. Comic book specialist of French and Belgian classics, including all of Tintin.

Paper +, 9 Rue du Pont-Louis-Philippe. Métro: Pont-Marie. Two shops of superb writing paper and equally superb recycled sheets of many hues.

La Papeterie, 203bis Boulevard St. Germain, 4548-0308. Métro: Bac. Panodia's clever briefcases, photo albums, files, and more.

Pylones, 57 Rue St. Louis-en-l'Ile, 4634-0502. Métro: Pont-Marie. Stupendous latex animal bracelets and gadgets, the latest being visor caps and suspenders.

Rougier et Plé, 13–15 Boulevard des Filles-du-Calvaire, 4272-8290. Métro: Filles-du-Calvaire. Supply house for handicrafts of every sort.

La Route du Tibet, 3 Rue des Fossés-St. Jacques, 4633-1016. Métro: Luxembourg. Handcrafted articles from Tibet: carpets, textiles, silk shirts, bags, dolls, and jewelry.

Science, Art et Nature, 87 Rue Monge, 4707-5370. Métro: Censier-Daubenton. Butterflies and insects from the world over as well as nets and equipment for their preservation.

Sennelier, 3 Quai Voltaire, 4260-2938. Métro: Bac. The largest stock of art supplies in Paris.

Soco, 8 Place des Petits-Pères, 4260-1280. Métro: Bourse. Briefcases and handbags for the entire family made of leather or canvas, plastified or not. 250 francs ($40) and up.

CHAPTER 18

To Drink and Buy Wine

Wine Bars

1st arrondissement
Aux Bons Crus, 7 Rue des Petits-Champs. Métro: Pyramides. Inexpensive. Good cold snacks. Closed Saturdays and Sundays.

Bar du Caveau, 17 Place Dauphine. Métro: Pont-Neuf. Newspapers presented on a stick as in the past. Claret is recommended. Closed Saturdays and Sundays.

La Cave des Halles, 34 Rue Coquillère. Métro: Halles. Snacks and daily specials. Closed Sundays and Mondays.

Juvenile's, 47 Rue de Richelieu. Métro: Pyramides. Owner is Williamson of Willi's Wine Bar. Specialty here is Spanish and Portuguese wines and *tapas*; roast beef, too. Wine by the bottle to go. Closed Sundays.

Le Rubis, 10 Rue du Marché St. Honoré. Métro: Pyramides. Specialty of Beaujolais and Burgundy. Cold cuts alongside. Lean on the wine kegs. When the Beaujolais Nouveau arrives in mid-November, the atmosphere is delirious. Closed Saturdays and Sundays.

Bar du Sommelier, Hôtel Intercontinental, 3 Rue Castiglione. Métro: Tuileries. Comfortable and expensive.

Taverne Henri IV, 13 Place du Pont-Neuf. Métro: Pont-Neuf. Good choice of wines and sandwiches; also wine to go. The waiters are marathoners, New York included. Closed Saturdays and Sundays.

Willi's Wine Bar, 13 Rue des Petits-Champs, 4261-0509. Métro: Pyramides. Wide variety of excellent quality wines. Pleasant restaurant, medium-priced. See Chapter 13. Closed Saturdays and Sundays.

2nd arrondissement
La Côte, 77 Rue de Richelieu. Métro: Bourse. Another two marathon runners. House-bottled wine. Closed Saturdays and Sundays.

Au Duc de Richelieu, 110 Rue de Richelieu. Métro: Richelieu-Drouot. Very Parisian. Open until 3 A.M. Specialty is Beaujolais.

L'Entre-Deux-Verres, 48 Rue Sainte-Anne. Métro: Pyramides. Bordeaux from the family's vines and culinary specialties of the Southwest. Wine-tasting on Tuesdays. Closed Saturdays, Sundays, and August.

4th arrondissement
Le Coude Fou, 12 Rue du Bourg-Tibourg. Métro: Hôtel-de-Ville. Good selection of little-known wines. Inexpensive. See Chapter 5, Itinerary 1.

Au Franc Pinot, 1 Quai de Bourbon, 4329-4798. Métro: Pont-Marie. In lovely, 17th-century house along the Seine. Comfortable bar with good Loire Valley wines. Elegant restaurant alongside. Reserve for dinner. See Chapter 3. Closed Sundays and Mondays.

La Tartine, 24 Rue de Rivoli. Métro: St. Paul. Plain and inexpensive, with a vast selection of wines. Trotsky, it seems, lifted his elbow onto the marble counter here. Closed Tuesdays.

Verre à Soif, 2 Rue des Hospitalières-Saint Gervais. Métro: St. Paul. Attractive bar with selection of wines from all over the world, including California. Interesting menu, too.

5th arrondissement
Le Café de la Nouvelle Mairie, 19 Rue des Fossés-Saint-Bernard. Métro: Cardinal-Lemoine. Touraine wines and daily specials. Closed Saturday nights and Sundays.

6th arrondissement
L'Ecluse, 15 Quai des Grands Augustins. Métro: St. Michel. A classic, now owned by Nicolas wines. See Chapter 3.

Millésimes, 7 Rue Lobineau. Métro: Mabillon, Odéon. A real neighborhood bar with an excellent selection of wines from all over the world. Original, cold snacks. Closed Sundays.

Le Pain et le Vin, 95 Boulevard de Montparnasse. Métro: Vavin. Some thirty-five wines to choose from, plus sandwiches.

Le Petit Bacchus, 13 Rue du Cherche-Midi. Métro: Sèvres-Babylone. Attractive bar with Steven Spurrier's selection of wines. Good cheese and bread (Poilane) from excellent bakery across the street.

7th arrondissement
Le Sancerre, 22 Avenue Rapp, 4551-7591. Métro: Ecole-Militaire. Specialty of same name direct from their vineyards to their bistro in Paris. Snacks, too. For a table at lunch time, call ahead and reserve. Closed Saturday afternoons and Sundays.

8th arrondissement
Le Bistro du Sommelier, 97 Boulevard Haussmann, 4265-2485. Métro: St. Augustin. More a restaurant than a wine bar. First-class selection of wines. Closed Saturday mornings and Sundays.

Les Domaines, 56 Rue François Ier. Métro: Georges V. Good Touraine wines. Elegant. Meals, too. Closed Sundays.

Ma Bourgogne, 133 Boulevard Haussmann. Métro: St. Augustin. High temple of Beaujolais bottled by the house. Moderately priced. Closed Saturdays and Sundays.

Le Val d'Or, 28 Avenue Franklin-Roosevelt. Métro: St. Philippe-du-Roule. Short list of quality wines. Good snacks. Cellar restaurant is classic. Closed Sundays.

9th arrondissement
Cave Drouot, 8 Rue Drouot. Métro: Richelieu-Drouot. Wines bottled by the house. Cheese from the Pyrenees. Closed Saturdays and Sundays.

L'Oenothèque, 20 Rue Saint-Lazare. Métro: Notre-Dame-de-Lorette. Restaurant, bar, and wine shop on the expensive side. Closed Saturdays, Sundays, and August.

11th arrondissement
Jacques Mélac, 42 Rue Léon-Frot. Métro: Charonne. Picturesque proprietor, good selection, and low prices. Closed Sundays and Mondays.

1929, 90bis Rue de la Roquette. Métro: Voltaire. Mixture of neon, sono, and good wine. Closed Sunday nights.

La Nuit des Rois, 3 Rue du Pasteur-Wagner. Métro: Bastille. A champagne bar, from 150 francs ($25) and up per bottle. Champagne also served by the glass.

14th arrondissement
Aux Vins des Rues, 21 Rue Boulard. Métro: Denfert-Rochereau. Next to a lively street market. Beaujolais and Macon on the wine list, charcuteries on the menu. Closed Sunday mornings and Mondays.

16th arrondissement
Les Caves Angevines, 2 Place Léon-Deubel. Métro: Porte-de-St. Cloud. Good white wines bottled in the cellar and Lyonaise daily specials.

17th arrondissement
Pétrissans, 30bis Avenue Niel, 4227-5203. Métro: Pereire. Century-old bistro frequented in other times by Verlaine, Tristan Bernard, and Céline. Champagne from the vines of the Pétrissans. Excellent choice of wines and daily specials. For lunch, call ahead and reserve. Closed Saturdays and Sundays.

20th arrondissement
Cave des Envierges, 11 Rue des Envierges. Métro: Pyrénées. Bar and shop with very good choice of little known wines. Inexpensive.

Accessories

Wine maps of France from the *Revue du Vin de France*, 65 Rue Montmartre, 75002 Paris, 4236-2083. Métro: Bourse. 9 A.M.–1 P.M. and 2–6 P.M. weekdays. About 50 francs each.

Wine books and maps: *La Maison Rustique,* 22 Rue Jacob. Métro: St.-Germain-des-Près, Mabillon. 9:30 A.M.–6:30 P.M. Closed Sundays. Large collection of contemporary books, including many in English. See Chapter 4.

Old and rare books and maps: *Librairie Gourmande,* 4 Rue Dante. Métro: Maubert-Mutualité. 10 A.M.–7 P.M. Closed Sunday afternoons.

Wine books, maps, accessories: *Le Verre et l'Assiette,* 1 Rue Val-de-Grâce. Métro: Port-Royal. 10 A.M.–12:30 P.M. and 2:30–7 P.M. Closed Sundays and Monday mornings. Books, accessories, some selected wines as well as a taster's kit. Publishers of a monthly newsletter, (120 francs $20 a year), which goes with a five percent rebate on purchases.

Everything for the Table and the Cellar
Académie du Vin, Cité Berryer, 25 Rue Royale. Métro: Madeleine, Concorde. 10 A.M.–7 P.M. Closed Saturdays and Sundays. Englishman Steven Spurrier's bilingual shop. Books, accessories, and games.

Bain Marie, 12 Rue Boissy d'Anglas. Métro: Concorde. 10 A.M.–7 P.M. Closed Sundays. Chic shop, new and antiques, books, glasses, and games.

L'Esprit et le Vin, 65 Boulevard Malesherbes. Métro: St. Augustin. 10 A.M.–7 P.M. Closed Sundays and Monday mornings. Many of their own creations.

Lescene Dura, 63 Rue de la Verrerie. Métro: Hôtel-de-Ville. 9:30 A.M.–1 P.M. and 2–6:30 P.M. Closed Sundays. Supplier to the trade as well as retail.

L'Arlequin, 13 Rue des Francs-Bourgeois, 4278-7700. Métro: Hôtel-de-Villes. 12–7 P.M. Tuesdays through Saturdays. Sold by the glass. Glasses and Carafes, 19th century.

Crystal

Doria, 4 Rue Bourbon-le-Château. Métro: St. Germain-des-Près, Mabillon. 10 A.M.–1 P.M. and 2–7 P.M. Closed Sundays, Mondays, and August. René Lalique and Baccarat crystal only.

Lalique, 11 Rue Royale. Métro: Concorde. 9:30 A.M.–12 P.M. and 2–6 P.M. Closed Sundays. Celebrated Lalique crystal.

Glassware Galore
Rue de Paradis. Métro: Poissonière.

30: *Cristalleries de St. Louis*, 4770-2570. 9 A.M.–5:30 P.M. Closed Saturdays and Sundays. Collection and mini-museum.

30bis: *Baccarat*, 4770-6430. 9 A.M.–5:30 P.M. Closed Sundays. Old, new, and mini-museum.

34: *Madronet* for quality items.

Modern glassware: *Quartz Diffusion*, 12 Rue des Quatre Vents. Métro: Odéon, Mabillon. 10:30 A.M.–7 P.M. Closed Sundays and Monday mornings. Both one-of-a-kind and series of contemporary designers of glassware.

Original glassware: *Rosenthal*, 37 Rue des Capucines. Métro: Madeleine, Opéra. 10 A.M.–7 P.M. Closed Sundays. Glasses by Mario Bellini.

Scandinavian glassware: *Scandi Boutique*, 3 Rue de Rivoli. Métro: St. Paul. 10 A.M.–7 P.M. Closed Sundays. Ittala and Kosta Boda glasses and carafes.

When choosing wine glasses, make sure they are clear, not tainted, and made of crystal or fine glass. The best form is the "tulip," which allows for concentration of the aroma and also airs the wine. Stemmed glasses are recommended so as to be able to hold the glass without warming it. Whatever the glass, it should be filled to between one-third and one-half of its widest part.

When choosing carafes, the body of the carafe should be round and wide, so that when half or one-third filled, the wine may air. The neck should be long and narrow, and the carafe should have a glass stopper.

Wine Tasting

Some merchants offer wine for tasting.

LeGrand Filles et Fils, 1 Rue de la Banque, 4260-0712. Métro: Palais-Royal. 8:30 A.M.–8:30 P.M. Closed Sundays and Mondays. 12 Galérie Vivienne. Métro: Bourse. 9 A.M.–12:30 P.M. and 2–6:30 P.M. Closed Sundays and Mondays. Tasting of different wine each week. See Chapter 10.

Club Amical du Vin, 10 Rue de La Cerisaie, 4273-3305. Métro: Bastille. 9:30 A.M.–12:30 P.M. and 2:30–7:30 P.M. Closed Sundays and Mondays. Tasting on Saturdays.

Club Amical du Vin, 292 Rue St. Jacques, 4634-6978. Métro: Port Royal, Luxembourg. 10 A.M.–1 P.M. and 3–8 P.M. Closed Sundays and Mondays. Tasting on Saturdays.

Cave Miard, 9 Rue des Quatre Vents, 4354-9930. Métro: Odéon, Mabillon. 10 A.M.–1:30 P.M. and 4–8:30 P.M. Closed Sundays and Mondays. Tasting Fridays and Saturdays.

Hédiard, 21 Place de la Madeleine. 4266-0484. Métro: Madeleine. The famous deluxe grocery store organizes wine-tasting sessions throughout the year. To be invited, send request to: Hédiard Press Service, 5 Rue Jules-Ferry, 92400 COUR-BEVOIE.

Le Relais du Vignoble, 4 Rue de Roussillon, 4344-2572. Métro:

Dugommier. 11 A.M.–7 P.M. Closed Saturday afternoons, Sundays, and Mondays. Large warehouse. Tasting of several wines at all times.

Cave des Gobelins, 56 Avenue des Gobelins, 4331-6679. Métro: Gobelins, Place d'Italie. 8 A.M.–1 P.M. and 3–8 P.M. Wine tasting on Saturdays.

Réserve et Sélection, 119 Rue du Dessous-des-Berges, 4583-6519. Métro: Chevaleret. 10:30 A.M.–7 P.M. Closed Sundays. Several wines always available for tasting.

Vignobles de France, 42 Quai d'Austerlitz, 4582-6800. Métro: Austerlitz. 8 A.M.–8 P.M. Enormous warehouse. Wine tasting on Saturdays in presence of winegrowers.

Caves de Passy, 3 Rue Duban, 4288-8556. Métro: Muette. 10 A.M.–1 P.M. and 4:30–7:30 P.M. Closed Sunday afternoons and Mondays. Wine tasting.

Centre de Distribution de Vins de Propriétés, 215 Rue d'Aubervilliers, 4209-6150. 10 A.M.–7 P.M. Closed Sunday afternoons. Métro: Porte-de-la-Chapelle. Wine tasting Saturdays and Sunday mornings.

CHAPTER 19

Best of Bars, Cafés, and Beer Halls*

There are hundreds of bars and sidewalk cafés in Paris. Let yourself be guided by your intuition. This list is in no way exhaustive.

1st arrondissement

Bar Vendôme on the patio, the tiny *Hemingway Bar,* Hôtel Ritz, 15 Place Vendôme. Métro: Tuileries, Opéra. 11–1 A.M. Both elegant and expensive—and so professional. See Chapter 9.

Flann O'Brien's, 6 Rue Bailleul. Métro: Louvre. No doubt about it, the general HQ of the Irish population of Paris. Imported beers and snacks.

*See Chapter 18 for wine bars.

Le Normandy, 7 Rue de l'Echelle. Métro: Palais-Royal. 11 A.M.–midnight. Comfortable leather armchairs to sink into.

2nd arrondissement

Celadon Bar, Hôtel Westminster, 13 Rue de la Paix. Métro: Opéra. 11 A.M.–midnight. Pretty and comfortable, in soft green. Guitarist on Friday evenings.

Le Chapman, 27 Rue Louis-le-Grand. Métro: Opéra. 11–2 A.M. Second drink on the house during happy hour, from 5–7 P.M.

Harry's Bar, 5 Rue Daunou. Métro: Opéra. 10:30–4 A.M. Top trap, wide selection, busy. See Chapter 13.

Kitty O'Shea, 10 Rue des Capucines. Métro: Opéra, Madeleine. 12 noon–1:30 A.M. Charming Irish pub serving beer from over the Channel. English-speaking staff. Snacks.

4th arrondissement

Brasserie de l'Ile St. Louis, 55 Quai de Bourbon. Métro: Pont-Marie. Until 1:30 A.M. Closed Wednesdays, Thursdays for lunch, and August. Good for beer and sauerkraut and sausages. See Chapter 3.

Le Flore en l'Ile, 42 Quai d'Orléans. Métro: Pont-Marie. Charming quayside café and restaurant on Ile St. Louis across from Notre-Dame. See Chapter 3.

Ma Bourgogne, 19 Place des Vosges. Métro: St. Paul. Open until 12:30 A.M. summer, 11 P.M. the rest of the year. Right on the Place des Vosges. See Chapter 5, Itinerary 1.

La Perla, 26 Rue François Miron. Métro: St. Paul. An inviting neighborhood bar and restaurant serving Mexican specialties. See Chapter 5, Itinerary 2.

5th arrondissement

La Chope, Place Mouffetard. Métro: Monge. Wide sidewalk terrace on pleasant village square.

La Geueze, 19 Rue Soufflot. Métro: Luxembourg, Cluny. 12 P.M.–2 A.M. Closed Sundays. Student hangout next to Sorbonne. Specialties are beer, sandwiches, and daily blue plates.

6th arrondissement

Le Bélier, L'Hôtel, 13 Rue des Beaux-Arts. Métro: St. Germain-des-Près. Open twenty-four hours a day every day. Astonishing setting of fountain, birds, and decorous plants in the house that served as Oscar Wilde's last abode. The restaurant, too, is welcoming. See Chapter 4.

Closerie des Lilas, 171 Boulevard de Montparnasse. Métro: Port-Royal. 10:30–2 A.M. Wonderful garden surroundings. Good drinks and good memories. On the expensive side. See Chapter 13.

Les Deux Magots, 6 Place St. Germain-des-Près. Métro: St. Germain-des-Près. 8–2 A.M. The classic Left Bank café with large winter and summer terraces to keep a check on passers-by. The heart of St. Germain-des-Près after World War II. It was for a long time Sartre et de Beauvoir's standby. See Chapter 4.

L'Entr'acte, 14 Rue Jacob. Métro: St. Germain-des-Près, Mabillon. Welcome atmosphere for a drink or nightcap. See Chapter 4.

Le Flore, 172 Boulevard St. Germain. Métro: St. Germain-des-Près. 8–1:30 A.M. Closed July. Another large sidewalk area. Also a classic. See Chapter 4.

Lipp, 151 Boulevard St. German. Métro: St. Germain-des-Près. Open until 2 A.M. Closed July. An institution. Frequented by politicians, writers, and would-be's. The second floor dining room is for tourists. The inner sanctum is on the ground floor.

Le Mazet, 61 Rue St. André-des-Arts. Métro: Odéon. Until 2 A.M. Closed Sundays. Hangout for young, English-speaking "on-the-road" crowd. There is usually someone around to play the guitar. Good draft beer. See Chapter 4.

La Palette, 43 Rue de Seine. Métro: Odéon, Mabillon. Nice outdoor terrace in the warmer months. On the inside, the second room is classified a "historic monument." See Chapter 4.

Au Petit Suisse, 17 Rue de Vaugirard. Métro: Luxembourg, Odéon. Just a nice neighborhood café facing south.

Pub St. Germain, 17 Rue de l'Ancienne-Comédie. Métro: Odéon. Open twenty-four hours a day, every day. A landmark devoted to 450 brands of beer, twenty-four on draft, which would seem to be some sort of world record. See Chapter 4.

Rhumerie Martiniquaise, 166 Boulevard St. Germain. Métro: St. Germain-des-Près, Mabillon. Punch actually is served in this curious theatre box. A great vantage point.

7th arrondissement

Le Bourbon, Hôtel Sofitel, 32 Rue St. Dominique. Métro: Invalides. Open twenty-four hours a day every day. Perfect cocktails, calm and discreet.

Le Lénox, 9 Rue de l'Université. Métro: St. Germain-des-Près. 5 P.M.–1 A.M. Small and comfortable sunken bar in small and comfortable hotel.

The Twickenham, 70 Rue des Saints-Pères. Métro: Sèvres-Babylone. 11–2 A.M. Closed Saturday nights, Sundays, and August. Headquarters for a literary crowd from the publishing houses in the quarter. Rugby fans most welcome. Typically English beer and décor.

8th arrondissement

Le Fouquet's, 99 Avenue des Champs-Elysées. Métro: Georges V. 9–2 A.M. Chic sidewalk café fancied by the press and personalities. A landmark.

La Maison d'Allemagne, 45 Rue Pierre-Charron. Métro: Franklin-Roosevelt. 8:30 A.M.–11 P.M. Closed Sundays. Wide variety of German beers. Pleasant bar and good food. On the expensive side.

The Regency, Hôtel Prince-du-Galles, 33 Avenue George V. Métro: Georges V. Open until 2 A.M. On Friday and Saturday nights, the very English bar becomes a cabaret with live entertainment. Warm ambience.

9th arrondissement

Le Café de la Paix, 5 Place de l'Opéra. Métro: Opéra. A very famous, elegant café. On the expensive side, but very well situated. See Chapter 9.

Au Général LaFayette, 52 Rue LaFayette. Métro: Cadet. 11–3 A.M. Closed Saturday mornings and Sundays. Nice, old-fashioned beer hall with a sidewalk café. Good plain food, too.

12th arrondissement

Le Train Bleu, second floor, Gare de Lyon, 20 Boulevard Diderot. Métro: Gare de Lyon. 11 A.M.–10 P.M. Sumptuous 19th-century background. Comfortable armchairs and the sense of travel.

14th arrondissement

La Coupole, 102 Boulevard de Montparnasse. Métro: Vavin. 8–2 A.M. Recently renovated by new owners, this most Parisian of Parisian café-restaurants remains true to a century of tradition. Both sidewalk and inside café.

Le Dôme, 108 Boulevard du Montparnasse. Métro: Vavin. Member of the group of Montparnasse cafés frequented by the artists and writers of the 1920s (Select, Coupole, Closerie des Lilas). Completely renovated and still very popular.

15th arrondissement

Hôtel Hilton, 18 Avenue de Suffren. Métro: Bir-Hakeim. *Bar Suffren:* 11 A.M.–midnight. Very pleasant hotel bar. *Cocktail Corner*, 6 P.M.–2 A.M. From the 10th floor is a supreme view of Eiffel Tower.

16th arrondissement

Bar du Raphaël, 17 Avenue Kléber. Métro: Kléber. 11 A.M.–midnight. A little stuffy and expensive but lovely and refined.

17th arrondissement

Lionel Hampton Bar, Hôtel Méridien, 81 Boulevard Gouvion-Saint-Cyr. Métro: Porte Maillot. Live jazz every night in relaxed, open-ended bar and patio.

18th arrondissement

Le Tire-Bouchon, 9 Rue Norvins. Métro: Abbesses. Show Thursdays, Fridays, and Saturdays at 9 P.M. Closed from May to September. Drinks 10 francs ($3.50) and up. Every day during the day this is a crêpe shop. Also a piano bar.

CHAPTER 20

Good Food with Charm

Restaurants are difficult to classify. However, since people will go anywhere for good food, I have grouped them by price rather than location. Within the price category they are listed by *arrondissement*, then alphabetically.

There are five categories: *inexpensive* is under 100 francs ($18); *moderate* is 100 to 200 francs ($18–35); *expensive* is 200 to 300 francs ($35–50); *very expensive* is 300 to 500 francs ($50–85); and *luxury* is 500 and more ($85 and more). Let it be said that food in Paris will never be bad, just more or less delicious. *Bon appetit!*

Inexpensive

1st arrondissement
Lescure, 7 Rue de Mondovi, 4260-1891. Closed Saturday nights, Sundays, and July. Métro: Concorde. Hearty food, bistro atmosphere.

4th arrondissement
Aquarius, 54 Rue Sainte-Croix de la Bretonnerie, 4887-4871. Métro: Hôtel-de-Ville. Pleasant vegetarian restaurant.

Le Faste-Fou, 36 Boulevard Henri IV, 4272-1709. Métro: Bastille. Menu changes every day. Brunch on Saturdays and Sundays.

Piccolo Teatro, 6 Rue des Ecouffes, 4272-1779. Métro: St. Paul. Agreeable vegetarian restaurant. Try the apple crumble.

5th arrondissement
Le Boute Grill, 12 Rue Boutebrie, 4354-0330. Métro: St. Michel. Tunisian couscous served in wooden bowls in typical setting.

Perraudin, 157 Rue St. Jacques, 4633-1575. Métro: Cardinal-Lemoine. Closed Saturdays. Family style with Sunday brunch.

6th arrondissement
Chez Wadja, 10 Rue de la Grande-Chaumière. Métro: Vavin. Closed Sundays. Canteen for students and down-and-out artists. Wadja's home cooking warms the heart. No reservations.

Le Petit St. Benoît, 4 Rue St. Benoît. Métro: St. Germain-des-Près. Closed Saturdays, Sundays, and August. A unique neighborhood bistro of which there are few nowadays. No reservations.

Polidor, 41 Rue Monsieur-le-Prince, 4326-9534. Métro: Odéon. Another authentic bistro, in operation since 1845.

7th arrondissement
Babkine, 30 Rue Pierre-Leroux, 4273-2834. Métro: Vaneau. Closed Saturday evenings, Sundays, and August. Fixed-price delight.

Le Balisier, 20 Rue Rousselet, 4734-6629. Métro: Vaneau. Closed Saturdays for lunch, Sundays, and August. Astonishing fixed-price menus, wine included.

Le Crick, 10 Rue de Bellechasse, 4705-9866. Métro: Solférino. Closed Mondays. For a good snack. No reservations.

Nara, 12 Rue de Bellechasse, 4705-2063. Métro: Solférino. Closed Mondays and first half of August. Korean cooking. Close to Orsay Museum.

8th arrondissement
American Pershing Hall, 49 Rue Pierre-Charron, 4225-3817. Métro: Franklin-Roosevelt. American Legion's restaurant. Brunch, too.

9th arrondissement
Chartier, 7 Rue du Faubourg Montmartre, 4770-8629. Métro: Rue Montmartre. Really special: lovely, lively canteen-type hall from the 19th century.

14th arrondissement
Le Jéraboam, 72 Rue Didot, 4539-3913. Métro: Plaisance. Closed Sundays and Mondays. All-you-can-eat hors-d'oeuvres table.

15th arrondissement
Les Artistes, 98 Boulevard de Grenelle, 4577-7970. Métro: La Motte-Picquet. Closed Sundays. Italian-style.

Le Commerce, 51 Rue du Commerce, 4575-0327. Métro: LaMotte-Picquet. A steal.

17th arrondissement
Stefany, 5 Avenue des Ternes, 4267-7912. Métro: Ternes. Amid the flowers and plants, interesting dishes.

Moderate

1st arrondissement
L'Amanguier, 110 Rue de Richelieu, 4296-3779. Métro: Richelieu-Drouot. Prettily decorated, straightforward food.

Les Cartes Postales, 7 Rue Gomboust, 4261-0293. Métro: Pyramides. Closed Sundays. Japanese cook trained by the best French chefs offers interesting menus at reasonable prices.

Le Louchebem, 31 Rue Berger, 4233-1299. Métro: Louvre. Closed Sundays. All the beef you can eat.

Prunier-Madeleine, 9 Rue Duphot, 4260-3604. Métro: Madeleine. This is an institution, expensive. However, in the ground floor dining corner, a special menu at 150 francs ($25) is served from 11 A.M. to 1 A.M. and features everything from an apéritif to coffee and all the wine you can drink.

Willi's Wine Bar, 13 Rue des Petits-Champs, 4261-0509. Métro: Pyramides. Wonderful wines and good fixed-price menu, wine included.

2nd arrondissement
Le Brissemoret, 5 Rue St. Marc, 4236-9172. Métro: Bourse. Closed Saturdays and Sundays. Old bistro, old specialties cooked slowly on the wood stove.

3rd arrondissement
La Guirlande de Julie, 25 Place des Vosges, 4887-9407. Métro: St. Paul. Closed Mondays and Tuesdays. Located on Paris's first square. Simple cuisine, reasonably priced.

4th arrondissement
Au Tibourg, 31 Rue du Bourg-Tibourg, 4278-5744. Métro: Hôtel-de-Ville. Closed Sundays. Friendly Greek restaurant.

Le Bistrot de Clémence, 4 Quai d'Orléans, 4633-0836. Métro: Pont-Marie. Agreeably situated on the river. Home cooking.

La Canaille, 4 Rue Crillon, 4278-0971. Métro: Arsenal. Hangout of young crowd. Regular art exhibits, good food, and conversation.

L'Excuse, 14 Rue Charles V, 4277-9897. Métro: St. Paul. Closed Sundays. Charming, good, and moderately priced.

Jo Goldenberg, 7 Rue des Rosiers, 4887-2016. Métro: St. Paul. Eastern European specialties and delicatessen.

Le Maraîcher, 5 Rue Beautrellis, 4271-4249. Métro: Bastille. Closed Sundays. Sophisticated décor and inventive food.

L'Oulette, 38 Rue des Tournelles, 4271-4333. Métro: Chemin-Vert. Closed Saturdays for lunch and Sundays. Sensational fixed price menus. French southwestern cuisine.

5th arrondissement
L'Atelier du Maître Albert, 1 Rue du Maître Albert, 4633-0644. Métro: Maubert-Mutualité. Fireplace, velvet trappings, and pleasant food.

La Bouteille d'Or, 9 Rue Quai Montebello, 4054-5758. Métro: Maubert-Mutualité. Family cooking.

Chieng-Mai, 12 Rue Frédéric-Sauton, 4325-4545. Métro: Maubert-Mutualité. Closed Sundays and August. One of the best Thai menus in Paris.

La Marée Verte, 9 Rue de Pontoise, 4325-8941. Métro: Maubert-Mutualité. Closed Sundays, Mondays, and August. Interesting fish dishes.

Table d'Harmonie, 19 Rue du Sommerard, 4354-5947. Métro: Cluny. Closed Saturdays for lunch and Sundays. At the piano an adept of Fats Waller; in the kitchen a fine chef.

6th arrondissement

Le Bélier, L'Hôtel, 13 Rue des Beaux-Arts, 4325-2722. Métro: St. Germain-des-Près. Delicious and very elegant.

Le Chat Grippé, 87 Rue d'Assas, 4354-7000. Métro: Raspail. Closed Saturday for lunch and August. A butcher shop become first-rate bistro.

Naka, 5 Rue Bernard-Palissy, 4549-3876. Métro: St. Germain-des-Près. Closed Sundays and Mondays. Inventive cuisine in small, friendly locale a stone's throw from St. Germain-des-Près.

Vagenende, 142 Boulevard St. Germain, 4326-1914. Métro: Mabillon, Odéon. Beautiful 1900s décor, classified a historic monument.

7th arrondissement

Chez Ribe, 15 Avenue de Suffren, 4566-5379. Métro: Bir-Hakeim. Closed Sundays and August. Market-fresh menu changes every day. Comfortable.

La Grenelle d'Asie, 124 Rue de Grenelle, 4551-7723. Métro: Solférino. Fine Chinese cuisine, warm, pleasant décor.

L'Oeillade, 10 Rue St. Simon, 4222-0160. Métro: Bac. Closed Saturdays for lunch, Sundays, and holidays. Good fixed-price menus, pleasant décor.

Le Télégraphe, 41 Rue de Lille, 4015-0665. Métro: Bac. Former rest home for postal employees. Worth a try, if only for the magnificent 1900s décor.

Thoumieux, 79 Rue St. Dominique, 4705-4975. Métro: LaTour-Maubourg. Closed Mondays. Good French country cuisine and a 50-franc ($9) fixed-price menu.

8th arrondissement
Dynastie Thaï, 101 Rue La Boétie, 4289-0905. Métro: Franklin-Roosevelt. Exotic mirrors, Victorian statues, and charming service for excellent Thai food.

La Maison du Valais, 20 Rue Royale, 4260-2272. Métro: Concorde. Closed Sundays. Swiss specialties made with cheese. Try the first floor for that warm, mountain-inn feeling.

Yvan, 1bis Rue Jean-Mermoz, 4359-1840. Métro: Franklin-Roosevelt. Closed Saturdays at noon and Sundays. Elegant, interesting fixed-price menus.

9th arrondissement
Pagoda, 50 Rue de Provence, 4874-8148. Métro: Chausée-d'Antin. Closed Sundays and August. First-class Khmer cuisine from Cambodia.

10th arrondissement
Brasserie Flo, 7 Cour des Petites-Ecuries, 4770-1359. Métro: Chateau-d'Eau. Popular brasserie of the 1900s.

The New Port, 79 Rue du Faubourg St. Denis, 4824-1936. Métro: Château-d'Eau. Closed Saturdays for lunch and Sundays. Pleasant, especially for fixed-price fish dinners. Expensive à la carte.

11th arrondissement
Astier, 44 Rue Jean-Pierre-Timbaud, 4357-1635. Métro: Parmentier. Closed Saturdays, Sundays, and August. Excellent value with charm.

Chardenoux, 1 Rue Jules-Vallés, 4371-4952. Métro: Charonne. Closed Saturdays for lunch, Sundays, and August. Off the beaten track, a real 1900s bistro with reasonable prices.

12th arrondissement
Le Square Trousseau, 1 Rue Antoine-Vollon, 4343-0600. Métro: Ledru-Rollin. Closed Sundays, Mondays, and August. Attractive bistro run by young couple with new ideas for traditional fare.

13th arrondissement
Boeuf Bistrot, 4 Place des Alpes, 4582-0809. Métro: Place d'Italie. Closed Saturdays for lunch and Sundays. Beef and disc jockey.

15th arrondissement
Ashoka, 5 Rue du Dr. J. Clémenceau, 4532-9646. Métro: Vaugirard. Delightful Indian specialties, including tandoori, in colonial setting.

Aux Trois Chevrons, 148 Avenue Félix-Faure, 4554-1226. Métro: Balard. Closed Saturdays for lunch and Sundays. Charming restaurant with fine cuisine. Market and season determine the menu, presented on a blackboard.

La Barrail, 17 Rue Falguière, 4322-4261. Métro: Falguière. Superb quality for the price. Great chocolate desserts.

Au Boeuf Gros Sel, 299 Rue Lecourbe, 4557-1633. Métro: Balard. Closed Mondays for lunch, Sundays, and August. Succulent traditional stews.

Le Clos des Morillons, 50 Rue des Morillons, 4828-0437. Métro: Convention. Closed Saturdays for lunch and Sundays. Excellent fixed-price meals. Many fish specialties and perfect pastry.

Les Fêtes Gourmandes, 51 Boulevard Garibaldi, 4734-3141. Closed Mondays for lunch and Tuesdays. Superbly inventive cuisine. Soufflé specialist. Fabulous desserts.

16th arrondissement

Le Scheffer, 22 Rue Scheffer, 4727-8111. Métro: Passy. Closed Sundays. Checkered tablecloths and good bistro food.

Le Totem, 1 Place du Trocadéro, 4727-7411. Métro: Trocadéro. Closed Sunday evenings and Tuesdays. A grill with a view of Eiffel Tower.

17th arrondissement

Le Bistrot d'à côté, 10 Rue Gustave-Flaubert, 4267-0581. Métro: Pereire. Closed Saturdays for lunch and Sundays. The super bistro of lyonnaise cooking and pitchers of Côte du Rhône.

Le Bistrot de l'Etoile, 13 Rue Troyon, 4267-2595. Métro: Etoile. Closed Saturdays for lunch, Sundays, and July. Swish bistro for solid fare: pot-au-feu, lamb stew, and macaroni with cheese. The owner is none other than Guy Savoy, one of the two or three top French chefs.

Le Congrès, 80 Avenue de la Grande-Armée, 4574-1724. Métro: Porte-Maillot. The freshest oysters plus charcoal-broiled meats.

Epicure 108, 108 Rue Cardinet, 4763-5091. Métro: Malesherbes. Closed Saturdays for lunch and Sundays. Epicurean food at bistro prices.

18th arrondissement

Da Graziano, 83 Rue Lepic, 4606-8477. Métro: Abbesses. Closed February. Italian specialties on the fixed-price menu. More expensive à la carte.

Grain de Folie, Rue de La Vieuville. Métro: Abbesses. Cute little restaurant with carefully prepared dishes. Steamed vegetables.

20th arrondissement

Le Bistro du 20e, 44 Rue du Surmelin, 4897-2030. Métro: Pelleport. Closed Saturdays, Sundays, and July. A bit out of the way, this old delicatessen was made into a restaurant. Excellent fixed-price menu, wine included, for 150 francs ($25).

Le Courtil, 15 Rue St. Blaise, 4370-0932. Métro: Porte-de-Montreuil. Closed Sundays, Mondays, and August. If you visit the Charonne church and cemetery, you could stop here to prolong the charm. Jazz duo on Tuesday nights.

Royal Bangkok, 4 Rue du Cher, 4636-4624. Métro: Gambetta. Fine Thai in pleasant surroundings.

Expensive

1st arrondissement

Au Pied de Cochon, 6 Rue Coquillère, 4236-1175. Métro: Les Halles. Open twenty-four hours a day every day of the year. Specialties are pigs' feet, raw oysters, and memories of the old Halles.

Joe Allen, 30 Rue Pierre-Lescot, 4236-7013. Métro: Etienne-Marcel. For spare ribs and fried chicken.

Pharamond, 24 Rue de la Grande-Truanderie, 4233-0672. Métro: Etienne-Marcel. Closed Sundays and Mondays for lunch. Regional dishes—tripe and andouillette with pea purée, etc.—in ravishing Art Nouveau setting.

Le Poquelin, 17 Rue Molière, 4296-2219. Métro: Palais-Royal. Closed Saturdays for lunch, Sundays, and August. Creative cuisine: duck liver salad, braised salmon with sweet and sour sauce, and more.

2nd arrondissement

Le Celadon, 15 Rue Daunou, 4703-4042. Métro: Opéra. Closed

Saturdays, Sundays, and August. Elegant and refined from start to finish.

La Corbeille, 154 Rue Montmartre, 4026-3087. Métro: Montmartre. Closed Saturdays for lunch and Sundays. Non-smoking sector. Décor reminiscent of southern Italy. The savors of Provence in the cuisine are featured, like lobster ravioli with a squash sauce. Taster's menu with wine is excellent value.

Vishnou, 11bis Rue Volney, 4297-5654. Métro: Madeleine. Closed Mondays for lunch and Sundays. Pungent Indian specialties and exotic ambience.

4th arrondissement
Bofinger, 3–7 Rue de la Bastille, 4272-8782. Métro: Bastille. Art Nouveau brasserie where first draft beer ever was served. Specialties include sauerkraut and sausages.

Wally, 16 Rue Le Regrattier, 4325-0139. Métro: Pont-Marie. Closed Sundays. Algerian specialties served under what could well be a Saharan tent.

5th arrondissement
La Timonerie, 35 Quai de la Tournelle, 4325-4442. Métro: Maubert-Mutualité. Closed Sundays and Mondays. Delicate cuisine and elegant décor.

6th arrondissement
Chez Marie, 25 Rue Servandoni, 4633-1206. Métro: St. Sulpice. Closed Saturdays for lunch and Mondays. Picturebook French bistro. Delectable.

7th arrondissement
Le Bourdonnais, 113 Avenue de La Bourdonnais, 4705-4796. Métro: Ecole-Militaire. Refined ambience and cuisine. For dessert, why not try pear gratin with butter honey sauce?

Chez Muriel et Isabelle, 94 Boulevard de LaTour-Maubourg, 4551-3796. Métro: Ecole-Militaire. Closed Saturdays, Sundays, and August. A small house of flowers and garden for interesting cuisine, i.e. stewed rabbit with ginger and candied oranges, trout with rhubarb purée, and more.

Le Florence, 22 Rue du Champ-de-Mars, 4551-5269. Métro: Ecole-Militaire. Closed Sundays, Mondays, and August. Italian cuisine in ravishing surroundings.

8th arrondissement
Au Jardin du Printemps, 32 Rue du Penthièvre, 4359-3291. Métro: St. Philippe-du-Roule. Closed Sundays and August. Amazingly inventive Asian cuisine.

Baumann Marbeuf, 15 Rue Marbeuf, 4720-1111. Métro: Franklin-Roosevelt. Closed August. About the best grilled beef this side of the Atlantic.

Cactus Charly, 68 Rue de Ponthieu, 4562-0177. Métro: Franklin-Roosevelt. Steaks and hamburgers. Country and western bar, live music.

La Fermette Marbeuf 1900, 5 Rue Marbeuf, 4720-6353. Métro: Franklin-Roosevelt. Magnificent and authentic 1900s décor, beautiful food. In the evenings there is a 180 francs ($30) menu that includes such delights as chicken liver and sweetbreads tourte with wild mushrooms.

Marshal's Bar et Grill, 63 Avenue Franklin-Roosevelt, 4563-2122. Métro: St. Philippe-du-Roule. New York steaks and caesar salads.

9th arrondissement
Au Petit Riche, 25 Rue Le Peletier, 4770-6868. Métro: Le Peletier. Closed Sundays and holidays. Opened in 1880, the series of intimate dining rooms still are fashionable. Classic cooking.

Cartouche Edouard VII, 18 Rue Caumartin, 4742-0882. Métro: Havre-Caumartin. Basque cuisine in very comfortable English-style bar.

11th arrondissement
Perry Brothers, 20 Passage des Panoramas, 4508-8919. Métro: Montmartre. Closed Saturdays and Sundays. Very pretty dining room, inventive dishes by Welsh team.

12th arrondissement
La Gourmandise, 271 Avenue Daumesnil, 4343-9441. Métro: Porte Dorée. Closed Saturdays for lunch, Sundays, Easter, and August. Of excellent quality are the filet of sole with curry sauce and mango-spiced ravioli, among other dishes. Neighborhood atmosphere.

14th arrondissement
L'Assiette, 181 Rue du Château, 4322-6486. Métro: Pernéty. Closed Mondays, Tuesdays, and August. Lulu's place. Delicious Basque specialties.

Le Bar à Huitres, 112 Boulevard du Montparnasse, 4320-7101. Métro: Vavin. Modern oyster bar.

15th arrondissement
Aux Senteurs de Provence, 295 Rue Lecourbe, 4557-1198. Métro: Balard. Closed Sundays, Mondays, and August. Bouillabaisse in particular and fish in general.

Pierre Vedel, 19 Rue Duranton, 4558-4317. Métro: Boucicaut. Closed Saturdays and Sundays. Cuisine from the south by one of Georges Brassens' gang. Tuna with green tomatoes and peppers, fricassee of snails with sorrel and garlic croutons.

16th arrondissement
Al Mounia, 16 Rue de Magdebourg, 4727-5728. Métro: Iéna.

Closed Sundays and mid-July through the end of August. Divine Moroccan cuisine.

Vi Foc, 33 Rue de Longchamp, 4704-9681. Métro: Boissière. Closed August. Among the best Chinese-Vietnamese restaurants.

17th arrondissement
Les Béatilles, 127 Rue Cardinet, 4227-9564. Métro: Malesherbes. Closed Saturdays for lunch, Sundays, and August. Bright white setting for *haute cuisine* such as wild mushroom soup served with grilled scallops, pigs feet with turnips and parsley juice, and bitter chocolate desserts.

Chez Georges, 273 Boulevard Pereire, 4574-3100. Métro: Porte-Maillot. Closed August. Family bistro, good hearty food, very Parisian ambience.

La Toque, 16 Rue de Tocqueville, 4227-9775. Métro: Villiers. Closed Saturdays, Sundays, and August. Excellent quality for the price, as the French say. Lamb filets cooked with thyme and served with an eggplant pudding are an example.

Very Expensive

4th arrondissement
Au Franc Pinot, 1 Quai de Bourbon, 4329-4698. Métro: Pont-Marie. Closed Sundays and Mondays. Genuine old bistro on the quay, beautifully prepared food and good wines. Also wine bar.

5th arrondissement
La Bûcherie, 41 Rue de la Bûcherie, 4354-7806. Métro: Maubert-Mutualité. Good food in a lovely country inn across from Notre Dame. Lamb and eggplant, veal and tarragon, and more.

Miravile, 25 Quai de la Tournelle, 4634-0778. Métro: Maubert-Mutualité. Closed Saturdays for lunch and Sundays. The salt air of Brittany and its sea produce at its best. Lobster served with cream of lentils, apple caramel with prunes and cinnamon are among the favorites.

7th arrondissement

Arpège, 84 Rue de Varenne, 4551-4733. Métro: Varenne. Closed Saturdays for lunch, Sundays, and August. Young chef already renowned for his creative cuisine. Crab-stuffed cabbage with mustard sauce, hare with wild mushrooms and minced nuts, raspberry macaroons, and sweet tomatoes stuffed with vanilla.

Le Dauphin, Sofitel, 32 Rue St. Dominque, 4555-9180. Métro: Invalides. Beautifully presented, very creative dishes from southern France. Cold vegetable omelet with bits of grilled salmon, sweetbread and shrimp terrine served with orange-flavored onion bread.

Duquesnoy, 6 Avenue Bosquet, 4705-9678. Métro: Ecole-Militaire. Closed Saturdays for lunch, Sundays, and August. Astute cuisine of a master chef. His pressed duck and iced nougat with honey are pure marvels.

Jules Verne, second floor, Eiffel Tower, 4555-6144. Métro: Ecole-Militaire. Exceptional view of the city. Gourmet cooking, such as frog and snail purée with an herb bouillon, and peach gratin with currant sauce.

8th arrondissement

Au Petit Montmorency, 5 Rue Rabelais, 4225-1119. Métro: Franklin-Roosevelt. Closed Saturdays, Sundays, and August. Absolutely charming décor and welcome, and most inventive cuisine possible. Truffled soufflé with scallops, steak soup of turtle, and baby veal with sage.

12th arrondissement

Au Pressoir, 257 Avenue Daumesnil, 4344-3821. Métro: Michel-Bizot. Closed Saturdays, Sundays, and August. A little out of the way, but such culinary enchantment! Warm goose liver served with bitter cherries, and filet mignon with truffle sauce and homemade noodles.

14th arrondissement

La Cagouille, 12 Place Constantin-Brancusi, 4322-0901. Closed Sundays, Mondays, and August. Beautiful food from the sea.

15th arrondissement

La Maison Blanche, 82 Boulevard Lefebvre, 4828-3883. Métro: Porte-de-Versailles. Closed Saturdays for lunch, Sundays, and Mondays. Superbly inventive cuisine. For example: warm oysters with leek sauce, paper-thin sheets of coffee-flavored caramel, or candied pears with ginger.

16th arrondissement

Le Petit Belon, 38 Rue Pergolèse, 4500-2366. Métro: Argentine. Closed Saturdays, Sundays, and August. Tastefully decorated dining room and visible kitchen on the other side of glass partition. Crab pie with green lemon, and warm duck liver served with spices and fruit compotes.

Le Toit de Paris, 94 Avenue Paul Doumer, 4524-5537. Métro: La Muette. Closed Saturdays for lunch, and Sundays. Elegance with a view of the rooftops of Paris. Try the Brittany pigeon roasted in a crust of heavy salt, for example.

Luxury

1st arrondissement

Carré des Feuillants, 14 Rue de Castiglione, 4286-8282. Métro: Tuileries. Closed Saturdays for lunch and Sundays. One of most reputable restaurants of Paris. A Gascon chef's specialties include asparagus cooked over the vapors of duck, wild salmon topped with cream of sea urchin sauce, and more.

Le Grand Véfour, 17 Rue de Beaujolais, 4296-5627. Métro: Palais-Royal. Closed Saturdays for lunch, Sundays, and August. An historic monument of old world elegance. 18th-century allegoric ceiling and perfect cuisine. Specially priced luncheon menu. Poached turbot with a hollandaise sauce, rack of lamb and potato purée, and magnificent desserts.

4th arrondissement
L'Ambroisie, 9 Place des Vosges, 4278-5145. Métro: St. Paul. Closed Sundays, Mondays, and August. Creative and fashionable *haute cuisine*. Sweetbreads in a saboyon of capers, rayfish and cabbage soup, and chocolate pie are among the specialties.

6th arrondissement
Jacques Cagna, 14 Rue des Grands-Augustins, 4326-4939. Métro: St. Michel. Closed Saturdays, Sundays, and August. An exquisite 17th-century tavern with wonderful food. Shellfish with creamed lobster sauce or beef served with potato purée topped with a marrow or shallot sauce.

16th arrondissement
Robuchon, 32 Rue de Longchamp, 4727-1227. Métro: Boissière. Closed Saturdays, Sundays, and July. One of the finest and most-enchanting restaurants in the world. Booked solid for months in advance. Between 600 and 1200 francs ($100 and $200).

Vivarois, 192 Avenue Victor-Hugo, 4504-0431, Métro: Pompe. Closed Saturdays, Sundays, and August. Another magnificent chef. Royal hare served with slices of quince, fowl with morels, and more.

17th arrondissement

Guy Savoy, 18 Rue Troyon, 4380-4061. Métro: Etoile. Closed Saturdays, Sundays, and the second half of July. The chic surroundings of master chef Guy Savoy. Blinis with juniper served with smoked salmon and sour cream, smoked eel with green beans and an onion sauce, and many other specialties.

18th arrondissement

A. *Beauvilliers,* 52 Rue Lamarck, 4254-5442. Métro: Lamarck-Caulaincourt. Closed Sundays, Mondays for lunch, and the first half of September. One of the prettiest restaurants in Paris, and with such fare: rabbit stew with mussels, spices and new potatoes, and baby lamb roasted with tarragon and served with beet leaves. Fixed-price luncheon menu is more reasonably priced.

CHAPTER 21

Super Pastry Shops and Tearooms

plus snacks, brunch, ice cream, and exquisite chocolate

Pastry shops, bakeries, chocolate craftsmen, tearooms, brunches *à l'Américaine* or *à la* French are to be found on every block. Truly, nothing is inedible and much is memorable. Some shops have several functions but have been listed only under the essential category.

1st arrondissement

Bread and Pastry
Cador, 2 Rue de l'Amiral-de-Coligny. Métro: Louvre. 10 A.M.– 7:15 P.M. Closed Mondays and August.

Flo Prestige, 42 Rue du Marché-Saint-Honoré. Métro: Pyramides. 8 A.M.–midnight. Pastry, catering, and takeout.

Rageneau, 202 Rue St. Honoré. Métro: Louvre. 8 A.M.–7:30 P.M. Closed Saturdays, Sundays, and July.

Régence, 14 Rue Duphot. Métro: Madeleine. 6 A.M.–10 P.M.

Tearooms
Angelina-Rumpelmayer, 226 Rue de Rivoli. Métro: Tuileries. 10 A.M.–7 P.M. Classic and elegant, a landmark.

Fanny Tea, 20 Place Dauphine. Métro: Pont-Neuf. 1–7:30 P.M. Closed Mondays and August. Old-fashioned tea shop on a quiet, dreamy square. Yves Montand and Simone Signoret used to live across the way.

Rose Thé, 91 Rue St. Honoré. Métro: Palais-Royal. 12–6:30 P.M. Closed Saturdays and Sundays. Another calm and absolutely charming spot for tea or a snack.

Toraya, 10 Rue St. Florentin. Métro: Concorde. 10 A.M.–7 P.M. Closed Sundays. Exotic ambience of a Japanese tearoom.

Verlet, 256 Rue St. Honoré. Métro: Palais-Royal. Delicious odor of grilled coffee in this coffee shop and tearoom. A high mark for authenticity.

Chocolate
Côte de France, 25 Avenue de l'Opéra. Métro: Pyramides. 9:30 A.M.–7 P.M. Closed Sundays and Monday mornings. Impeccable French chocolate.

Godiva, 237 Rue St. Honoré. Métro: Tuileries. Closed Sundays. Belgian chocolate.

2nd arrondissement

Bread and Pastry

Au Duc de Praslin, 33 Rue Vivienne. Métro: Bourse. 9 A.M.–7 P.M. Closed Saturdays and Sundays.

Au Panetier, 10 Place des Petits-Pères. Métro: Bourse. 8 A.M.– 7 P.M. Closed Saturdays and Sundays. Bread recipes of the past prepared over wood fires.

Stohrer, 51 Rue Montorgueil. Métro: Sentier. 7 A.M.–8 P.M. Closed Mondays. Founded in 1730 by Louis XV's pastry chef and still renowned!

Tearooms

A Priori Thé, 36–37 Galérie Vivienne. Métro: Bourse. An American tearoom serving homemade pies, cheesecake, brownies, as well as lunch. See Chapter 10.

L'Arbre à Cannelle, 57 Passage des Panoramas. Métro: Montmartre or Richelieu-Drouot. Excellent cakes, tortes, and luncheon menu in Napoleon III setting. See Chapter 10.

Chocolate

Ballotin, 14 Rue Montorgueil. Métro: Les Halles. 9:30 A.M.–8 P.M. (–11 P.M. Fridays and Saturdays). Closed Monday mornings. Modern.

3rd arrondissement

Bread and Pastry

Brocco, 180 Rue du Temple. Métro: République. 6:30 A.M.–7:30 P.M. Very pretty shop with authentic turn-of-century décor.

Onfroy, 34 Rue de Saintonge. Métro: République. 8:15 A.M.– 1:30 P.M. and 3–8 P.M. Closed Saturday afternoons and Sundays.

Tearooms

Galérie Gourmande, 38 Rue de Sévigné. Métro: St. Paul. 12–7 P.M. Closed Mondays. Très chic and very good.

Marais Plus, 20 Rue des Francs-Bourgeois. Métro: St. Paul. 10 A.M.–midnight. Closed Sunday nights. Tea shop, bookshop, gift shop, and Sunday brunch. See Chapter 5, Itinerary 1.

Les Mille-Feuilles, 2 Rue Rambuteau. Métro: Rambuteau. Noon until midnight. Closed Sundays and Mondays. Newly decorated, refreshingly so.

Le Petit Salé, 97 Rue Vieille-du-Temple. Métro: Filles-du-Calvaire. 12–10 P.M. Closed Monday nights and Tuesdays. Just behind the Picasso Museum.

Chocolate

La Maison des Bonbons, 46 Rue de Sévigné. Métro: St. Paul. 10 A.M.–7 P.M. Closed Sundays. A candy store.

4th arrondissement

Bread and Pastry

Clichy, 5 Boulevard Beaumarchais. Métro: Bastille. 8 A.M.–7:30 P.M. Closed Mondays. Paul Bugeat, owner of this shop, teaches a course on pastry at Yale!

Finkelsztajn, 27 Rue des Rosiers. Métro: St. Paul. 9 A.M.–1:30 P.M. and 2:30–7:30 P.M. Closed Mondays and Tuesdays. Specialty is Eastern European breads and sweets. See Chapter 5, Itinerary 1.

Pottier, 4 Rue de Rivoli. Métro: St. Paul. 8 A.M.–1:30 P.M. and 3–7:30 P.M. Closed Monday and Tuesday. Chocolate is their thing.

Tearooms

La Charlotte en l'Ile, 24 Rue St. Louis-en-l'Ile. Métro: St. Paul. 2–8 P.M. Closed Mondays and Tuesdays. Intimate décor and good chocolate cake. See Chapter 3.

Les Enfants Gâtés, 43 Rue des Francs-Bourgeois. Métro: St. Paul. 9 A.M.–7 P.M. Closed Tuesdays. Comfortable old leather armchairs welcome an intellectual, local crowd. Several formulas for brunch. See Chapter 5, Itinerary 3.

Eurydice, 10 Place des Vosges. Métro: St. Paul. 12–7 P.M. Closed Mondays and Tuesdays.

Les Fous de l'Ile, 33 Rue des Deux-Ponts. Métro: Pont-Marie. 12–11 P.M. Airy, pleasant, and comfortable. Brunch. See Chapter 3.

Le Jardin de Thé, 10 Rue Brisemiche. Métro: Hôtel-de-Ville. 12–7 P.M. (–11:30 P.M. in summer). Closed Tuesdays. The nicest tearoom in the vicinity of Pompidou Center.

Le Loir dans la Théière, 3 Rue des Rosiers. Métro: St. Paul. 12–7 P.M. Closed Mondays and August. Tranquil dormouse in the teapot looking through the mirror. See Chapter 5, Itinerary 1.

Mariage Frères, 30–32 Rue du Bourg-Tibourg. Métro: Hôtel-de-Ville. 11 A.M.–7:30 P.M. Closed Mondays. Three hundred varieties of tea on sale, tearoom and cakes, and tea ice cream. Authentic and expensive. See Chapter 5, Itinerary 1.

Ice Cream

Berthillon, 31 Rue St. Louis-en-l'Ile. Métro: Pont-Marie. 10 A.M.–8 P.M. Closed Mondays and Tuesdays. The best French ice cream in Paris. See Chapter 3.

Snacks, Brunch

Chez Daisy, 54 Rue des Rosiers. Métro: St. Paul. 12–3 P.M. and 7–11:30 P.M. A wow of a Middle Eastern luncheonette.

Chez Marianne, 2 Rue des Hospitalières-St. Gervais. Métro: St. Paul. 11 A.M.–11 P.M. Closed Fridays. Both sit-down and takeout felafel and food.

L'Ebouillanté, 6 Rue des Barres. Métro: St. Paul, Pont-Marie. 12–9 P.M. Closed Mondays. For crêpes and Tunisian *briks.*

Chocolate

Chocaine, 9 Rue St. Merri. Métro: Hôtel-de-Ville. 11 A.M.–8 P.M. Alsatian specialties.

5th arrondissement

Bread and Pastry

Ad Dar, 8–10 Rue Frédéric-Sauton. Métro: Maubert-Mutualité. 8 A.M.–midnight. Lebanese pastry.

La Fournée, 21 Rue St. Jacques. Métro: Cluny. 7:30 A.M.–8:30 P.M. Closed Mondays.

Lerch, 4 Rue du Cardinal-Lemoine. Métro: Cardinal-Lemoine. 7 A.M.–1:30 P.M. and 3–7 P.M. Closed Mondays and Tuesdays. Alsatian specialties.

Tearooms

Café of the Paris Mosque, 19 Rue Geoffroy-St. Hilaire. Métro: Monge. 10 A.M.–9:30 P.M. Mint tea in superb surroundings.

Le Fourmi Ailée, 8 Rue Fouarre. Métro: Maubert-Mutualité. 12–7 P.M. Closed Tuesdays. Tea and books.

Le Satay, 10 Rue St. Julien-le-Pauvre. Métro: St. Michel. Excellent teas plus good chocolate and cakes in a tropical setting. See Chapter 3.

Tea Caddy, 14 Rue St. Julien-le-Pauvre. Métro: St. Michel. 12–7 P.M. Closed Tuesdays. A lovely, cozy shop for pies, scones, buns, muffins, and tea. See Chapter 3.

Chocolate

Passion et Chocolat, 134 Rue Mouffetard. Métro: Censier-Daubenton, Gobelins. 9:30 A.M.–7:30 P.M. Closed Sunday afternoons and Mondays. Belgian chocolate.

6th arrondissement

Bread and Pastry

La Bonbonnière de Buci, 12 Rue de Buci. Métro: Mabillon, St. Germain-des-Près. 8 A.M.–8 P.M. Closed Tuesdays. See Chapter 4.

Fournil de Pierre, 64 Rue de Seine. Métro: Mabillon, St. Germain-des-Près. 8:30 A.M.–7:30 P.M. Closed Sunday afternoons and Monday mornings. See Chapter 4.

Gérard Mulot, 2 Rue Lobineau. Métro: Mabillon, St. Germain-des-Près. 7 A.M.–8 P.M. Closed Wednesdays. One of my absolute favorites.

Poilâne, 8 Rue du Cherche-Midi. Métro: Sèvres-Babylone. 7 A.M.–8 P.M. Closed Sundays. Poilâne's bread is sold all over the city; it originates, warm, here.

Vieille France, 14 Rue de Buci. Métro: Mabillon, St. Germain-des-Près. 9 A.M.–8 P.M. Closed Mondays. See Chapter 4.

Tearooms

A la Cour de Rohan, Cour de Commerce, 59–61 Rue St. André-des-Arts. Métro: Odéon. 12–7:30 P.M. Closed Mondays and August. The most satisfying tea shop imaginable. Décor, china, cakes and pies, and Friday afternoon organ concerts. Lunch, too.

Dalloyeau, 2 Place Edmond-Rostand. Métro: Luxembourg. 9:30 A.M.–6:40 P.M. One of the top pastry shops. Also serves lunch. See Chapter 6.

L'Heure Gourmande, 22 Passage Dauphine. Métro: Odéon. 11 A.M.–7 P.M. Closed Sundays and August. Good teas and good coffee in a cobblestone alley from yesteryear. Brunch.

Ice Cream

Baskin-Robbins, 1 Rue du Four. Métro: Mabillon. 12–8 P.M. (–midnight Fridays and Saturdays). Closed Sundays. American recipes made in Europe.

LGM, 57 Rue St. André-des-Arts. Metro: Odéon. Open all day every day from March to October.

Chocolate

Chocotruffe, 39 Rue du Cherche-Midi. Métro: Sèvres-Babylone. 10 A.M.–7:30 P.M. Closed Sundays and Mondays.

7th arrondissement

Bread and Pastry

Dalloyeau, 64 Rue de Grenelle. Métro: Bac. 10 A.M.–7:30 P.M. Closed Sundays. One of several sublime shops across the city. See Chapter 8.

Gérard Beaufort, 51 Avenue du Suffren. Métro: Champ-de-Mars. 8:30 A.M.–8 P.M. Closed Saturdays, Sundays, and August.

Millet, 103 Rue St. Dominique. Métro: Ecole-Militaire. 9 A.M.–7 P.M. Closed Sunday afternoons, Mondays, and August. Shop where the president of French pastry chefs officiates.

Peltier, 66 Rue de Sèvres. Métro: Vaneau. 9:30 A.M.–8 P.M. Closed Mondays. Another great pastry chef.

Poujaran, 20 Rue Jean-Nicot. Métro: La Tour-Maubourg. 8:30 A.M.–8:30 P.M. Closed Sundays and August. Basque cakes are the specialty.

Pradier, 32 Rue de Bourgogne. Métro: Chambre-des-Députés. 8 A.M.–8 P.M. Closed Mondays.

Tearooms
Christian Constant, 26 Rue du Bac. Métro: Bac. 8 A.M.–8 P.M. A delight visually and pastry-wise. No artificial ingredients whatsoever.

Les Deux Abeilles, 198 Rue de l'Université. Métro: Alma-Marceau. 9 A.M.–7 P.M. Closed Sundays. Atmosphere and good fruit crumbles.

La Nuit des Thés, 22 Rue de Beaune. Métro: Bac. Elegant, expensive.

Snacks
Rollet-Pradier, 6 Rue de Bourgogne. Métro: Chambre-des-Députés. See Chapter 8.

Chocolates
Aux Chocolats de Puyricard, 27 Avenue Rapp. Métro: Ecole-Militaire. 9:30 A.M.–1 P.M. and 2–7:30 P.M. Closed Sundays. The least expensive of the first-quality chocolates.

Debauve et Gallais, 30 Rue des Sts. Pères. Métro: St. Germain-des-Près. 10 A.M.–12:30 P.M. and 2–7 P.M. Closed Sundays and Mondays. Originally were chocolate-treating pharmacists!

Richard, 258 Boulevard St. Germain. Métro: Solférino. 10 A.M.–7 P.M. Closed Sundays and Monday mornings. Beautiful chocolate presented with art.

8th arrondissement

Bread and Pastry

A *la Cigogne*, 61 Rue de l'Arcade. Métro: St. Lazare. 8 A.M.–7 P.M. Closed Sundays and August. Quality Alsatian pastry.

Dalloyeau, 99–101 Rue du Faubourg St. Honoré. Métro: St. Philippe-du-Roule. 9:30 A.M.–7:15 P.M. One of the finest.

Fauchon, 28 Place de la Madeleine. Métro: Madeleine. 9:45 A.M.–7 P.M. Closed Sundays and Mondays. Famous deluxe grocery store with wonderful pastry adjunct.

Saint-Ouen, 111 Boulevard Haussmann. Métro: Miromesnil. 8 A.M.–8 P.M. Closed Sundays. Interesting bread, too.

Tearooms

Costa Diva, 27 Rue Cambacérès. Métro: Miromesnil. 11:30 A.M.–6:30 P.M. Closed Sundays. Classic setting and inventive dishes.

Ladurée, 16 Rue Royale. Métro: Concorde, Madeleine. 8:30 A.M.–7 P.M. Closed Sundays. An institution on the Parisian scene.

Maison du Chocolat, 52 Rue François Ier. Métro: Georges V. 9:30 A.M.–7 P.M. Closed Sundays. Chocolate brews fit for kings.

Paris-Vierzon, 24 Rue Boissy d'Anglas. Métro: Madeleine. Decorated in the style of a transatlantic liner.

Chocolate
Maison du Chocolat, 225 Rue du Faubourg St. Honoré. Métro: Ternes. 9:30 A.M.–7 P.M. Closed Sundays. Chocolates made in the downstairs kitchen by one of the best artisans in France.

La Marquise de Sévigné, 32 Place de la Madeleine. Métro: Madeleine. 9:30 A.M.–7 P.M. Closed Sundays. A classic.

Paul B, 4 Rue Marbeuf. Métro: Franklin-Roosevelt. 10 A.M.–7 P.M. Closed Sundays and Monday mornings. Shop divided into three sections: bitter, flavored, and milk chocolate.

9th arrondissement

Bread and Pastry
Bourdaloue, 7 Rue Bourdaloue. Métro: Notre-Dame-de-Lorette. 8 A.M.–7:30 P.M. Closed Sundays.

Daniel Dupuy, 13 Rue Cadet. Métro: Cadet. 8 A.M.–8 P.M. Natural breads with no preservatives.

J. Caron, 26 Rue du Faubourg Montmartre. Métro: Montmartre. Everything is baked in a wood-burning stove, there to be seen.

La Tour des Délices, Passage Jouffroy, 10 Boulevard Montmartre. Métro: Richelieu-Drouot, Rue Montmartre. Enticing Oriental pastry.

Yoshio Chiba, 29 Rue Vignon. 9 A.M.–7 P.M. Métro: Havre-Caumartin. Closed Sundays and August. A venerable Japanese chef of French pastry.

Tearooms

Tea Follies, 6 Place Gustave-Toudouze. Métro: St. Georges. 12–10 P.M. Ownership is French-English. Sidewalk on the square. Watercolors inside. Brunch on Sundays.

Snacks

Les Menus Plaisirs, 28 Passage Verdeau. Métro: Montmartre, Le Peletier. 12–7 P.M. Closed Saturdays and Sundays. Wonderful homemade tourtes, pies, and welcome. See Chapter 10.

Chocolate

La Bonbonnière de la Trinité, 4 Place Estienne-d'Orves. Métro: Trinité. 9 A.M.–7 P.M. Closed Sundays. Famous for its bitter chocolate.

Fouquet, 36 Rue Laffitte. Métro: Notre-Dame-de-Lorette. 9:30 A.M.–6:30 P.M. Closed Saturdays and Sundays. Jams, candy, and chocolate of the finest, all made on the premises.

Tanrade, 18 Rue Vignon. Métro: Madeleine. 9:15 A.M.–12 P.M. and 1:30–6:30 P.M. The best candied chestnuts in Paris.

10th arrondissement

Bread and Pastry

Mauduit, 54 Rue du Faubourg St. Denis. Métro: Chateau-d'Eau. 7:15 A.M.–7:30 P.M. Closed Sunday afternoons, Mondays, and August.

Tholoniat, 47 Rue du Chateau-d'Eau. Métro: Chateau-d'Eau. 8 A.M.–7:30 P.M. Closed Wednesdays.

Chocolate

Le Lys Rouge, 63 Rue Chabrol. Métro: Poissonnière. 10 A.M.–7 P.M.

11th arrondissement

Bread and Pastry

Barbey, 10 Avenue de la République. Métro: République. 8:30
A.M.–8 P.M. Closed Sundays and Mondays.

Au Bon Pain d'Autrefois, 45 Rue Popincourt. Métro: St. Am-
broise. 6 A.M.–8 P.M. Closed Sundays. Lovely shop classified
with historic monuments.

Couderc, 6 Boulevard Voltaire. Métro: République. 8:30 A.M.–8
P.M. Closed Mondays, Tuesdays, and August. Chocolate specialists.

Le Palais des Dames, 58bis Rue de Montreuil. Métro: Boulets-
Montreuil. 11 A.M.–7:30 P.M. Closed Sundays, Mondays, and
Tuesday mornings. American pastry prepared right in front of
you.

Tearooms

Thé Troc, 46 Rue Jean-Pierre Timbaud. Métro: Parmentier. 9
A.M.–12 P.M. and 2–8 P.M. Closed Sundays and August. An air
of the Orient.

Chocolate

Léonidas, 5 Boulevard Voltaire. Métro: République. Closed Sundays. Inexpensive Belgian chocolate.

12th arrondissement

Bread and Pastry

Saffers, 24 Place de la Nation. Métro: Nation. 8:30 A.M.–8 P.M.
Closed Mondays.

Chocolate

Aux Gourmandises, 97 Rue Claude Decaen. Métro: Porte-de-

Charenton. 9 A.M.–8 P.M. Closed Sundays and Mondays. Original gift baskets of sweets and appetizers.

13th arrondissement

Bread and Pastry
Auge, 60 Rue Bobillot. Métro: Place-d'Italie. 7 A.M.–1 P.M. and 2–7:30 P.M.

Moisan, 114 Rue de Patay. Métro: Porte-d'Ivry. 7:30 A.M.–7:30 P.M. Closed Wednesdays.

Tearooms
Chamarre, 90 Boulevard Auguste-Blanqui. Métro: Glacière. 8 A.M.–7:30 P.M. Closed Mondays. A range of cholesterol-free cakes.

14th arrondissement

Bread and Pastry
Guibert, 66 Avenue Jean Moulin. Métro: Alésia.

Le Moulin de la Vièrge, 105 Rue Vercingétorix. Métro: Pernéty. 7:30 A.M.–8 P.M. Closed Sundays. Stone-ground flour and natural leavening. Breads cooked in wood-stowed oven.

Saibon, Place Brancusi. Métro: Gaîté. Fabulous bread on beautiful, modern square designed by architect Bofill.

Ice Cream
Calabrese, 15 Rue d'Odessa. Métro: Montparnasse. 10–12 midnight. Real Italian ice cream.

Chocolate
La Vicomté, 100 Boulevard Brune. Métro: Porte-d'Orléans.

15th arrondissement

Bread and Pastry
Fischer, 68 Rue du Commerce. Métro: Commerce. 8 A.M.–7:30
P.M. Closed Mondays and August.

Hellegouarch, 185 Rue de Vaugirard. Métro: Volontaires. 8:30
A.M.–7:30 P.M. Closed Mondays and August.

Max Poilâne, 87 Rue Brancion. Métro: Convention. 7 A.M.–8
P.M. Closed Mondays. *Natural* is the by-word.

Le Moulin de la Vièrge, 166 Avenue de Suffren. Métro: Sèvres-
Lecourbe. 7:30 A.M.–8 P.M. Closed Sundays. Same as in 14th
arrondissement.

La Petite Marquise, 50 Avenue de LaMotte-Picquet. Métro:
Champ-de-Mars. 8:30 A.M.–8 P.M. Closed Tuesdays and August.

Tearooms
Je thé . . .me, 4 Rue d'Alleray. Métro: Vaugirard. 10:30 A.M.–7
P.M. Closed Sundays and Mondays in summer. A grocery store
become a tea shop with its former fixtures. Pleasant.

Chocolate
Boucher, 202 Rue de la Convention. Métro: Convention. 9:15
A.M.–1 P.M. and 2:15–7:30 P.M. Closed Sundays and Mondays.
Tremendous variety of homemade chocolates.

16th arrondissement

Bread and Pastry
Chatton, 125 Avenue Victor Hugo. Métro: Pompe. 9 A.M.–7
P.M.

Coquelin Aîné, 65 Rue de Passy. Métro: La Muette. 9 A.M.–7:30 P.M. Closed Sunday afternoons and Mondays.

Lenôtre, 44 Rue d'Auteuil. Métro: Michelange-Auteuil. 9:15 A.M.–7:15 P.M. Known the world over as the tops.

Malitourne, 80 Rue de Chaillot. Métro: Iéna. 8:30 A.M.–2:30 P.M. and 4–7:30 P.M. Closed Sunday afternoons and Mondays. A new menu of pastry every day.

Sineau, 79 Rue de la Tour. Métro: La Muette. 9 A.M.–7 P.M. Closed Mondays and August. Elegant student hangout.

Tearooms
Boissier, 184 Avenue Victor-Hugo. Métro: Pompe. 9 A.M.–7 P.M. Closed Saturday afternoons and Sundays. Attractive and moderately priced.

Carette, 4 Place de Trocadéro. Métro: Trocadéro. 8 A.M.–7 P.M. Closed Tuesdays and August. Well located on the place.

Les Champs-Mesnil, 15 Rue Mesnil. 4755-9644. Métro: Victor-Hugo. 7 A.M.–7:30 P.M. Closed Sundays. Only natural products used—no coloring and no preservatives. Reserve for lunch.

Au Régal, 4 Rue Nicolo. Métro: La Muette. 9 A.M.–11 P.M. Closed Sundays, Russian tearoom and restaurant.

Chocolate
Le Confiseur d'Auteuil, 30 Rue d'Auteuil. Métro: Eglise-d'Auteuil. 9 A.M.–7:30 P.M. Closed Sunday afternoons and Mondays. Old-fashioned shop with the best candy-covered walls.

Régis, 89 Rue de Passy. Métro: La Muette. 10 A.M.–7 P.M. Closed Sundays, Monday mornings, and August. Excellent chocolate.

17th arrondissement

Bread and Pastry
Gros, 5 Rue Pierre-Demours. Métro: Terner, 7 A.M.–1:30 P.M. and 3–7:30 P.M. Closed Sundays.

Tearooms
Aux Délices, 39 Avenue de Villiers. Métro: Malesherbes. 9 A.M.–6:45 P.M. Closed Mondays. Beautiful, though solemn, décor. Lunch also is served.

Le Stübli, 11 Rue Poncelet. Métro: Ternes. 10 A.M.–6:30 P.M. Closed Sundays and Mondays. Genuine Austrian pastry.

18th arrondissement

Bread and Pastry
Jandré, 76 Rue Duhesme. Métro: Jules-Joffrin. 9 A.M.–7:30 P.M. Former pastry chef of the governor of Canada.

Le Pain complet de Paris, 59bis Rue du Mont-Cénis. Métro: Jules-Joffrin. Natural whole-wheat flour.

Pâtisserie de Montmartre, 81 Rue du Mont-Cénis. Métro: Jules-Joffrin. 9 A.M.–7:45 P.M.

La Savoyarde, 34 Rue Lamarck. Métro: Lamarck-Caulincourt. 7:30 A.M.–8 P.M. Closed Thursdays.

Tearooms
L'Invité, 1bis Rue Félix-Ziem. Métro: Lamarck-Caulaincourt. Closed Sundays and Monday mornings. Original cakes.

Patachou, Place du Tertre. Métro: Abbesses. Open all day every day, with a unique view of Paris. See Chapter 11.

Le Téléphone, 38 Rue Lepic. Métro: Abbesses. South American artifacts and fruit teas.

20th arrondissement

Bread and Pastry
Lambert et Séguin, 10 and 140 Rue du Jourdain. Métro: Jourdain. Closed Mondays.

Riem-Becker, 89 Avenue Gambetta. Métro: Gambetta. 8:30 A.M.–7:30 P.M.

CHAPTER 22

In the Evening

Prices are based on a dollar exchange rate of approximately 6 francs to one dollar.

The Classics

Crazy Horse Saloon, 12 Avenue Georges V. 4723-3232. Métro: Alma-Marceau. Two shows weekdays: 9 and 11:35 P.M. Three shows Friday and Saturday: 8, 10:30 P.M., and 12:50 A.M. From $35 to $80 with drinks. Reserve. The best of the girlie shows in totally renovated hall. Striptease.

Folies Bergères, 32 Rue Richer. 4246-7711. Métro: Cadet. Two shows nightly: 9 and 11:30 P.M. Closed Mondays. From $15 to $60. Reserve. The theatre that feted Josephine Baker has discovered a new star from Broadway, Yolanda Graves, to be seen amid masses of feather, sequins, and rhinestones.

Le Lido, 116 Avenue des Champs-Elysées. 4563-1161. Métro: Georges V. Dinner and revue: 8 P.M. $90. Revue and champagne: 10 P.M. and midnight, $60. Reserve. Well-timed, well-balanced show of the famed long-legged beauties.

Moulin Rouge, 82 Boulevard de Clichy. 4606-0019. Métro: Blanche. Dinner and revue: 8 P.M. $90. Revue and champagne: 10 P.M. and midnight, $60. Reserve. The ultimate in French cancan, unchanged since the war.

Le Paradis Latin, 28 Rue du Cardinal Lemoine. 4325-2828. Métro: Cardinal-Lemoine. Dinner and show: 8 P.M. $90. Show and champagne: 10 P.M. $60. Reserve. Eiffel designed the theatre a hundred years ago. The show is shades of a Hollywood extravaganza.

Piano Bars, Dance Halls, Nightclubs

Le Bar Platinum, Hôtel Méridien-Montparnasse, 19 Rue du Commandant-Mouchotte. Métro: Montparnasse-Bienvenue. 12 P.M.–2 A.M. Music begins at 10:30 P.M. except Sundays. Quality New Orleans and electric guitar.

Le Bilboquet, 13 Rue St. Benoît. Métro: St. Germain-des-Près. One of the first cellar jazz clubs after World War II. Every night until 3 A.M. Drinks: $15.

La Calavados, 40 Avenue Pierre Ier de Serbie. 4720-3139. Métro: Alma-Marceau. 10:30 P.M.–6 A.M. Closed Sundays. Pianist Joe Turner is there with the oldies after midnight.

L'Escale, 5 Rue Monsieur-le-Prince. Métro: Odéon. 11 P.M.– 4 A.M. Minute cellar devoted to live Latin American music. $10–$15 a drink.

L'Eustache, 37 Rue Berger. Métro: Halles. Concert at 10:30 P.M. Closed Sundays. Live jazz, relaxed atmosphere. Drinks: $7.

Gibus, 18 Rue du Faubourg du Temple. Métro: République. 11 P.M. on. Closed Sundays and Mondays. Dance hall of the rockers. Entrance fee and one drink: $7; Friday and Saturday: $12.

Le Katmandou, 21 Rue du Vieux-Colombier. Métro: Sèvres-Babylone, Saint-Sulpice. 11 P.M. until dawn. The best known of the women's bars. Drinks: $15.

Lapin Agile, 22 Rue des Saules. 4606-8587. Métro: Lamarck-Caulaincourt. 9 P.M.–2 A.M. Closed Mondays. Show and drink: $15. See Chapter 11.

Latitudes, 7–11 Rue Saint-Benoît. Métro: St. Germain-des-Près. Piano bar in spacious, modern setting. Comfortable and chic. Concerts Thursday, Friday, and Saturday evenings: $15.

La Locomotive, 90 Boulevard de Clichy. Métro: Blanche. 11 P.M.–dawn. Closed Monday. Vast and varied hangout of the younger set: shops, bars, exhibits and, of course, dance podiums and much music. Weekdays with a drink: $10; weekends: $15.

Le Magnetic Terrace, 12 Rue de la Cossonnerie. Métro: Les Halles. Deluxe cellar and live be-bop. Closed Sundays. Cover: $20.

La Main Jaune, Porte de Champerret, Square de l'Amérique Latine. Métro: Champerret. Dancing. Live music. Change of theme every evening. Mondays: soul, funk, rhythm and blues. Wednesdays: langorous Latin music. Wednesday, Saturday, and Sunday afternoons: 2:30–7 P.M. and Friday and Saturday nights from 10 P.M. to dawn: rollerskating. Monday and Friday afternoons: tea dancing.

Montana, 28 Rue St. Benoît. Métro: St. Germain-des-Près. Classic jazz from pianist René Urtrager in cellar club. 10:30 P.M.–2 A.M. Bar: $15, club: $20.

Pau Brasil, 32 Rue de Tilsitt. 4227-3139. Métro: Charles-de-Gaulle. 8 P.M.–2 A.M. Closed Sundays. Brazilian dinner-dance club. Show at 10:30 P.M. No limit on the twelve sorts of meat wheeled among the tables. About $50 for dinner.

Le Petit Journal, 71 Boulevard St. Michel. 4326-2859. Métro: Luxembourg. Concert 10 P.M.–1 A.M. Closed Sundays. Traditional jazz in a relaxed atmosphere. Dinner: $35, drinks: $15.

Le Petit Opportun, 15 Rue des Lavandières-Sainte Opportune. Métro: Châtelet. Concert 11 P.M. Minute, vaulted cellar devoted to live jazz. First drink: $20, second: $10.

La Poste, 34–37 Rue Duperré. 4280-6616. Métro: Pigalle. Dinner and show until 2 A.M. Closed Sundays. Most elegant supper club of Paris run by torch singer Rochelle Robertson of L.A. Located in former town house of composer Georges Bizet. Dinner: $50, cocktails: $10.

Le Real Scoop, 24 Rue Pasquier. Métro: Madeleine. Piano bar and singer: 10:30 P.M., except Sundays. Drinks: $10.

Studio A, 51 Rue de Ponthieu. Métro: Franklin-Roosevelt. 11 P.M.–5 A.M. Fridays and Saturdays. Fashionable disco. Young clientele. Cover and a drink: $15.

Trottoirs de Buenos Aires, 37 Rue des Lombards. Métro: Châtelet. 10:30 P.M.–1 A.M. Closed Mondays. Two shows nightly at 8:30 and 10:30 P.M. Tango lessons in the afternoon. Live music and dancing. The attraction is the tango. Entrance fee: $15.

Concerts, Shows

For the weekly program of theatre, shows, and films, see *L'Officiel des Spectacles* on sale at all newspaper stands for two francs.

Galérie 55, The English Theater of Paris, 55 Rue de Seine. 4326-6351. Métro: Odéon, Mabillon. 8:30 P.M. except Sundays and Mondays. See Chapter 4.

New Morning, 7–9 Rue des Petites-Ecuries. Métro: Chateau-d'Eau. Concerts nightly of best American and English jazz groups to come through Paris. Starting times vary. Reservations at the FNAC: Forum des Halles; 22 Avenue de Wagram (Métro: Etoile); 153bis Rue de Rennes (Métro: Montparnasse).

Paris Opera, Place de la Bastille. Métro: Bastille. Opera.

Paris Opera-Garnier, Place de l'Opéra. 4742-5371. Métro: Opéra. Classical ballet.

Châtelet, Théâtre Musical de Paris, Place du Châtelet. Métro: Châtelet. Concerts of all types.

Théâtre de la Ville, 2 Place du Châtelet. Métro: Châtelet. Varied shows, theatre, ballet, and concerts.

Théâtre Renaud-Barrault, Rond-Point des Champs Elysées. Métro: Franklin-Roosevelt. Sunday morning concerts of classical music at 11 A.M. Seventy francs. No reservations.

Concerts in a number of churches occur regularly, especially during the summer season. Mostly classical music. Some are free. See *Officiel des Spectacles* for programs and schedules.

Discount Tickets to Theatres

Kiosk alongside Madeleine Church (west side) for discount tickets. Métro: Madeleine. 12:30 to 8 P.M. for all weekday shows; 12 noon for afternoon shows on Saturdays and Sundays and 2 P.M. for evening shows. Same-day tickets only: one-half price.

Théâtre Français, Place du Palais-Royal. Métro: Palais-Royal. French classical theater. One-half hour before each show, 112 seats are sold for $3 apiece at ticket window in the Rue Montpensier.

CHAPTER 23

Keeping Yourself Trim

Prices are based on a dollar exchange rate of approximately six francs to one dollar.

Cycle Rental

Bicyclub de France
8 Place Porte–de–Champerret   4766-5592
Métro: Champerret
Operates from middle of March to end of November.
$10 a day plus $5 membership and insurance fee.
Passport required.

Paris Vélo-Rent-a-Bike
2 Rue Fer à Moulin   4337-5922
Métro: Censier-Daubenton, Gobelins
Operates year round.
From $15 to $25 a day plus guarantee of $150 to $200.

Exercise Classes

American Church
65 Quai d'Orsay   4705-0799
Métro: Invalides, Alma-Marceau
Bus: 28, 42, 49, 63, 80, 82

Hours and days vary. Call following numbers for information:

Gymnastics: 4753-4246 or 4578-9131
Karate: 4338-1276
Kung fu: 4577-4471
Tai chi: 4577-4471
Yoga: 4608-4855

Golf

Rennes-Raspail
149 Rue de Rennes   4544-2435
Métro: Montparnasse
8 A.M.–midnight weekdays, 9 A.M.–9 P.M. Saturdays and Sundays.
Putting green, bunkers and driving range.
$7.50 for half hour. Reserve.

Jogging

Along the quays of the Seine.

Luxembourg Gardens—métro: Luxembourg, St. Sulpice
Outside track.

Park Montsouris—métro: Cité-Universitaire

Champ-de-Mars—métro: Ecole-Militaire

Park Monceau—métro: Monceau

Buttes Chaumont Park—métro: Buttes-Chaumont, Botzaris

Roller Skating

Buttes-Chaumont Rink
30 Rue Edouard Pailleron   4239-8610
Métro: Bolivar
Open every day and Thursday, Friday, and Saturday evenings.
Hours vary. Adults: $3.50
Children: $2.50
Skate rental: $2.50

Main Jaune
Place de la Porte-de-Champerret   4763-2647
Métro: Champerret
2:30–7 P.M. Wednesdays, Saturdays, and Sundays.
$7 with a drink. $1.50 skate rental.
10 P.M. until dawn Fridays and Saturdays.
$12 with a drink. $2.50 skate rental.

Squash

Maine
37 Avenue du Maine   4538-6620
Métro: Montparnasse
8 A.M.–11 P.M. (–8 P.M. Saturdays and Sundays).
6 courts and exercise room.
40 minutes: $10.

Rennes-Raspail
149 Rue de Rennes   4544-2435
Métro: Montparnasse
8 A.M.–midnight. 9 A.M.–9 P.M. Saturdays and Sundays.

7 courts.
Half-hour: $9. Reserve.

Swimming

Buttes-Chaumont pool
30 Rue Edouard-Pailleron   4239-8610
Métro: Bolivar
From 12 noon every day, plus Wednesday and Sunday mornings
from 8 A.M.
Adults: $3. Children $2.50.

Hôtel Nikko
61 Quai de Grenelle, 4th Fl.   4475-2545
Métro: Javel
10 A.M.–9 P.M. Closed Sundays.
$4.

Jean Taris
36 Rue Thouin   4325-5403
Métro: Censier-Daubenton

St. Germain market
Rue Clément   4329-0815
Métro: St. Germain-des-Près, Mabillon.
Closed Mondays.
$1.50.

Pontoise
19 Rue de Pontoise   4354-0623
Métro: Maubert-Mutualité
$3.

Suzanne Berlioux
10 Place de la Rotonde   4236-9844

Métro: Les Halles
$3.

Tennis

Luxembourg Gardens courts
Métro: Luxembourg, St. Sulpice, Vavin
Six outdoor hard courts: 8 A.M. until dusk.
Half-hour: $2. No reservations. See Chapter 6.

Municipal Sports Center
7 Avenue Paul-Appell
Métro: Porte-d'Orléans
Nine outdoor hard courts: 8 A.M. until dusk.
Half-hour: $2. No reservations. Avoid weekends.

CHAPTER 24

Back to Class

Prices are based on a dollar exchange rate of approximately six francs to one dollar.

Art Classes

Martine Moisan
6–8 Galérie Vivienne
75002 PARIS   4297-4665

Métro: Bourse

Let Paris be your studio for a weekend. Martine Moisan, painter and gallery owner, will take you in hand, rain or shine, for drawing and painting lessons: in a bistro, along the river, on a market square, or in front of Maillol's stone nudes. Lessons, lunch, and all art supplies cost $150. There are reduced prices for couples and families.

Le Rouvray
1 Rue Fréderic-Sauton
75005 PARIS   4325-0045

Métro: Maubert Mutualité

Patchwork lessons in the very heart of old Paris. American folk art has crossed the Atlantic with Diane de Obaldia, who will instruct you, in English, afternoons or for a weekend. The cost is $70 for three sessions, supplies included.

Cooking Classes

Association Culturelle Franco-Chinoise
38 Rue de la Tour
75016 PARIS   4520-7409

Métro: Passy

Learn to make a Chinese dish—and partake—all in one lesson—for $20.

Bibiane Deschamps
17 Rue de Grenelle
75007 PARIS   4548-7235

Métro: Sèvres-Babylone, Bac

Traditional French cuisine. Each class is devoted to a different dish and dessert. The cost is $22.

Le Cordon Bleu
8 Rue Léon-Delhomme
75007 PARIS   4856-0606

Métro: Vaugirard

Daily demonstrations at the world-famous cooking school from 9:30–11:30 A.M., 1:30–4 P.M., and 4–6:30 P.M. Cost $22.

Ecole de Cuisine du Chef Hubert
48 Rue de Sèvres
75007 PARIS   4296-0888

Métro: Sèvres-Babylone

All the dishes are prepared and the dinner takes place. Cost is $60. Classes are Wednesdays at 6:30 P.M.

Ecole de Cuisine de Varenne
34 Rue St. Dominique
75007 PARIS   4705-1016

Métro: Invalides

Afternoon demonstrations with famous chefs. Bilingual.

Marie-Blanche de Broglie
18 Avenue de LaMotte-Picquet
75007 PARIS   4551-3634

Métro: Ecole-Militaire

Regional and *nouvelle* cuisine. One-day session costs $70. Bilingual. Princess de Broglie organizes week-long courses at her château in Normandy in August and at the beginning of September.

Paris en Cuisine
49 Rue de Richelieu
75001 PARIS   4261-3523

Métro: Pyramides

Robert Noah, American chef and food enthusiast who has lived and worked in France for almost twenty years, organizes a number of classes and demonstrations in English. Demonstration in kitchens of top Paris restaurants (three Wednesday afternoons) costs $50. Walking tour of restaurant kitchens (Thursday mornings) costs $42.

Other longer and more gastronomic possibilities are available. Write for brochure in English.

Wine Classes

L'Académie du vin
Cité Berryer
25 Rue Royale
75008 PARIS   4265-0982

Métro: Madeleine, Concorde

Three sessions by writers and oenologists. Cost is $180 with wine tasting. Comparative tasting sessions are Mondays at 7 P.M.—$37 for the session. Bilingual.

Centre d'Information, de Documentation et de Dégustation
45 Rue Liancourt
75014 PARIS   4327-6721

Métro: Denfert-Rochereau

Weekdays 11 A.M., 3 and 6 P.M. Three sessions, three hours each cost $110. In French.

L'Ecole du Vin
17 Passage Foubert
75013 PARIS   4589-7739

Métro: Tolbiac

Weekend course with tasting. Roughly $110. Bilingual.

La Maison de la Vigne et du Vin de France
21 Rue François Ier
75008 PARIS   4720-2076

Métro: Franklin-Roosevelt

Information center for French wines. Wednesdays and Thursdays from 5:30 to 7:30 P.M. and on Saturday mornings a two-part course includes half lecture and half tasting. Roughly $25 a session, all expenses included. In French. Register early.

CHAPTER 25

Children's Paris

Museums

Children's Museum of Modern Art
14 Avenue de New-York   4723-6127
Métro: Trocadéro
10 A.M.–5:40 P.M.
10 A.M.–8:30 P.M. Wednesdays
Closed Mondays and holidays.

Shows and workshops especially conceived for children. Parents also welcome. Check with museum for exact time of workshops.

Discovery Palace
Grand Palais, Avenue Franklin-Roosevelt   4359-1821
Métro: Franklin-Roosevelt   4074-8000
10 A.M.–6 P.M.
Closed Mondays
Planetarium shows at 2, 3:15, 4:30 P.M.

Somewhat old-fashioned hands-on museum, especially when compared to the new Science City at La Villette. Wonderful space voyage at the Planetarium.

Grévin Museum
10 Boulevard Montmartre   4770-8505
Métro: Montmartre
10 A.M.–7 P.M.
Forum des Halles (on balcony)   4026-2850
Métro: Châtelet
10 A.M.–6:45 P.M.
1–8 P.M. Sundays and holidays.

The original museum of wax replicas of celebrated people is constantly updated. At the mini-museum at the Halles, the sound and light show of the 1890s is worthwhile.

Museum of Man
Chaillot Palace, 17 Place du Trocadéro   4553-7060
Métro: Trocadéro
9:45 A.M.–5:15 P.M.
Closed Tuesdays and holidays.

Presentations of man from his beginnings across five continents, emphasizing his customs, skills, art, and evolution. Recently renovated. Many life-size exhibits in natural habitat.

Museum of Mechanical Musical Instruments
Impasse Berthaud (across the street from Pompidou Center)
Métro: Rambuteau
2–7 P.M. Saturdays, Sundays, and holidays only.

The private collection of this charming museum's director, including the first nickelodeons, mechanical pianos, and a wonderful animated jazz band. Steven Spielberg has signed the visitor's book here.

Museum of Natural History and Plant Garden
57 Rue Cuvier,   4336-5426   Other entrance:
Métro: Jussieu   Quai St. Bernard
11 A.M.–6:30 P.M.   Métro: Austerlitz
Menagerie-Vivarium
9 A.M.–5 P.M. (–6 P.M. in summer)
Temporary exhibits are closed Tuesdays and holidays.

Many fine permanent exhibits feature mastodons and dino-
sauria, ferns, and fossils billions of years old. Plant perfume
exhibits. Precious stones. Beautiful butterflies and insects: entrance at 45 Rue Buffon. The mineralogical exhibits of giant
crystals are magnificent.

There also is a menagerie, originally from the Royal Menagerie at Versailles. Kiki, the giant turtle from the Seychelles
Islands, arrived here in 1878.

Science City, Cité des Sciences et de l'Industrie
30 Avenue Corentin-Cariou, Parc de la Villette   4642-1313
Métro: Porte-de-la-Villette   4005-0607
10 A.M.–6 P.M.
Closed Mondays.

Vast complex of the future, a hands-on museum, plus a
planetarium. Permanent and temporary exhibitions. Nonstop
cinema, science news, inventorium, geode with giant hemi-
spheric movie screen, and more.

Port de la Villette: The *Argonaute,* a submarine of the French
Navy, harbored here after twenty-four years of active duty. Transported by barge from the Mediterranean to Le Havre, then
pushed down the Seine, it traveled through the Parisian canals to
la Villette.

Parks and Zoos

Aquarium
Chaillot Palace Gardens
Place du Trocadéro
Métro: Trocadéro

See Chapter 12.

Bagatelle Park
Bois de Boulogne   4624-6700
Métro: Pont-de-Neuilly
8:30 A.M.–8 P.M.

Lovely flower gardens in a park.

Buttes-Chaumont Park
5 Rue Botzaris
Métro: Buttes-Chaumont or Botzaris

A lake and falls, a romantic spot. Also puppet shows.

Cousteau's Ocean Park
Forum des Halles, Place Carrée   4028-9898
Métro: Les Halles
10 A.M.–7:30 P.M. Wednesdays, Saturdays and Sundays.
12–7:30 P.M. other days.
Closed Fridays.
$15 for adults, $9 for children.

Georges-Brassens Park
Rue des Morillons
Métro: Convention

Formerly grounds of slaughterhouses. Rock-climbing, puppet
theatre, vineyard, and a herb garden.

Jardin d'Acclimatation
Bois de Boulogne   4067-9080
Métro: Porte-Maillot, Sablons, Neuilly
10 A.M.–6 P.M.

Created in 1860. There are still a few animals: brown bears, farm animals, peacocks, birds, and monkeys. Emphasis is now on merry-go-round and rides, games, and puppets. Some amusements are free, some are not.

Visit Musée en herbe, where shows change. Entrance at Porte-des-Sablons, métro Sablons.

The baby train at Porte-Maillot operates on Wednesdays, Saturdays, Sundays, and holiday afternoons as well as during vacation periods.

Jardin des Halles
105 Rue Rambuteau   4508-0718
Métro: Les Halles
Closed Mondays.

For seven- to eleven-year-olds, a miniature adventure land.

Luxembourg Gardens
6th arrondissement
Métro: Luxembourg, St.-Sulpice, Vavin
See Chapter 6.

Paris Zoo
53 Avenue de St. Maurice   4343-8495
Métro: Porte-Dorée
9 A.M.–5 P.M. (–6 P.M. in summer)

Undergoing restoration. This was once the largest zoo in Europe. Has a panda offered by Mao in 1971 and other rare creatures.

Vincennes Floral Park
Bois de Vincennes   4343-9295
Métro: Chateau-de-Vincennes and bus 112
9:30 A.M.–6 P.M.

All sorts of activities: merry-go-round, rides, old train, nature walks, a real farm, flower gardens, children's theatre, and more.

Other

Boat rides
See Chapter 2.

Eiffel Tower
Champ-de-Mars   4555-9111
Métro: Bir-Hakeim
10 A.M.–11 P.M.

See Chapter 12.

English Theater of Paris
Gallery 55
55 Rue de Seine   4326-6351
Métro: Mabillon, St. German-des-Près
3 P.M. Wednesdays and Saturdays
Summertime and Christmas holidays: every day except Sundays and Mondays.

English-language theatre's show for children. Telephone for reservations 11 A.M.–7 P.M.

Grand Arch
1 Parvis de la Défense   4778-1333
9 A.M.–6 P.M.
RER: Défense
See Chapter 14.

Puppet shows

Marionnettes des Champs-Elysées   4257-4334
Rond-Point des Champs-Elysées
Métro: Champs-Elysées-Clemenceau
3, 4, 5 P.M. Wednesdays, Saturdays, Sundays, and during school
vacations.

Marionnettes du Luxembourg   4326-4647
Luxembourg Gardens
Métro: Vavin, St. Sulpice, Gare-de-Luxembourg
See Chapter 6.

Marionnettes de Montsouris
Parc Montsouris at Avenue Reilles-Rue Gazan intersection
Métro: Cité-Universitaire
3:30, 4:30 P.M. Wednesdays
3, 4 P.M. Saturdays

Chinese marionnettes
Kwok On Museum
41 Rue des Franc-Bourgeois
Métro: St. Paul
10 A.M. and 2:30 P.M. weekdays.
Combined show and museum visit. See Chapter 5, Itinerary 3.

Roller-skating

Main Jaune
Place de la Porte-de-Champerret   4763-2647
Métro: Porte-de-Champerret
2:30–7 P.M. Wednesdays, Saturdays, and Sundays
$7 with a drink. $1.50 skate rental.

Buttes Chaumont Rink
30 Rue Edouard-Pailleron   4239-8610
Métro: Bolivar
Open every day and Thursday, Friday, and Saturday evenings.
Hours vary. $3.50 adults, $2.50 children. $2.50 skate rental.

Baby-sitting

Hotels usually are in contact with baby-sitting services. Here are a few addresses. Prices range from $4 to $6 an hour.

Ababa: 4549-4646
Allô Maman Poule: 4747-7878
Baby-Sitting Service: 4637-5124
Catholic Institute: 4548-3170
Kid Service: 4296-0416
Ludévic: 4553-9393
Sweetbriar College junior year in France: 4548-7930

CHAPTER 26

For the Curious

Tombs and Cemeteries

You do not have to be imbued with necrolatry to appreciate
Parisian cemeteries. They are neither sad nor morbid. In fact,
they rather beget earthly peace, even lightness of heart. They
definitely are bucolic. Try any of these for an experience.

Père-Lachaise

Entrance: Corner of Boulevard Menilmontant and Rue de la
Roquette or Rue des Rondeaux and Avenue de Père-
Lachaise.

Métro: Père-Lachaise, Gambetta

Bus: 26, 61, 69, 76

Hours: 8:30 A.M.–5 P.M.

The largest single plot of land in Paris, Père-Lachaise, or
Father Lachaise, was named after Louis XIV's confessor. He was

a powerful man in the 17th century and received here—in a rest home of the Jesuits—those who sought his intervention with the King. It is rumored that he was not adverse to giving certain female petitioners a trial run before presentation to the monarch. In the early 18th century the area was converted into a cemetery, but Parisians were reluctant to place their loved ones here. An intensive promotional campaign was designed and, with the help of the supposed remains of Molière and La Fontaine, as well as Héloïse and Abélard, the cemetery soon became stylish.

It is impossible to know how many thousands have been buried at Père-Lachaise over the centuries. Among the most famous are Oscar Wilde, Balzac, Proust, Colette, David, Delacroix, Ingres, Pissarro, Modigliani, Marie Laurencin, Chopin, Sarah Bernhardt, Piaf, Isadora Duncan, Simone Signoret, Richard Wright, and Gertrude Stein.

In the northeast corner is the Federalists' Wall, where the people of the commune made their last stand in 1871 and were mowed down. The wall is visited every May Day by delegations of workers.

Père-Lachaise is a beautiful place with no trace of uniformity. On the contrary, under its 12,000 trees, imagination is the ruler. Areas 7 and 96 are almost exclusively inhabited by Jewish graves. Area 85 contains the remains of what was a Muslim cemetery and which at one time contained a mosque. It is now occupied by a columbarium.

St. Vincent Cemetery
See Chapter 11.

Montparnasse Cemetery
Address: 3 Boulevard Edgar Quinet

Metro: Raspail

Bus: 28, 58, 68

Hours: 8 A.M.–5:30 P.M.

A street runs right through the cemetery. I have attended burials here as women from the neighborhood have passed through with their shopping bags and children have jogged along with their books in their knapsacks. Among the personalities present are St. Saëns, Baudelaire, Bourdelle, Jean-Paul Sartre, Brancusi, Maria Montez (remember her?), and Guy de Maupassant.

Charonne Cemetery
Address: 4 Place St. Blaise

Métro: Gambetta, Porte-de-Bagnolet

Bus: 26, 76

Very far off the beaten track, this little cemetery circles a small village church, partially hidden from sight by its surrounding mounds. Its tower dates from the 12th century Romanesque period, while other parts were rebuilt in the 15th, 18th, and 19th centuries.

Despite the charm of the place, no truly famous people are buried here. Unfortunately, the church and its yard are surrounded by monstrosities.

Pantheon
Address: Place du Panthéon

Métro: Cardinal-Lemoine

Bus: 21, 27, 38, 84, 85, 89

Hours: 10 A.M.–4 P.M. (–6 P.M. in summer)
      Closed Tuesdays and holidays

The Pantheon originally was built as a church following a vow made by Louis XV as he lay at death's door. It now houses the remains of the great men of France in its crypt: Voltaire, Gambetta, Rousseau, Hugo, Zola, Braille, Jaurès, and Jean Moulin among others.

Catacombs

Address: 1 Place Denfert-Rochereau, 4322-4763.

Métro: Denfert-Rochereau

Bus: 38, 68

Visits: 2–4 P.M. every day except Mondays and holidays.
9–11 A.M. Saturdays and Sundays.

Since 1785 the bones amassed in numerous Parisian cemeteries have been deposited in the Catacombs. Its land was riddled with mine shafts and galleries and was, therefore, an ideal spot to scatter some five or six million skeletons. During World War II French Resistance fighters made the Catacombs their headquarters.

If you have a flashlight, take it along. Dress warmly and keep a stiff upper lip!

Sewers

Address: Place de la Résistance
Left Bank side of Alma Bridge

Metro: Alma-Marceau

Bus: 42, 63, 80, 92

Hours: 3–8 P.M. Wednesdays through Sundays.

The Paris sewer system was a gigantic undertaking of engineering. Here again, dress warmly.

CHAPTER 27

Holidays and Special Events

In addition to normal national and religious holidays like Easter, Christmas, New Year's Day, and Bastille Day, the French celebrate—and most often close shop on—Easter Monday, May Day (May 1st), Victory Day 1945 (May 8), Ascension Day or Holy Thursday (fortieth day after Easter), Whitsunday Monday (Pentecost: the seventh Sunday after Easter), Assumption Day (August 15), All Saints Day (November 1st), and Armistice Day 1918 (November 11).

Bastille Day, July 14, is the French national day in celebration of the French Revolution. There is dancing in the streets of Paris on the night of the 13th in particular and the 14th on a lesser scale. Orchestra locations you can count on include the courtyards of the city's fire brigades, the Bastille, Champ-de-Mars, St. Catherine Place in the Marais, the top of the Rue du Montagne Sainte Geneviève behind the Panthéon, and Montmartre. On the morning of the 14th, there is a military parade on the

Champs-Elysées. Fireworks visible from the Seine, near Trocadéro, are displayed in the evening.

Beaujolais Nouveau arrives in town at one minute past midnight on the third Thursday of November.

Horseracing: check newspaper for days and times.

Auteuil Race Track: Métro: Porte-d'Auteuil
Bus: 52, PC

Longchamp Race Track: Métro: Porte-d'Auteuil and 244n bus
Porte-Maillot and 244 bus

St. Cloud Race Track: Métro: Pont-de-Neuilly and bus 141 or 144

Vincennes Race Track: RER—Joinville-le-Pont

Music Night occurs on the first day of summer (June 21). Parisians take to the streets with their musical instruments, individually and in groups. Unabashedly, they produce both classical and modern sounds until far into the night. On squares in different quarters, orchestras play and people dance.

Paris Fair is an extensive commercial fair with products from all over France, including wines, food, and handicrafts. The fair runs for ten days at the end of April and beginning of May. Located at the Porte-de-Versailles.

Paris Marathon occurs the last Sunday in April. Starting point: Place de la Concorde at 10 A.M.

Sound and Light Shows, in English, are held on summer evenings from April to October at the Invalides.

Tennis Opens: check newspapers for exact dates.

Roland Garros Stadium—Métro: Porte-d'Auteuil
Beginning of June

Bercy Omnisports Palace—Métro: Bercy
Bus: 24, 87
Last week October/first week November

Wine Festival at Montmartre takes place the first Sunday in October, after the local harvest.

CHAPTER 28

Some Very Nice Hotels

Each of the following hotels is heartily recommended for varying reasons. Some are havens of calm, others ooze old world charm. Many are sophisticated or "international," and perhaps expensive, while others are pleasant and affordable. All are well situated.

The hotels have been arranged by quarter or *arrondissement*. 5, 6, 7, 13, 14, 15 are Left Bank, with 5 and 6 being the Latin Quarter; 7 an elegant, bourgeois fief. On the Right Bank *arrondissements* 1 and 2 are the most central, and good hotels are numerous (as in the 8th). 3 and 4 possess a few good hotels with charm (in the Marais). 16 and 17 are crossed by wide, tree-lined avenues and are particularly residential. In addition, the 16th is chic.

Keep in mind, when making reservations, that the busy season for hotels is September, October, and the beginning of November, plus March, May, and June. Should you reserve by letter, add the zip code. Paris is 750. The 1st *arrondissement* would be

75001 and the 16th would be 75016. We have not repeated "hotel" each time, so you use it when addressing your envelope. For telephone reservations remember there is a time change, so call at the end of the afternoon or in the evening. Nowadays, desk personnel speak English, at least enough to make a reservation.

The exchange rate has been calculated at six francs for one dollar.

1st arrondissement

Duminy-Vendôme, 3 Rue du Mont-Tabor, 4260-3280. Métro: Tuileries. Comfortable, quiet, well situated. $65–150.

Family Hôtel, 35 Rue Cambon, 4261-5484. Métro: Concorde. Former private town house transformed into an attractive hotel. Only twenty-five rooms. $50 to 80.

Intercontinental, 3 Rue de Castiglione, 4260-3780. Métro: Tuileries. True to its name, this luxury hotel serves celebrities from all over the world. $200 and up.

Lotti, 7 Rue de Castiglione, 4260-3734. Métro: Tuileries. A discrete luxury hotel completely redecorated by new ownership, an Italian hotel chain. $200–300.

Meurice, 228 Rue de Rivoli, 4260-3860. Métro: Palais-Royal. Much old world charm at this luxury hotel. $250 and up.

Montana-Tuileries, 12 Rue St. Roch, 4260-3510. Métro: Pyramides. Small hotel, comfortable, well located. $70–110.

Régina, 2 Place des Pyramides, 4260-3110. Métro: Tuileries, Palais-Royal. Enormous rooms, with period furniture. $110–350.

Ritz, 15 Place Vendôme, 4260-3830. Métro: Opéra, Tuileries. The most perfect hotel in Paris, veritable little palace. $400 and up.

St. James and Albany, 202 Rue de Rivoli, 4260-3160. Métro: Palais-Royal. Sprawling hotel, completely redone in contemporary international style. Top floor mansards are the nicest. $100–400.

Saint Romain, 7 Rue St. Roch, 4260-3170. Métro: Pyramides. Small hotel, completely renovated, in peaceful street. $65–100.

2nd arrondissement
Westminster, 13 Rue de la Paix, 4261-5746. Métro: Opéra. One of the Warwick chain of hotels. Pleasant, well-run hotel. $200–300.

3rd arrondissement
Chevaliers, 30 Rue de Turenne, 4272-7347. Métro: Chemin-Vert. Totally renovated in tones of beige. Small hotel. $70–80.

Pavillon de la Reine, 28 Place des Vosges, 4297-9640. Métro: Chemin-Vert. Newly opened, charming hotel. $125–350.

4th arrondissement
Célestins, 1 Rue Charles-V, 4887-8704. Métro: Bastille, Sully-Morland. Old-style furniture and charm. $50–60.

Deux Iles, 59 Rue St. Louis-en-l'Ile, 4326-1335. Métro: Pont-Marie. There are only eighteen rooms in this delightful hotel. $85–100.

Grand Hôtel Jeanne d'Arc, 3 Rue de Jarente, 4887-6211. Métro: St. Paul. Old-fashioned. $35.

Jeu de Paume, 54 Rue St. Louis-en-l'Ile. 4326-1418. Métro: Pont-Marie. An unforgettable dreamland. $100–125.

Lutèce, 65 Rue St. Louis-en-l'Ile, 4326-2352. Métro: Pont-Marie. Another ravishing hotel. $100.

Septième Art, 20 Rue St. Paul, 4277-0403. Métro: St. Paul. Pleasant hotel run by cinema enthusiasts. $35–65.

Sévigné, 2 Rue Malher, 4272-7617. Métro: St. Paul, Bastille. Reasonably priced: $35 with breakfast.

Vieux Marais, 8 Rue du Plâtre, 4278-4722. Mêtro: Hôtel-de-Ville, Rambuteau. Definite charm. $70 with breakfast.

There are three hostel-hotels in this quarter run by French youth organizations. Magnificent old residences have been totally renovated, tastefully fitted out and are so inexpensive as to blow minds. Turnover is rapid as there is a five-day limit on accommodations. Cost is $12 with breakfast.

Le Fauconnier, 11 Rue Fauconnier, 4274-2345. Métro: St. Paul. 17th-century town house.

Fourcy, 6 Rue du Fourcy, 4274-2345. Métro: St. Paul. 17th-century chateau.

Maubuisson, 12 Rue des Barres, 4272-7209. Métro: Hôtel-de-Ville, St. Paul. A gingerbread house.

5th arrondissement
Le Colbert, 7 Rue Hôtel-Colbert, 4325-8565. Métro: Maubert-Mutualité. A number of rooms look directly onto Notre Dame across the river. $80–200.

Elysa-Luxembourg, 6 Rue Gay-Lussac, 4325-3174. Métro: Luxembourg. Brand new hotel, bright, agreeably decorated. $40–100.

Esmeralda, 4 Rue St. Julien-le-Pauvre, 4354-1920. Métro: St. Michel, Cluny. The front rooms have view of St. Julien-le-Pauvre Church and Notre Dame. Small 17th-century structure with wonderful staircase. $35–65.

Grandes Ecoles, 75 Rue du Cardinal-Lemoine, 4326-7923. Métro: Cardinal-Lemoine. Charming country house surrounded by garden at the end of a cobblestone path. $45 with bath.

Notre-Dame Hôtel, 1 Quai St. Michel, 4354-2043. Métro: St. Michel. Recently renovated. A few of the upper-floor rooms look onto Notre Dame. $80–170.

6th arrondissement

Angleterre, 44 Rue Jacob, 4260-3472. Métro: St. Germain-des-Près. Very pretty patio surrounded by hotel; former British Embassy. $60–125.

Atelier Montparnasse, 49 Rue Vavin, 4633–6000. Métro: Vavin. Tiny, comfortable, family style hotel. $75–120.

Danemark, 21 Rue Vavin, 4326-9378. Métro: Notre–Dame–des Champs. Tastefully decorated, well situated. $75–100.

Delavigne, 1 Rue Casimir-Delavigne, 4329-3150. Métro: Odéon. On a quiet street. $70–75.

Ferrandi, 92 Rue du Cherche-Midi, 4222-9740. Métro: Vaneau. Very comfortable. $60–90.

L'Hôtel, 13 Rue des Beaux-Arts, 4325-2722. Métro: St. Germain-des-Près, Mabillon. An absolute jewel of a hotel! $150–220.

Latitudes, 7-11 Rue St. Benoît, 4262-5353. Métro: St. Germain-des-Près. Modern hotel, very conveniently situated. $85–120.

Lutétia, 45 Boulevard Raspail, 4544-3810. Métro: Sèvres-Babylone. Elegant and sophisticated, one of few large hotels on the Left Bank. $140–270.

Madison, 143 Boulevard St. Germain, 4329-7250. Métro: St. Germain-des-Près. View of St. Germain-des-Près Church from front windows. Recently remodelled with taste. $80–150.

Maronniers, 21 Rue Jacob, 4325-3060. Métro: St. Germain-des-Près. Small hotel in quiet courtyard. $80.

Quality Inn, 92 Rue de Vaugirard, 4222-0056. Métro: St. Placide. Spacious, elegant. $80–110.

Relais Christine, 3 Rue Christine, 4326-7180. Métro: Odéon. Calm, expensive. $200.

Relais St. Germain, 9 Carrefour de l'Odéon, 4329-1205. Métro: Odéon. Small, argreeably sophisticated. $150–180.

Sainte-Beuve, 9 Rue Sainte-Beuve, 4548-2007. Métro: Notre-Dame-des-Champs. Comfort plus period furniture in brand-new hotel. $85–150.

Saints-Pères, 65 Rue des Saints-Pères, 4544–4500. Métro: St. Germain-des-Près. Comfortable rooms overlooking fine courtyard. $65–140.

La Villa, 29 Rue Jacob, 4634-6363. Métro: St. Germain-des-Près. The only hotel truly employing comtemporary design. $100–150.

7th arrondissement

Bellechasse, 8 Rue de Bellechasse, 4551-5236. Métro: Solférino. Bright and cheerful recent renovation. $80–110.

Bersolys Saint-Germain, 28 Rue de Lille, 4260-7379. Métro: Bac. Each room is dedicated to a different painter. Period furniture. $70–90.

Duc de Saint-Simon, 14 Rue de St. Simon, 4548-3566. Métro: Bac. Comfortably classic. $110–160.

Elysées-Maubourg, 35 Boulevard LaTour-Maubourg, 4556-1078. Métro: LaTour-Maubourg. A certain standing. Sauna on the premises. $80–110.

Jardins d'Eiffel, 8 Rue Amélie. 4705-4621. Métro: LaTour-Maubourg. Completely renovated. Sauna here as well, $70–80.

Lénox, 9 Rue de l'Université, 4296-1095. Métro: St. Germain-des-Près. Rooms are small but very tastefully decorated. Pleasant, quiet hotel. $65–90.

Montalembert, 3 Rue de Montalembert, 4548-6811. Métro: Bac. Rooms are spacious and pleasant. A classic. $80–130.

Résidence Orsay, 93 Rue de Lille, 4705-0527. Métro: Chambre-des-Députés. Plain but comfortable. $30–50.

Saxe-Résidence, 17 Avenue de Saxe, 4783-9829. Métro: Ségur. Spacious rooms, tranquil, relaxing. $60–70.

Sofitel-Paris Invalides, 32 Rue Saint-Dominique, 4555-9180. Métro: Solférino. Sophisticated. Fine bar. $200–250.

Solférino, 91 Rue de Lille, 4705-8354. Métro: Chambre-des-Députés. Rooms are pleasant though small. $40–65.

Suède, 31 Rue Vaneau, 4705-0008. Métro: Varenne. Period furniture. Third floor and up has a view of the Prime Minister's gardens. $70–80.

Varenne, 44 Rue de Bourgogne, 4551-4555. Métro: Bac. A perfect charmer. $50–80.

8th arrondissement
Atala, 10 Rue Chateaubriand, 4562-0162. Métro: Georges V. Quiet. Good view of city from upper floors. $100–140.

Balzac, 6 Rue de Balzac. Métro: Georges V. Sophisticated. Impeccable. $210–300.

Bradford, 10 Rue St. Philippe-du-Roule, 4359-2420. Métro: St. Philippe-du-Roule. Spacious, tasteful, classic, $80–110.

Bristol, 112 Rue du Faubourg St.-Honoré. Métro: Miromesnil. Lovely and luxurious. $220–400.

Château Frontenac, 54 Rue Pierre-Charron, 4723-5585. Métro: Franklin-Roosevelt. International class. $85–140.

Crillon, 10 Place de la Concorde, 4265-2424. Métro: Concorde. Luxury hotel deluxe. $400–500.

Lancaster, 7 Rue de Berri, 4559-9043. Métro: Georges V. Class and charm. $230–350.

Mariott-Prince-de-Galles, 33 Avenue Georges V, 4723-5511. Métro: Georges V. Very elegant. $200–350.

Napoléon, 40 Avenue Friedland, 4766-0202. Métro: Etoile-Charles-de-Gaulle. Light, spacious rooms. $95–150.

Plaza-Athénée, 25 Avenue Montaigne, 4723-7833. Métro: Alma-Marceau. A white palace of elegance and sophistication. $300–1200.

Pullman-Saint-Honoré, 15 Rue Boissy d'Anglas, 4266-9362. Métro: Concorde. Recently remodelled and well located. $95–125.

Résidence Monceau, 85 Rue du Rocher, 4522-7511. Métro: Villiers. Newly renovated and pleasant. One price: $80.

San Régis, 12 Rue Jean-Goujon, 4359-4190. Métro: Champs-Elysées-Clemenceau. Classic, cheerful, authentic, and situated on a charming little square. $200–600.

La Trémoille, 14 Rue La Trémoille, 4723-2420. Métro: Alma-Marceau. Very lovely, with refined décor. $210–330.

9th arrondissement

Ambassador-Concorde, 16 Boulevard Haussmann, 4246-9263. Métro: Chaussée-d'Antin. Fine hotel completely renovated in varying styles. $160–220.

Bergère, 34 Rue Bergère, 4770-3434. Métro: Montmartre. Light, neat. $80–110.

Commodore, 12 Boulevard Haussmann, 4246-7282. Métro: Chaussée d'Antin. Art Déco style, with spacious rooms. $110–200.

Gotty, 11 Rue de Trévise, 4770-7912. Métro: Montmartre. Pleasant and bright. $90–100.

La Havane, 44 Rue de Trévise, 4770-7912. Métro: Cadet. Small, agreeable, and moderately priced. $45–80.

Léman, 20 Rue de Trévise, 4246-5066. Métro: Montmartre. Delightful and harmonious. $60–120.

Moulin-Rouge, 39 Rue Fontaine, 4282-0856. Métro: Blanche. Tastefully furnished. $80–90.

Pré, 10 Rue Pierre-Semard, 4281-3711. Métro: Poissonnière. Quiet and agreeable $60–85.

10th arrondissement

Claret, 44 Boulevard de Bercy, 4628-4131. Métro: Bercy. For wine lovers, next door to wine dealers warehouses. A bright, new hotel. $50–85.

Grand Hôtel de Cognac, 8 Cours de Vincennes, 4345-1353. Métro: Nation. Plain, neat and moderately priced. $45–55.

Urbis, 12 Rue Louis-Blanc, 4201-2121. Métro: Colonel-Fabien. Small and comfortable. Several rooms overlook St. Martin Canal. $65–190.

11th arrondissement

Nouvel Hôtel, 24 Avenue du Bel-Air, 4343-0181. Métro: Nation. Flowered wallpaper and tranquility. $30–65.

14th arrondissement

La Loire, 39 Rue du Moulin-Vert, 4540-6688. Métro: Alésia, Plaisance. Calm and pleasant. $40–50.

15th arrondissement

Wallace, 89 Rue Fondary, 4578-8330. Métro: Emile-Zola. Totally renovated, colorful, calm, and original. $40–80.

16th arrondissement

Alexander, 102 Avenue Victor-Hugo, 4553-6465. Métro: Victor-Hugo. Old-fashioned elegance. $100–140.

Ambassade, 79 Rue Lauriston, 4553-4115. Métro: Boissière. The most pleasant rooms are on the courtyard. $55–80.

Bouquet de Longchamp, 6 rue du Bouquet de Longchamp, 4704-4171. Métro: Trocadéro. Charming hotel on a quiet street. $50–90.

Garden-Elysée, 12 Rue St. Didier, 4755-0111. Métro: Trocadéro. All rooms face the garden and patio. $135–200.

Hameau de Passy, 48 Rue de Passy, 4288-4755. Métro: La Muette. Set in a garden; total calm. $30.

Longchamp, 68 Rue de Longchamp, 4727-1348. Métro: Trocadéro. Quiet and comfortable. $80–90.

Majestic, 29 Rue Dumont-d'Urville, 4500-8370. Métro: Kléber. Refined, traditional, and comfortable. $100–150.

Park Avenue et Central Park, 57 Avenue Raymond-Poincaré, 4553-4460. Métro: Victor-Hugo. Modern and original, with kitchenettes in the Park Avenue wing. $120–220.

Passy-Eiffel, 10 Rue de Passy, 4225-5566. Métro: Passy. Beams and naive paintings. $65–80.

Queen's Hôtel, 4 Rue Bastien-Lepage, 4288-8985. Métro: Michelange-Auteuil. Each room is devoted to a different contemporary artist. $35–80.

Raphaël, 17 Avenue Kléber, 4502-1600. Métro: Kléber. A richly decorated luxury hotel. $150–900.

Résidence Bassano, 15 Rue de Bassano, 4723-7823. Métro: Georges V. Art déco surroundings plus sauna and jacuzzi on premises. $125–160.

Résidence du Bois, 16 Rue Chalgrin, 4500-5059. Métro: Argentine. Lavish manor house. $200–250.

17th arrondissement

Banville, 166 Boulevard Berthier, 4267-7016. Métro: Champerret. No two rooms are alike; all are charming. $80–90.

Etoile-Park Hôtel, 10 Avenue MacMahon, 4267-6963. Métro: Etoile-Charles-de-Gaulle. Very fashionable décor. $55–100.

Etoile-Pereire, 146 Bouleuard Pereire, 4267-6000. Métro: Pereire. Recently renovated, calm, and pleasant. $70–140.

Saint-Ferdinand, 36 Rue Saint-Ferdinand, 4272-6666. Métro: Porte-Maillot. Spacious, pleasant rooms. $100–120.

18th arrondissement

Caulincourt, 2 Square Caulaincourt, 4606-4299. Métro: Lamarck-Caulaincourt. Old-fashioned and simple. $20.

Coeur de la Butte, 42 Rue Berthe, 4255-3750. Métro: Pigalle. Quiet family-type hotel. $35.

Résidence Montmartre, 10 Rue Burq, 4606-4528. Métro: Abbesses, Blanche. Calm and well situated. $40.

Tim Hôtel, 11 Place Emile-Goudeau, 4255-7479. Métro: Abbesses. Renovated hotel on romantic square of Montmartre. $55.

Index